Weight Watchers®
NEW INTERNATIONAL
COOKBOOK

Weight Watchers®

NEW INTERNATIONAL
COOKBOOK

Photography by Aaron Rezny

NAL BOOKS

NEW AMERICAN LIBRARY

NEW YORK AND SCARBOROUGH, ONTARIO

WEIGHT WATCHERS is a registered trademark of
Weight Watchers International, Inc.

NAL BOOKS TRADEMARK REG. U.S. PAT. OFF. AND FOREIGN COUNTRIES
REGISTERED TRADEMARK—MARCA REGISTRADA
HECHO EN HARRISONBURG, VA., U.S.A.

SIGNET, SIGNET CLASSIC, MENTOR, PLUME, MERIDIAN,
and NAL BOOKS are published *in the United States* by
New American Library, 1633 Broadway, New York,
New York 10019, *in Canada* by The New American Library
of Canada, Limited, 81 Mack Avenue,
Scarborough, Ontario M1L 1M8

Library of Congress Cataloging-in-Publication Data
Main entry under title:

Weight Watchers new international cookbook.

   Includes index.
   1. Reducing diets — Recipes.   2. Cookery,
International.   I. Weight Watchers International.
RM222.2.W322   1985   641.59   85-13443
ISBN 0-453-00011-3

First Printing, December, 1985

1 2 3 4 5 6 7 8 9

PRINTED IN THE UNITED STATES OF AMERICA

Contents

ACKNOWLEDGMENTS

This book represents the collaboration of many talented people who shared their knowledge and expertise to accomplish a very challenging task. A world of thanks is given to Nina Procaccini, Bianca Brown, Christy Foley-McHale, and Judi Rettmer for the many hours spent developing, adapting, and testing the recipes. We extend our grateful appreciation to Eileen Pregosin, Patricia Barnett, Harriet Pollock, Elizabeth Resnick, and April Rozea for researching, writing, and editing the text. For their patience and cooperation in devoting their secretarial skills to typing and revising the manuscript, we extend our gratitude to Isabel Fleisher, Lola Sher, and Angela Talley. And a special thank-you to Michael Grand for his cheerful, invaluable assistance in photography.

WEIGHT WATCHERS INTERNATIONAL, INC.

Introduction

If you've ever asked yourself, "How in the world can I lose weight and still enjoy Deep-Dish Apple Pie, Shrimp with Lobster Sauce, Tostadas, Couscous, and Arroz con Pollo?" then this book is for you! For Weight Watchers International, the world-famous authority on weight control, has adapted an intriguing collection of over 300 international recipes (representing the cuisines of over 40 countries) to meet the guidelines of the Food Plan. Just as a wide and exciting range of taste experiences greet the traveler with an adventurous appetite, so the weight-conscious cook can delight her family and friends with culinary treats from other countries without ever leaving home. Some cooking techniques have been adapted to make the recipes more convenient to use, some hard-to-find foods have been replaced with ones that are more readily available, and some ingredients have been modified to conform to the requirements of the Food Plan. Yet all the recipes are still a true reflection of the classic and best-loved dishes of each area. Now you can discover new flavors, new textures, new menu combinations, and, at the same time, a new you!

The Weight Watchers organization's culinary journey around the world has been inspired by timely interest in the classic cuisines of other countries. The recipes provide a broad spectrum of traditional favorites; some flavors may be familiar, others will afford new interest and excitement. So, if you're searching for a new and different recipe, a simple yet unique cooking technique, or interesting information on the culinary background of some areas of the world, travel through these pages and arrive at your calorie-conscious destination.

You'll find that countries within each chapter have been grouped together according to their geographic proximity or similar culinary influences. To give you a head start on meal planning, a suggested menu that will give you the flavor of a typical meal has been included in each chapter. (An asterisk next to a dish means that the recipe appears in the section.) Of course, you have the flexibility to be creative and adjust the menu to your own personal taste; just be sure to keep the Food Plan requirements in mind. So, be daring...be brave. Study the recipes and menu suggestions and treat yourself to new taste appeal for everyday meals or elegant dinner parties.

Most dishes are easy to prepare; a few may be exotic and more time-consuming, but are worth the challenge.

The pleasure derived from good food is a feeling shared by people around the world. So, all of our recipes have been simmered with care, blended with ingenuity, and served with pride in order to enhance your enjoyment of fine food, international cooking, and, at the same time, help you in your weight-loss efforts.

The World of Ingredients

When following the recipes in this book, in order to achieve the best results keep these points in mind:

• Always take time to measure and weigh ingredients carefully; this is vital to both recipe results and weight control. Don't try to judge portions by eye.

To weigh foods, use a scale.

To measure liquids, use a standard glass or clear plastic measuring cup. Place it on a level surface and read markings at eye level. Fill the cup just to the appropriate marking. To measure less than ¼ cup, use standard measuring spoons.

To measure dry ingredients, use metal or plastic measuring cups that come in sets of four: ¼ cup, ⅓ cup, ½ cup, and 1 cup. Spoon the ingredients into the cup, then level with the straight edge of a knife or metal spatula. To measure less than ¼ cup, use standard measuring spoons and, unless otherwise directed, level as for measuring cup.

To measure a dash, as a guide consider a dash to be about ¹⁄₁₆ of a teaspoon (½ of a ⅛-teaspoon measure or ¼ of a ¼-teaspoon measure).

- In any recipe for more than one serving it is important to mix ingredients well and to divide evenly so that each portion will be the same size.

- The herbs used in these recipes are dried unless otherwise indicated. If you are substituting fresh herbs, use approximately four times the amount of dried (e.g., 1 teaspoon chopped fresh basil instead of ¼ teaspoon dried basil leaves). If you are substituting ground (powdered) herbs for dried leaves, use approximately half the amount of dried (e.g., ¼ teaspoon ground thyme instead of ½ teaspoon dried thyme leaves).

- If you are substituting fresh spices for ground, generally use approximately eight times the amount of ground (e.g., 1 teaspoon minced ginger root instead of ⅛ teaspoon ground ginger).

- Generally, dried herbs and spices should not be kept for more than a year. Date the container at the time of purchase and check periodically for potency. Usually, if the herb (or spice) is aromatic, it is still potent; if the aroma has diminished, the recipe may require a larger amount of the seasoning.

- Unless otherwise specified, the raisins used in our recipes are dark seedless raisins.

- We've used fresh vegetables unless otherwise indicated. If you substitute frozen or canned vegetables, it may be necessary to adjust cooking times accordingly.

- When vegetable oil is called for, oils such as safflower, sunflower, soybean, corn, cottonseed, peanut, or any of these combined may be used. Since olive oil and Chinese sesame oil have distinctive flavors, they have been specifically indicated. There are two types of sesame oil: light and dark. The light oil is relatively flavorless and may be used as a substitute for any other vegetable oil. When sesame oil is specified, use the dark variety. This product, made from toasted sesame seeds, has a rich amber color and a characteristic sesame flavor.

- Hot chili peppers are indigenous to many of the cuisines of the world and add a typical fiery touch. However, chili peppers require special handling; their volatile oils can make your skin and eyes burn. Wear rubber gloves and be careful not to touch your face or eyes while working with these peppers. Before continuing with the recipe, thoroughly wash your hands, knife, and cutting board to remove all traces of the pepper.

Using the Exchange and Nutrition Information

Each recipe in this book is followed by an Exchange Information statement. This statement provides information as to how one serving of the item prepared from that recipe fits into the Weight Watchers food plan. If you are following the Food Plan, be aware that some of the recipes use ingredients from the Personal Choice™ series. You will find the Exchange Information useful when preparing menus as it will help you keep track of your Exchanges. If you make any changes in the recipes, be sure to adjust the Exchange Information accordingly.

Since many people are concerned about nutrition, on each recipe we have also included the per-serving nutrition analyses for calories, protein, fat, carbohydrate, sodium, and cholesterol. These figures were calculated using the most up-to-date data available; they will change if the recipe is altered, even if the substitution in ingredients does not affect the Exchange Information.

Using Recipe Symbols

 This symbol on recipes indicates that they can be prepared in 30 minutes or less.

 This symbol on recipes indicates that they can be prepared in 30 minutes to 1 hour.

Africa

For a culinary adventure, go on an African table-hopping safari. The variety of flavors will astound you. In coastal North Africa, for instance, which reflects Mediterranean tastes, couscous (semolina) is a national dish. Our easily prepared version pairs the grain with its traditional partner, a zesty stew.

"Zesty" is the word for most African cuisine, since dishes are usually livened up with potent spices. A typical example is Sambal, a vegetable relish that includes hot chili peppers, one of the world's fieriest foods. In Ethiopia, to provide a soothing contrast to such torrid dishes, people routinely serve Injera, their special bread.

One of the most popular meats isn't wild game but domestic lamb. Try our Tagine, an unusual Moroccan lamb stew mixed with prunes, or Bobotie, a South African lamb casserole.

Yams are raised throughout South Africa, probably originally brought there from South America; our Yam Salad is a refreshing way to serve them. (You can substitute sweet potatoes if you wish.) Another prime crop is peanuts, known locally as groundnuts. They flavor an array of dishes, including our adaptation of Nigerian Peanut Soup, a transglobal way to utilize that American favorite, peanut butter.

In another across-the-world exchange, centuries ago Portuguese traders introduced a strange-looking fruit from their Brazilian colonies. African natives named it "banana," and today both bananas and pineapples, which also crossed the sea to Africa, thrive on the Ivory Coast. Banana Fritters, a West African specialty, can make the windup of your meal an international treat.

African Adventure

Moroccan Tomato and Pepper Salad*

Couscous*

Banana Fritters*

West African Pineapple Quencher*

Nigerian Peanut Soup ⏱

MAKES 2 SERVINGS

With a touch of chili pepper, peanut butter is transformed into a truly interesting soup.

2 packets instant chicken broth and seasoning mix
2 cups water
1½ small dried green chili peppers, finely chopped
¼ cup each diced green bell pepper and onion
3 tablespoons chunky-style peanut butter

In 1-quart saucepan dissolve broth mix in water; add chili peppers and bring mixture to a boil. Stir in bell pepper and onion and return to a boil. Reduce heat to low, cover, and let simmer until vegetables are tender, about 10 minutes. Reduce heat to lowest possible temperature; add peanut butter and cook, stirring constantly, until peanut butter is melted and mixture is well blended.

Each serving provides: 1½ Protein Exchanges; ¾ Vegetable Exchange; 1½ Fat Exchanges; 10 calories Optional Exchange
Per serving: 162 calories; 8 g protein; 12 g fat; 8 g carbohydrate; 983 mg sodium; 0 mg cholesterol

Ingelegde

Flounder, scrod, and cod are all excellent choices for this South African pickled fish.

FISH

8 ounces firm white fish fillets, cut into 2-inch pieces
½ cup water
1 tablespoon lemon juice
3 peppercorns
1 bay leaf
Dash salt

SAUCE

2 teaspoons vegetable oil
½ cup sliced onion
½ teaspoon all-purpose flour
¼ cup water
1 tablespoon lemon juice
1½ teaspoons each granulated sugar and malt vinegar or cider vinegar
¼ teaspoon each curry powder and salt
Dash pepper

GARNISH

Lemon twists and parsley sprigs

To Prepare Fish: Using paper towels, pat fish dry. In small nonstick skillet combine water, lemon juice, and seasonings and bring to a boil. Reduce heat and add fish; cover and let simmer until fish flakes easily when tested with a fork, 1 to 2 minutes. Using slotted spoon, remove fish to a bowl; set aside. Discard cooking liquid.

To Prepare Sauce: Wipe same skillet clean; add oil and heat. Add onion and cook until translucent. Sprinkle with flour and stir quickly to combine; cook, stirring constantly, for 1 minute. Gradually stir in water; add lemon juice, sugar, vinegar, and seasonings and, stirring constantly, bring to a boil. Reduce heat and cook until mixture thickens slightly. Pour sauce over fish and gently toss to combine; cover

| (CONTINUED) | with plastic wrap and refrigerate until chilled. Just before serving, toss again and garnish with lemon and parsley.

Each serving provides: 3 Protein Exchanges; ½ Vegetable Exchange; 1 Fat Exchange; 20 calories Optional Exchange
Per serving with flounder: 166 calories; 22 g protein; 6 g fat; 9 g carbohydrate; 432 mg sodium; 57 mg cholesterol
With scrod or cod: 165 calories; 21 g protein; 5 g fat; 9 g carbohydrate; 423 mg sodium; 57 mg cholesterol |

Yam Salad ⏱

| **MAKES 2 SERVINGS**

South Africa gives us this unique way of using yams. | **6 ounces peeled cooked yams or sweet potatoes, cut into cubes**
¼ cup diced green bell pepper
2 tablespoons each diced onion and celery
2 teaspoons peanut or vegetable oil
1½ teaspoons lemon juice
¼ teaspoon salt
Dash pepper

In salad bowl combine yams, pepper, onion, and celery; set aside.

In small bowl combine remaining ingredients; pour over salad and toss to coat with dressing. Serve immediately or cover and refrigerate. Bring to room temperature and toss again before serving.

Each serving provides: 1 Bread Exchange; ½ Vegetable Exchange; 1 Fat Exchange
Per serving: 142 calories; 2 g protein; 5 g fat; 24 g carbohydrate; 325 mg sodium; 0 mg cholesterol |

Couscous

This is the national dish of Algeria, Tunisia, and Morocco. The word "couscous" refers to both the finished stew and the grain that is used in this dish. A coussoussière is the vessel that is traditionally used to prepare this hearty African entrée.

STEW

1 tablespoon olive oil, divided
1 whole chicken (3 pounds), cut into 8 pieces and skinned
1½ cups each diagonally sliced carrots, sliced onions, and cubed pared rutabaga (1-inch cubes)
1 cup water
1 tablespoon ground coriander
2 packets instant chicken broth and seasoning mix
2 small garlic cloves, minced
½ teaspoon each crushed red pepper and ground turmeric
1 pound drained canned chick-peas (garbanzo beans)
1½ cups sliced zucchini

COUSCOUS

3 ounces uncooked couscous (dry precooked semolina)
1 cup boiling water
½ cup golden raisins
1 tablespoon plus 2 teaspoons margarine
½ teaspoon each ground turmeric and salt

To Prepare Stew: In 5-quart saucepot or Dutch oven heat 1½ teaspoons oil over medium-high heat. Add half of the chicken pieces and cook until browned on all sides; remove chicken from skillet. Repeat procedure with remaining oil and chicken pieces, returning all chicken to skillet. Add carrots, onions, rutabaga, water, coriander, broth mix, garlic, pepper, and turmeric to chicken; stir to combine and bring to a boil. Reduce heat to low, cover, and let simmer until chicken and vegetables are tender, 20 to 25 minutes. Stir in chick-peas and zucchini and let simmer until thoroughly heated, 10 to 15 minutes longer.

To Prepare Couscous and Serve: In medium bowl combine all ingredients for couscous and stir to combine; let stand for 5 minutes.

Using slotted spoon, arrange chicken pieces and vegetables on warmed serving platter, leaving a well in

(CONTINUED)	center. Spoon couscous into well and pour some of the juices from stew over chicken and vegetables; serve remaining juices with couscous.
	Each serving provides: 3 Protein Exchanges; ½ Bread Exchange; 1½ Vegetable Exchanges; 1 Fat Exchange; ½ Fruit Exchange; 3 calories Optional Exchange Per serving: 296 calories; 22 g protein; 7 g fat; 34 g carbohydrate; 636 mg sodium (estimated); 50 mg cholesterol

Sambal

MAKES 2 SERVINGS *Serve this spicy vegetable relish from South Africa with saltines or crispbread.*	**2 large cucumbers, pared, seeded, and grated** **½ teaspoon each salt and cider vinegar** **¼ cup thinly sliced scallions (green onions)** **1 tablespoon seeded and minced hot red chili pepper** **1½ teaspoons each lemon juice and soy sauce** **Dash ground or crushed red pepper (optional)** In small bowl combine cucumbers, salt, and vinegar and let stand for 30 minutes. Transfer to colander or sieve and squeeze out as much liquid as possible from cucumber mixture. In medium bowl combine cucumbers, scallions, chili pepper, lemon juice, and soy sauce and mix well. Let marinate at room temperature for 30 minutes. Stir again, transfer to serving dish, and, if desired, sprinkle with red pepper. Each serving provides: 2½ Vegetable Exchanges Per serving: 48 calories; 3 g protein; 0.3 g fat; 11 g carbohydrate; 895 mg sodium; 0 mg cholesterol

Moroccan Tomato and Pepper Salad

MAKES 2 SERVINGS

Enjoy this dish as an appetizer or side dish.

1 medium green bell pepper
1 medium tomato, blanched, peeled, seeded, and diced
½ medium cucumber, pared, seeded, and diced
1 tablespoon plus 1½ teaspoons lemon juice
1 tablespoon water
2 teaspoons olive oil
1½ teaspoons minced fresh parsley
½ teaspoon seeded and minced green chili pepper
¼ teaspoon paprika
⅛ teaspoon each ground cumin and minced fresh garlic

On baking sheet broil bell pepper 3 inches from heat source, turning frequently, until charred on all sides; transfer pepper to brown paper bag and let stand until cool enough to handle, 15 to 20 minutes.

Fit strainer into medium bowl and peel pepper over bowl; remove and discard stem end and seeds, allowing juice from pepper to drip into bowl. Cut pepper into strips and add to bowl with juice; add tomato and cucumber and toss to combine.

In measuring cup or small bowl combine remaining ingredients; mix well. Pour over vegetables in bowl and toss to coat with dressing; cover with plastic wrap and refrigerate for at least 30 minutes.

Each serving provides: 2½ Vegetable Exchanges; 1 Fat Exchange
Per serving: 76 calories; 2 g protein; 5 g fat; 8 g carbohydrate;
14 mg sodium; 0 mg cholesterol

Bobotie

MAKES 4 SERVINGS

This lamb casserole is a South African specialty.

15 ounces ground lamb
1 cup diced onions
1 garlic clove, minced
1 slice white bread, made into crumbs
¼ cup raisins
2 tablespoons lemon juice
2 teaspoons curry powder
1 cup skim milk, divided
4 eggs
¼ teaspoon each salt and pepper, divided

Form lamb into large patty; place on rack in broiling pan and broil until rare, turning once, 2 to 3 minutes on each side. Let cool slightly, then crumble.

In 10-inch nonstick skillet combine lamb, onions, and garlic and cook, stirring occasionally, until onions are tender; stir in bread crumbs, raisins, lemon juice, and curry powder and remove from heat.

In small bowl combine ½ cup milk, 2 eggs, and ⅛ teaspoon each salt and pepper, mixing well; stir into lamb mixture. Spray shallow 1-quart casserole with nonstick cooking spray and spread lamb mixture in bottom. In same bowl combine remaining ½ cup milk, 2 eggs, and ⅛ teaspoon each salt and pepper; mix well and pour over lamb mixture. Bake at 350°F. until top is browned and mixture is set, 40 to 45 minutes. Remove from oven and let stand for 5 minutes before serving.

Each serving provides: 4 Protein Exchanges; ½ Vegetable Exchange; ½ Fruit Exchange; ¼ Milk Exchange; 20 calories Optional Exchange
Per serving: 341 calories; 33 g protein; 15 g fat; 19 g carbohydrate; 331 mg sodium; 360 mg cholesterol

Skewered Kefta

MAKES 2 SERVINGS, 2 SKEWERS EACH

These Moroccan lamb kabobs are redolent with spices.

10 ounces ground lamb
2 tablespoons minced onion
1 tablespoon chopped fresh parsley
1 tablespoon chopped fresh mint or 1½ teaspoons dried
¼ teaspoon each ground cumin, ground marjoram, salt, and pepper
2 teaspoons olive oil
1 teaspoon lemon juice
½ garlic clove, minced
¼ teaspoon paprika

In medium bowl combine lamb, onion, parsley, mint, cumin, marjoram, salt, and pepper; mix well. Divide lamb mixture into 4 equal portions. Form each portion into a sausage shape, pressing each onto a 12-inch wooden or metal skewer; transfer skewers to rack in broiling pan.

In measuring cup or small bowl combine oil, lemon juice, garlic, and paprika; using pastry brush, brush oil mixture over keftas, coating all sides. Broil, turning once, until keftas are browned on all sides, 5 to 6 minutes on each side.

Each serving provides: 4 Protein Exchanges; ⅛ Vegetable Exchange; 40 calories Optional Exchange
Per serving: 283 calories; 31 g protein; 16 g fat; 2 g carbohydrate; 351 mg sodium; 113 mg cholesterol

Tagine

Prunes add interest to this Moroccan lamb stew.

10 ounces lamb for stew (1½-inch cubes)
1½ teaspoons each margarine and olive or vegetable oil
⅛ teaspoon each ground cinnamon and ground ginger
Dash each ground turmeric and crushed whole saffron
½ cup water
1 tablespoon each chopped fresh cilantro (Chinese parsley) and Italian (flat-leaf) parsley
1 cup chopped onions
4 large pitted prunes, diced
2 teaspoons honey
Dash each salt and pepper
½ teaspoon sesame seed, toasted

On rack in broiling pan broil lamb, turning once, until rare, 2 to 3 minutes on each side.

In 1½-quart saucepan combine margarine and oil and heat until margarine is bubbly and hot; add lamb and spices and stir to combine. Cook over medium heat for 5 minutes, stirring frequently; gradually pour in water. Add cilantro and parsley and stir to combine; bring to a boil. Reduce heat to low, cover, and let simmer for 30 minutes. Stir in onions and let simmer, covered, for 10 minutes longer; add prunes, honey, salt, and pepper and cook, uncovered, until prunes are plumped and lamb is tender, about 15 minutes longer. Serve each portion sprinkled with ¼ teaspoon sesame seed.

Each serving provides: 4 Protein Exchanges; 1 Vegetable Exchange; 1½ Fat Exchanges; 1 Fruit Exchange; 25 calories Optional Exchange
Per serving: 396 calories; 33 g protein; 18 g fat; 26 g carbohydrate; 187 mg sodium; 113 mg cholesterol

Green Mealie Bread

MAKES 6 SERVINGS

Serve this delicious South African steamed corn pudding either hot or at room temperature.

3 cups frozen whole-kernel corn, thawed
3 eggs
2 tablespoons each unsalted margarine, melted, and all-purpose flour
1 tablespoon granulated sugar
2 teaspoons double-acting baking powder
Dash salt

In blender container combine corn, eggs, and margarine and process until pureed, scraping down sides of container as necessary (mixture will be slightly lumpy). Add remaining ingredients and, using an on-off motion, process until combined.

Preheat oven to 375°F. Spray 7⅜ x 3⅝ x 2¼-inch loaf pan with nonstick cooking spray; pour in corn mixture and smooth top. Cover pan with double thickness of foil; crimp edges to sides of pan to seal. Place pan in 13 x 9 x 2-inch baking pan and fill baking pan with boiling water to a depth of about 1 inch; bake in middle of center oven rack for 1 hour (until knife, inserted in center of bread, comes out clean). Remove pan from oven and loaf pan from water bath; remove foil and let stand for 10 minutes. Run a knife around edges of bread and unmold onto serving plate. To serve, cut into 6 equal slices.

Each serving provides: ½ Protein Exchange; 1 Bread Exchange; 1 Fat Exchange; 20 calories Optional Exchange
Per serving: 159 calories; 6 g protein; 7 g fat; 21 g carbohydrate; 200 mg sodium; 137 mg cholesterol

Serving Suggestion: Top each portion of bread with 1 teaspoon warmed honey or maple syrup. Increase Optional Exchange to 40 calories.

Per serving: 179 calories; 6 g protein; 7 g fat; 27 g carbohydrate; 200 mg sodium; 137 mg cholesterol

Injera

MAKES 6 SERVINGS,
1 BREAD EACH

*This is the national
bread of Ethiopia and
is served with almost
every meal. It is
usually torn into
pieces and used to
scoop up food. Its
faintly sour but
soothing taste
cools off the
hot spicy dishes
it accompanies.*

6 ounces uncooked millet
1½ cups club soda (at room temperature)
1 egg
1 teaspoon double-acting baking powder
½ teaspoon baking soda

In blender container process millet in small batches until it resembles fine flour; remove to bowl and set aside.

In blender container combine club soda, egg, baking powder, and baking soda and, using an on-off motion, process until combined. Add ground millet and process at high speed into a smooth batter, about 1 minute. Pour into 4-cup measure, cover, and let stand at room temperature until fermented and foamy, about 1½ hours.

Spray 10-inch nonstick skillet with nonstick cooking spray and heat. Stir batter; pour ⅙ of batter (about scant ⅓ cup) into skillet and quickly swirl batter so that it covers entire bottom of pan. Cover skillet with tight-fitting lid and cook over high heat until bread is spongy and moist (it will have air holes), about 1 minute (do not brown bottom as edges will become crisp and bread will crack when folded); transfer to plate and let cool. Repeat procedure 5 more times, making 5 more breads. To serve, fold each bread into quarters.

Each serving provides: 1 Bread Exchange; 40 calories Optional Exchange
Per serving: 118 calories; 4 g protein; 2 g fat; 21 g carbohydrate;
   151 mg sodium; 46 mg cholesterol

West African Jollof Rice ⏱

MAKES 4 SERVINGS

A hearty rice with chicken, beef, and smoked ham.

7 ounces beef top or bottom round steak

2 tablespoons peanut or vegetable oil

1 pound 2 ounces chicken thighs, skinned, boned, and
   cut into 1-inch cubes

½ teaspoon each salt and pepper

1 cup each diced onions and drained canned whole
   tomatoes, seeded and chopped

¼ cup tomato paste

1 tablespoon seeded and minced hot green chili pepper

2 bay leaves

½ teaspoon ground ginger

3 cups water

5 ounces boneless "fully cooked" smoked ham,
   cut into cubes

4 ounces uncooked regular long-grain rice

4 packets instant chicken broth and seasoning mix

On rack in broiling pan broil steak, turning once, until rare, 2 to 3 minutes on each side. Remove from broiler and cut into 1-inch pieces; set aside.

In 12-inch nonstick skillet heat oil over high heat; add chicken, sprinkle with salt and pepper, and sauté until browned on all sides, 3 to 5 minutes. Remove from skillet and set aside.

To same skillet add onions and sauté until translucent; add tomatoes, paste, chili pepper, bay leaves, and ginger and cook over high heat, stirring constantly to prevent burning, until liquid has evaporated and mixture is a paste. Add water, steak, chicken, ham, rice, and broth mix and bring to a boil. Reduce heat, cover, and let simmer, stirring occasionally to prevent sticking, until rice is tender, about 30 minutes. Remove and discard bay leaves before serving.

Each serving provides: 4 Protein Exchanges; 1 Bread Exchange; 1¼
   Vegetable Exchanges; 1½ Fat Exchanges; 10 calories Optional Exchange
Per serving: 436 calories; 35 g protein; 17 g fat; 34 g carbohydrate;
   1,839 mg sodium; 94 mg cholesterol

Banana Fritters

MAKES 2 SERVINGS, 6 FRITTERS EACH

A dessert-type fritter from West Africa.

1 medium banana, peeled and cut into pieces
½ cup skim milk
1 egg
½ teaspoon vanilla extract
⅓ cup plus 2 teaspoons all-purpose flour
1½ teaspoons granulated sugar
2 teaspoons vegetable oil, divided
1 teaspoon confectioners' sugar

In blender container combine banana, milk, egg, and vanilla and process until pureed, scraping down sides of container as necessary. Add flour and sugar and process, stopping motor to scrape down sides of container as necessary; pour into bowl and let stand for 30 minutes.

In 12-inch nonstick skillet heat 1 teaspoon oil over high heat; stir batter and, using half of batter, drop mixture by tablespoonfuls into skillet, forming six 3½-inch fritters. Cook until bubbles appear on surface and bottom is browned; using pancake turner, turn fritters over. Cook other side briefly, just until browned; transfer to warmed serving plate and keep warm. Using remaining teaspoon oil and batter, repeat procedure, making 6 more fritters. Sprinkle an equal amount of confectioners' sugar over each fritter and serve warm.

Each serving provides: ½ Protein Exchange; 1 Bread Exchange; 1 Fat Exchange; 1 Fruit Exchange; ¼ Milk Exchange; 25 calories Optional Exchange
Per serving: 259 calories; 8 g protein; 8 g fat; 39 g carbohydrate; 67 mg sodium; 138 mg cholesterol

West African Pineapple Quencher

**MAKES 8 SERVINGS,
¾ CUP EACH**

*The sweetness of
pineapple with the
zing of clove and
orange.*

1 medium pineapple, cut in half lengthwise, pared,
    and cored (rinse and reserve peel)
4 to 6 whole cloves
½ cup water
Peel from 1 small orange, pith (white membrane) removed
1 quart boiling water
2 tablespoons granulated sugar
Garnish: mint sprigs

Cut 1 pineapple half into small pieces and transfer pieces to
large glass or stainless-steel bowl; wrap remaining fruit in
plastic wrap and refrigerate for use at another time. Stud
pineapple peel with cloves and add to bowl with pineapple.

   In small saucepan bring ½ cup water to a full boil; add
orange peel and cook for 2 minutes. Drain peel and add to
pineapple; add boiling water and sugar and stir to combine.
Cover with plastic wrap and let stand at room temperature
for 24 hours.

   Strain liquid, reserving liquid and fruit and discarding
pineapple peel with cloves and orange peel. In blender
container, in batches, process pineapple with liquid until
smooth; transfer to 2-quart pitcher, cover, and refrigerate
until chilled. Serve over ice in chilled glasses and garnish
each portion with a mint sprig.

Each serving provides: ½ Fruit Exchange; 15 calories Optional Exchange
Per serving: 46 calories; 0.3 g protein; 0.3 g fat; 12 g carbohydrate;
   0.8 mg sodium; 0 mg cholesterol

Australia and New Zealand

Australia, the country that's a continent in itself, reaps the bounty of both land and sea. Its vast extremes of temperature yield a wealth of varied produce ranging from apples, grown in the colder southern regions, to the lush fruits of tropical Queensland. Thousands of grazing acres result in an abundance of mutton and beef, and the encircling seas offer a diversity of seafood. All these are put to tasty use in dishes inherited from Australia's motherland, Britain, as well as in native specialties. Sample the land-sea combinations of Carpetbagger Steak, which combines beef and oysters, and Queensland Crab and Asparagus Soup.

Australians are partial to salads and make an unusual potato salad using Granny Smith apples (our version appears in this section). And for a century-old "down under" treat, serve Damper Bread, which originated with nineteenth-century "swagmen" (vagabonds) who cooked these unleavened round, flat cakes over campfires during their wanderings.

The "world's garden"—that's how New Zealand is touted by her proud inhabitants. Fruits and vegetables thrive in this beautiful land, and so does the lamb for which New Zealand is world-renowned. Game like venison is common, and seafood is plentiful, especially rock lobsters and oysters. Here, too, British culinary origins are evident, although sometimes mixed with native Maori dishes. But one of the foods for which New Zealand is now most famed came from China. Many years ago, voyagers from the Yangtze Valley introduced a fruit, which New Zealanders called the "Chinese gooseberry." Later, to differentiate it from other gooseberries, it was renamed "kiwi fruit," in honor of New Zealand's national bird. The fruit is used not only for desserts, but also as a meat tenderizer. And it's so highly regarded that New Zealanders often refer to themselves as "kiwis."

From A to Z Deliciously

Carpetbagger Steak*

"Down Under" Brussels Sprouts*

Tossed Salad

Damper Bread*

New Zealand Orangeade*

Cantaloupe Pie*

Tea

Queensland Crab and Asparagus Soup

MAKES 2 SERVINGS

A richly elegant, delicately flavored soup.

2 teaspoons reduced-calorie margarine
⅓ cup each chopped onion and diced celery
2 tablespoons finely chopped carrot
1 garlic clove, minced
½ teaspoon minced shallots
1 tablespoon all-purpose flour
2 cups skim milk
1 tablespoon dry sherry
½ bay leaf
½ teaspoon each salt, Worcestershire sauce, and grated lemon peel
⅛ teaspoon each white pepper and thyme leaves
3 ounces well-drained thawed frozen crab meat, flaked
½ cup sliced asparagus spears

In 1½-quart saucepan heat margarine over medium-high heat until bubbly and hot; add onion, celery, carrot, garlic, and shallots and sauté, stirring occasionally, until vegetables are softened, 2 to 3 minutes. Sprinkle with flour and stir quickly to combine; stirring constantly, gradually add milk and cook until sauce is smooth. Add remaining ingredients except crab meat and asparagus and bring to a boil. Reduce heat to low and add crab meat and asparagus; cover pan and cook, stirring occasionally, until soup is thickened and vegetables are tender, 20 to 30 minutes. Remove and discard bay leaf before serving.

Each serving provides: 1½ Protein Exchanges; 1¼ Vegetable Exchanges;
½ Fat Exchange; 1 Milk Exchange; 25 calories Optional Exchange
Per serving: 196 calories; 18 g protein; 3 g fat; 22 g carbohydrate;
854 mg sodium; 47 mg cholesterol

Scallops with Kiwi Fruit Sauce

MAKES 2 SERVINGS

Ginger root, lime juice, and lemon peel combine with kiwi fruit for a piquant sauce.

1 teaspoon each margarine and olive oil
10 ounces scallops
½ teaspoon minced pared ginger root
¼ teaspoon minced shallots
¼ cup each canned chicken broth and dry white wine
1 tablespoon lime juice (no sugar added)
¼ teaspoon grated lemon peel
Dash white pepper
2 teaspoons all-purpose flour, dissolved in 2 teaspoons water
1 medium kiwi fruit, pared, cut in half lengthwise, then sliced

In 10-inch nonstick skillet combine margarine and oil and heat over medium-high heat until margarine is bubbly and hot; add scallops and sauté, turning occasionally, until scallops are lightly browned, 3 to 4 minutes. Using slotted spoon, remove scallops to plate; set aside and keep warm.

In same skillet combine ginger and shallots and sauté until softened, about 1 minute; add broth, wine, lime juice, lemon peel, and pepper and stir to combine. Bring to a boil; add dissolved flour to skillet and stir quickly to combine. Reduce heat to low, cover, and let simmer, stirring occasionally, until sauce is smooth and thickened, 5 to 10 minutes. Return scallops to skillet; add kiwi fruit and cook until heated through, 2 to 3 minutes longer.

Each serving provides: 4 Protein Exchanges; 1 Fat Exchange; ½ Fruit Exchange; 45 calories Optional Exchange
Per serving: 215 calories; 23 g protein; 5 g fat; 14 g carbohydrate; 523 mg sodium; 50 mg cholesterol

Carpetbagger Steak ⏱

MAKES 2 SERVINGS

Australia's version of surf 'n' turf.

8 ounces boneless beef top loin steak
1 tablespoon plus 1 teaspoon reduced-calorie margarine
½ teaspoon minced shallots
2 tablespoons dry white wine
1 teaspoon each minced fresh parsley and lemon juice
6 small oysters, shucked

On rack in broiling pan broil steak 5 to 6 inches from heat source until done to taste (4 to 5 minutes on each side for rare; 6 to 7 minutes on each side for medium).

While steak is broiling, in 8-inch skillet heat margarine over medium-high heat until bubbly and hot; add shallots and sauté until golden, about 1 minute. Reduce heat to low and add wine, parsley, and lemon juice; add oysters and let simmer until oysters are firm to the touch, 2 to 3 minutes *(do not overcook)*.

To serve, arrange steak on serving plate and top with oyster sauce.

Each serving provides: 4 Protein Exchanges; 1 Fat Exchange; 15 calories Optional Exchange
Per serving: 241 calories; 30 g protein; 11 g fat; 2 g carbohydrate; 180 mg sodium; 92 mg cholesterol

Stuffed Steak Rolls

**MAKES 4 SERVINGS,
1 STEAK ROLL EACH**

*Serve steak "stuffed
and sauced" as
they do in
New Zealand.*

4 thin beef top or bottom round steaks (4 ounces each)
2 ounces Canadian-style bacon, diced
½ cup diced onion
3 tablespoons plain dried bread crumbs
2 tablespoons plus 2 teaspoons ketchup
⅛ teaspoon each salt and pepper
1 tablespoon plus 1 teaspoon all-purpose flour, divided
2 teaspoons vegetable oil
½ packet (about ½ teaspoon) instant beef broth and
    seasoning mix, dissolved in 1¼ cups hot water
1 tablespoon water

On rack in broiling pan broil steaks, turning once, until
rare, about 2 minutes on each side.

In 8-inch skillet combine bacon and onion and sauté until
onion is lightly browned; remove from heat and stir in
bread crumbs and ketchup. Sprinkle steaks evenly with salt
and pepper and spoon an equal amount of bacon mixture
onto center of each steak; roll steak to enclose filling and
secure with a toothpick. Sprinkle each steak roll with ½
teaspoon flour.

Preheat oven to 375°F. In 12-inch skillet that has a metal
or removable handle heat oil over medium-high heat; add
steak rolls and cook, turning, until well browned on all
sides. Pour dissolved broth mix over steak rolls and bring
to a boil. Cover skillet, transfer to oven, and bake until
steak is tender, about 1 hour.

Transfer steak rolls to a warmed serving plate, reserving
pan juices; remove toothpicks and keep steaks warm. In
small bowl combine water with remaining 2 teaspoons
flour, stirring to dissolve; stir into skillet. Stirring
constantly, bring mixture to a boil and cook just until
thickened, about 2 minutes; pour over steak rolls.

Each serving provides: 3½ Protein Exchanges; ¼ Vegetable Exchange;
    ½ Fat Exchange; 45 calories Optional Exchange
Per serving: 252 calories; 31 g protein; 9 g fat; 11 g carbohydrate;
    583 mg sodium; 85 mg cholesterol

Vegetable and Beef Casserole

MAKES 4 SERVINGS

A hearty stewlike casserole.

1¼ pounds boneless chuck steak
1¼ cups water, divided
½ cup dry red wine
1 bay leaf, broken in half
¼ teaspoon each thyme leaves, marjoram leaves, and salt
1 tablespoon plus 1 teaspoon vegetable oil
2 cups thinly sliced onions
1 tablespoon plus 1 teaspoon all-purpose flour
Dash pepper
1 cup each sliced carrots and celery (1-inch pieces)

On rack in broiling pan broil steak, turning once, until rare; cut into 1-inch pieces.

In medium bowl combine ½ cup water with the wine and seasonings; add chuck and toss to combine. Cover with plastic wrap and refrigerate for at least 8 hours.

Preheat oven to 350°F. Using slotted spoon, remove chuck from marinade, reserving marinade. In 10-inch skillet heat oil over medium-high heat; add onions and meat and sauté until onions are browned, 2 to 3 minutes. Transfer meat and onions to 2-quart casserole, reserving pan juices; set casserole aside.

In same skillet add flour to pan juices and stir to dissolve; cook, stirring, until flour is lightly browned. Gradually stir in reserved marinade; add pepper and remaining ¾ cup water and, stirring constantly, bring to a boil. Pour into casserole, cover, and bake for 1 hour. Add carrots and celery, cover casserole, and bake until meat is tender, about 1 hour longer. Remove bay leaf halves before serving.

Each serving provides: 4 Protein Exchanges; 2 Vegetable Exchanges; 1 Fat Exchange; 40 calories Optional Exchange
Per serving: 367 calories; 36 g protein; 15 g fat; 15 g carbohydrate; 252 mg sodium; 103 mg cholesterol

Cucumber-Lamb Stew

MAKES 2 SERVINGS

An unusual blend of cucumber with the famed local lamb.

10 ounces boneless lamb shoulder, cut into 1-inch cubes
1 teaspoon olive oil
½ cup small pearl onions
1 garlic clove, minced
½ cup each diced celery and sliced red bell pepper
1 cup water
1 packet instant beef broth and seasoning mix
½ bay leaf
½ teaspoon rosemary leaves
⅛ teaspoon pepper
Dash ground red pepper
1 medium cucumber, pared, seeded, and grated
1½ teaspoons cornstarch, dissolved in 1½ teaspoons water

On rack in broiling pan broil lamb 5 to 6 inches from heat source, turning once, until rare, 2 to 3 minutes on each side; set aside.

In 1½-quart saucepan heat oil over medium heat; add onions and garlic and sauté, stirring frequently, until onions are lightly browned, 2 to 3 minutes. Add celery and bell pepper and sauté until softened, 1 to 2 minutes; add water, lamb, broth mix, and seasonings and mix well. Reduce heat to low, cover, and let simmer, stirring occasionally, until lamb is fork-tender, 40 to 45 minutes. Stir in cucumber and dissolved cornstarch; cook, stirring constantly, until sauce thickens, 8 to 10 minutes. Remove and discard bay leaf before serving.

Each serving provides: 4 Protein Exchanges; 2½ Vegetable Exchanges; ½ Fat Exchange; 15 calories Optional Exchange
Per serving: 314 calories; 33 g protein; 14 g fat; 14 g carbohydrate; 501 mg sodium; 113 mg cholesterol

Lamb Chops with Pineapple-Mint Sauce

MAKES 2 SERVINGS

Mint sauce, traditionally served with lamb, is enlivened with a touch of pineapple.

2 teaspoons each margarine and minced shallots
1 garlic clove, minced
1 tablespoon all-purpose flour
½ cup canned beef broth
⅓ cup pineapple juice (no sugar added)
¼ cup canned chicken broth
1 tablespoon plus 1 teaspoon dry white wine
1 tablespoon each chopped fresh mint and lemon juice
¼ teaspoon salt
Dash pepper
½ teaspoon rosemary leaves
2 lamb chops (6 ounces each)

In 1-quart saucepan heat margarine over medium heat until bubbly and hot; add shallots and garlic and sauté until softened, about 1 minute. Sprinkle with flour and stir quickly to combine. Gradually stir in beef broth; add pineapple juice and chicken broth and cook, stirring constantly, until mixture is smooth. Add wine, mint, lemon juice, salt, and pepper and stir to combine. Reduce heat to low and let simmer, stirring occasionally, until sauce is thickened, 10 to 15 minutes.

While sauce is simmering, press ¼ teaspoon rosemary leaves into side edge (not surface) of each chop; transfer chops to rack in broiling pan and broil 5 to 6 inches from heat source, turning once, until done to taste (4 minutes on each side for rare; 6 minutes on each side for medium). Transfer to serving plate and top with sauce.

Each serving provides: 4 Protein Exchanges; 1 Fat Exchange; ½ Fruit Exchange; 40 calories Optional Exchange
Per serving: 308 calories; 34 g protein; 13 g fat; 11 g carbohydrate; 689 mg sodium; 113 mg cholesterol

New Zealand Bacon and Egg Pie

MAKES 4 SERVINGS

A New Zealand version of quiche.

CRUST
½ cup plus 2 tablespoons all-purpose flour
¼ teaspoon salt
2 tablespoons plus 2 teaspoons margarine
¼ cup plain low-fat yogurt

FILLING
4 ounces Canadian-style bacon, diced
2 medium tomatoes, each cut into quarters
3 ounces sharp Cheddar cheese, shredded
3 eggs
⅛ teaspoon each salt and pepper
1 cup evaporated skimmed milk

To Prepare Crust: Preheat oven to 400°F. In mixing bowl combine flour and salt; with pastry blender, or 2 knives used scissors-fashion, cut in margarine until mixture resembles coarse meal. Add yogurt and mix thoroughly. Form dough into a ball and roll between 2 sheets of wax paper, forming a circle about ⅛ inch thick. Fit dough into 9-inch pie plate; flute edges and, using tines of fork, prick bottom and sides of dough. Bake until golden brown, about 10 minutes; transfer to wire rack and let cool. Reduce oven temperature to 350°F.

To Prepare Pie: In small skillet cook bacon, stirring frequently, until lightly browned, 2 to 3 minutes. Arrange tomato wedges in bottom of cooled crust; top with bacon and sprinkle with cheese.

In medium bowl combine eggs, salt, and pepper and beat lightly; stir in milk. Pour into crust and bake for about 35 minutes (until knife, inserted in center, comes out clean). Remove from oven and let stand for 5 minutes.

Each serving provides: 2½ Protein Exchanges; ½ Bread Exchange; 1 Vegetable Exchange; 2 Fat Exchanges; ½ Milk Exchange; 40 calories Optional Exchange
Per serving: 402 calories; 24 g protein; 21 g fat; 28 g carbohydrate; 962 mg sodium; 245 mg cholesterol

Damper Bread

MAKES 12 SERVINGS,
1 SLICE EACH

*This bread may
be frozen as a
whole loaf or
as individually
wrapped slices.
When ready to
use, thaw at room
temperature.*

2¼ cups all-purpose flour
2 teaspoons double-acting baking powder
¼ teaspoon salt
¾ cup buttermilk
2 eggs, beaten
2 tablespoons margarine, melted

Preheat oven to 350°F. Into medium mixing bowl sift together flour, baking powder, and salt; using wooden spoon, stir in buttermilk, eggs, and margarine, stirring until thoroughly combined.

Spray 7⅜ x 3⅝ x 2¼-inch loaf pan with nonstick cooking spray; pour in batter and bake for 45 to 50 minutes (until top of bread is lightly browned and cake tester, inserted in center, comes out clean). Remove bread from pan and place on wire rack to cool. To serve, cut into 12 equal slices.

Each serving provides: 1 Bread Exchange; ½ Fat Exchange; 20 calories
Optional Exchange
Per serving: 122 calories; 4 g protein; 3 g fat; 19 g carbohydrate;
166 mg sodium; 46 mg cholesterol

"Down Under" Brussels Sprouts

MAKES 2 SERVINGS

Chestnuts and sherry dress up this fast and easy side dish.

1 teaspoon margarine
6 small chestnuts, peeled and cut into quarters
1 ounce Canadian-style bacon, chopped
¼ cup sliced mushrooms
1½ teaspoons minced shallots
1 cup cooked brussels sprouts, sliced
2 tablespoons canned chicken broth
1 tablespoon dry sherry
½ teaspoon grated lemon peel
¼ teaspoon salt
Dash pepper

In 9-inch nonstick skillet heat margarine over high heat until bubbly and hot; add chestnuts, bacon, mushrooms, and shallots and sauté, stirring occasionally, until mushrooms are lightly browned, 3 to 4 minutes. Add remaining ingredients and mix well to combine. Reduce heat to low and cook until all liquid evaporates, about 5 minutes.

Each serving provides: ½ Protein Exchange; ½ Bread Exchange; 1¼ Vegetable Exchanges; ½ Fat Exchange; 10 calories Optional Exchange
Per serving: 130 calories; 6 g protein; 4 g fat; 18 g carbohydrate; 560 mg sodium; 7 mg cholesterol

Granny Apple Potato Salad

MAKES 2 SERVINGS

Blue cheese and tart apple make this salad memorable.

1 tablespoon each buttermilk and lemon juice
2 teaspoons reduced-calorie mayonnaise
1½ teaspoons chopped fresh dill or ½ teaspoon dillweed
¼ teaspoon salt
⅛ teaspoon white pepper
1 ounce blue cheese, crumbled
6 ounces peeled cooked potatoes, diced
1 small Granny Smith apple, cored and diced
½ cup diced celery
1 ounce boiled ham, diced

In small mixing bowl combine buttermilk, lemon juice, mayonnaise, dill, salt, and pepper; stir in blue cheese and set aside.

In salad bowl combine potatoes, apple, celery, and ham; add dressing and toss to lightly coat. Cover with plastic wrap and refrigerate for at least 1 hour. Toss again just before serving.

Each serving provides: 1 Protein Exchange; 1 Bread Exchange;
½ Vegetable Exchange; ½ Fat Exchange; ½ Fruit Exchange;
5 calories Optional Exchange
Per serving: 181 calories; 8 g protein; 7 g fat; 23 g carbohydrate;
726 mg sodium; 20 mg cholesterol

Ribbon Pie

MAKES 8 SERVINGS

Coconut and vanilla pudding combine in this delicious Australian dessert.

CRUST

¾ cup all-purpose flour
¼ teaspoon salt
2 tablespoons plus 2 teaspoons margarine
¼ cup plain low-fat yogurt

FILLING

⅓ cup margarine*
2 tablespoons granulated sugar
3 eggs
3 tablespoons lemon juice
1 teaspoon grated lemon peel
2 cups skim milk
1 envelope (four ½-cup servings) reduced-calorie vanilla
    pudding mix
1 teaspoon unflavored gelatin
3 tablespoons shredded coconut, divided

To Prepare Crust: Preheat oven to 400°F. In mixing bowl combine flour and salt; with pastry blender, or 2 knives used scissors-fashion, cut in margarine until mixture resembles coarse meal. Add yogurt and mix thoroughly. Form dough into a ball and roll between 2 sheets of wax paper, forming a circle about ⅛ inch thick.

Fit dough into 9-inch pie plate; flute edges and, using tines of fork, prick bottom and sides of dough. Bake until lightly browned, about 15 minutes; transfer to wire rack and let cool.

To Prepare Pie: In double broiler cream margarine with sugar; beat in eggs, 1 at a time. Stir in lemon juice and lemon peel and cook over hot water, stirring constantly, until thickened, 2 to 3 minutes. Let cool slightly, then turn into cooled pie crust.

(CONTINUED) In 1-quart saucepan combine milk and pudding mix; sprinkle with gelatin and let stand for about 3 minutes to soften. Stir to combine and cook over medium heat until mixture comes to a boil; stir in 2 tablespoons plus 1½ teaspoons coconut and let cool until lukewarm, about 5 minutes. Spread over lemon mixture in pie crust; cover and refrigerate until set, at least 2 hours. Just before serving, sprinkle with remaining 1½ teaspoons coconut.

Each serving provides: ½ Bread Exchange; 3 Fat Exchanges; ½ Milk Exchange; 60 calories Optional Exchange
Per serving: 242 calories; 7 g protein; 14 g fat; 22 g carbohydrate; 268 mg sodium; 104 mg cholesterol

*If preferred, reduced-calorie margarine may be substituted in the filling; reduce Fat Exchange to 2 Exchanges.
Per serving: 207 calories; 7 g protein; 10 g fat; 22 g carbohydrate; 273 mg sodium; 104 mg cholesterol

Cantaloupe Pie

MAKES 6 SERVINGS

Try this uniquely different dessert from New Zealand.

CRUST
½ cup plus 2 tablespoons all-purpose flour
¼ teaspoon salt
3 tablespoons margarine
¼ cup plain low-fat yogurt

FILLING
2 tablespoons each cornstarch and cold water
1 teaspoon unflavored gelatin
3 eggs, separated
3 tablespoons granulated sugar
2 tablespoons lemon juice
½ teaspoon grated lemon peel
¾ cup boiling water
3 cups diced cantaloupe, divided

To Prepare Crust: Preheat oven to 400°F. In mixing bowl combine flour and salt; with pastry blender, or 2 knives used scissors-fashion, cut in margarine until mixture resembles coarse meal. Add yogurt and mix thoroughly. Form dough into a ball and roll between 2 sheets of wax paper, forming a circle about ⅛ inch thick. Fit dough into 9-inch pie plate; flute edges and, using tines of fork, prick bottom and sides of dough. Bake until lightly browned, about 15 minutes; transfer to wire rack and let cool.

To Prepare Pie: In double boiler combine cornstarch and cold water and stir to dissolve; sprinkle with gelatin and let stand to soften. Add egg yolks, sugar, lemon juice, and lemon peel; using wire whisk, gradually beat in boiling water. Cook over hot water, stirring constantly, until mixture thickens, about 5 minutes. Remove from heat and let cool.

In medium mixing bowl, using electric mixer, beat egg whites until stiff peaks form. Gently fold beaten whites and 2½ cups cantaloupe into cooled yolk mixture; spoon into cooled pie crust and refrigerate until set, at least

(CONTINUED)	3 hours. Decoratively arrange remaining ½ cup cantaloupe over surface of pie. Each serving provides: ½ Protein Exchange; ½ Bread Exchange; 1½ Fat Exchanges; ½ Fruit Exchange; 55 calories Optional Exchange Per serving: 208 calories; 6 g protein; 9 g fat; 26 g carbohydrate; 207 mg sodium; 138 mg cholesterol

New Zealand Orangeade

MAKES 2 SERVINGS *Especially delicious when made with freshly squeezed orange juice.*	**1½ cups orange juice (no sugar added)** **1 tablespoon each grated orange peel and lemon juice** **2 teaspoons honey** **½ teaspoon grated lemon peel** **¼ teaspoon each ground ginger and ground cinnamon** **2 whole cloves** **2 cups club soda or seltzer, chilled** In 1-quart saucepan combine orange juice, orange peel, lemon juice, honey, lemon peel, and spices and bring to a boil. Reduce heat to medium and cook, stirring occasionally, until liquid is reduced by half, about 5 minutes. Place sieve over 1-quart heatproof pitcher and pour orange juice mixture through sieve; discard solids. Cover and refrigerate until chilled, at least 30 minutes. Chill two 12-ounce glasses. Add club soda (or seltzer) to juice mixture and stir to combine; pour into chilled glasses. Each serving provides: 1½ Fruit Exchanges; 20 calories Optional Exchange Per serving: 112 calories; 1 g protein; 0.2 g fat; 28 g carbohydrate; 4 mg sodium; 0 mg cholesterol

Pumpkin-Baked Bread Pudding

MAKES 2 SERVINGS

Serving this Australian dessert in the pumpkin shell makes a unique, attractive presentation.

2-pound pumpkin*
1 tablespoon firmly packed dark brown sugar, divided
1 cup evaporated skimmed milk
1 egg
¼ teaspoon each vanilla extract and ground cinnamon
⅛ teaspoon ground nutmeg
2 tablespoons raisins
1 slice white bread, cut into ½-inch cubes

Preheat oven to 375°F. Using sharp knife, cut off stem end of pumpkin to make a lid; remove and discard seeds and stringy pulp from pumpkin. Sprinkle inside of pumpkin with 2 teaspoons sugar; replace lid. Place pumpkin in 9 x 9-inch baking dish and bake for 15 minutes.

While pumpkin is baking, in small mixing bowl combine milk, egg, vanilla, cinnamon, and nutmeg; stir in raisins and bread cubes. Remove baking dish from oven and discard pumpkin lid; fill inside of pumpkin with milk mixture and sprinkle with remaining teaspoon sugar. Pour water into baking dish to a depth of about 1½ inches; return dish to oven and bake until pumpkin is tender and a cake tester, inserted in center of pudding, comes out clean, about 1 hour.

Each serving provides: ½ Protein Exchange; ½ Bread Exchange;
2 Vegetable Exchanges; ½ Fruit Exchange; 1 Milk Exchange;
30 calories Optional Exchange
Per serving: 277 calories; 16 g protein; 4 g fat; 47 g carbohydrate;
248 mg sodium; 142 mg cholesterol

*A 2-pound pumpkin will yield about 2 cups cooked pumpkin.

Belgium, the Netherlands, and Luxembourg

Belgium scored a hit culinarily as well as culturally at the second New York World's Fair some years ago, where one of the most popular attractions was the Belgian waffle. Our "translation," Gaufres, is included here, and, unlike those World's Fair visitors, you won't have to wait in line to eat them.

Among Belgium's edible credits are her superlative vegetables, including what has become known as Belgian endive. We use it in Cream of Endive Soup and in Stuffed Endives au Gratin, as well as in colorful Beet and Endive Salad.

A classic Belgian entrée is Carbonnades. This French word originally meant meat grilled over charcoal *(carbon)*, but today it refers to a rich beef ragout made with beer. One of the most popular dishes in Belgium and in Holland, too, is Waterzooi. The name means "spouting water," but it's actually a stew made with either chicken (as in our recipe) or any freshwater fish. In the hilly northern regions and in neighboring Luxembourg, game like rabbit is plentiful. We offer an unusual dish, Rabbit Flemish Style, richly flavored with dried fruits.

In the Netherlands, foods tend to be simply prepared and wholesome. Fish is a favorite, particularly the herring sold by street vendors. Also welcomed are the famed Dutch cheeses—Edam and Gouda—which show up in one dish after another, including our Fish Fillets "Out of Oven." On chilly afternoons, skaters are happy to return to hearty soups like our Dutch Green Split-Pea Soup. And for a genuine "Dutch treat," savor our Saint Nicholas Spice Cookies, a traditional Christmas cookie that can help you get a gift from the scale!

A Flemish Feast

Cream of Endive Soup*

Chicken Waterzooi*
(Chicken in Creamed Broth)

Braised Endives

Tossed Salad

Gaufres*
(Waffles)

Coffee or Tea

Boerenkass Soup ⏱

This farmers' cheese soup is a blend of interesting flavors from the Netherlands.

2 teaspoons margarine, divided
¼ cup diced onion
1 cup small cauliflower florets
3 ounces pared potato, cut into ½-inch cubes
¼ cup each diced carrot and diced pared celeriac
   (celery root), ½-inch dice
2 cups water
2 packets instant chicken broth and seasoning mix
1½ ounces Canadian-style bacon, cut into 2 equal pieces
2 thin slices white bread (½ ounce each), toasted
1½ ounces Gouda cheese, thinly sliced

In 1½-quart saucepan heat 1 teaspoon margarine until bubbly and hot; add onion and sauté until softened. Add cauliflower, potato, carrot, and celeriac and sauté for 5 minutes. Add water and broth mix and stir to combine; bring to a boil. Reduce heat to low, cover, and let simmer until vegetables are tender-crisp, about 15 minutes.

In small skillet heat remaining teaspoon margarine until bubbly and hot; add bacon and sauté until lightly browned.

Pour soup into 2 individual flameproof crocks or bowls; add 1 piece of bacon to each portion of soup. Top each portion with a toast slice and top each slice of toast with ¾ ounce cheese; broil until cheese is bubbly, 2 to 3 minutes.

Each serving provides: 1½ Protein Exchanges; 1 Bread Exchange; 1¾ Vegetable Exchanges; 1 Fat Exchange; 10 calories Optional Exchange
Per serving: 261 calories; 15 g protein; 12 g fat; 25 g carbohydrate; 1,459 mg sodium; 35 mg cholesterol

Cream of Endive Soup

MAKES 2 SERVINGS

This creamy, hot soup is a Belgian variation on Vichyssoise.

2 teaspoons margarine, divided
2 medium Belgian endives (about 3 ounces each), trimmed, rinsed, and finely chopped
½ cup finely chopped leeks (white portion only)
2 cups skim milk
3 ounces pared potato, diced
¼ teaspoon salt
Dash white pepper

In 2-quart saucepan heat 1 teaspoon margarine over medium heat until bubbly and hot; add endives and leeks and stir to combine. Reduce heat to low, cover, and cook, stirring occasionally, until vegetables are softened, about 10 minutes. Add milk, potato, salt, and pepper and let simmer over low heat, uncovered, stirring frequently, until potato is very soft, about 40 minutes. Stir in remaining teaspoon margarine and serve.

Each serving provides: ½ Bread Exchange; 1½ Vegetable Exchanges; 1 Fat Exchange; 1 Milk Exchange
Per serving: 187 calories; 11 g protein; 4 g fat; 27 g carbohydrate; 452 mg sodium; 5 mg cholesterol

Dutch Green Split-Pea Soup

MAKES 2 SERVINGS

A stick-to-the-ribs cold-weather soup.

2 ounces Canadian-style bacon
2 cups water, divided
1½ ounces sorted uncooked green split peas, rinsed
6 ounces pared potatoes, diced
½ cup each chopped leeks and diced pared celeriac (celery root)
2 tablespoons celery leaves
4 ounces "precooked" kielbasa, sliced into ¼-inch-thick rounds
⅛ teaspoon summer savory leaves
Dash pepper

Cut bacon into small pieces and set aside. In 2-quart saucepan bring 1 cup water to a boil; add peas and boil for 3 minutes. Remove from heat, cover, and let stand for 1 hour.

Add remaining cup water and the bacon to saucepan and bring to a boil. Reduce heat, partially cover, and let simmer for 1 hour. Add potatoes, leeks, celeriac, and celery leaves and cook until vegetables are tender, about 30 minutes. Add kielbasa, savory, and pepper and cook until sausage is heated through.

Each serving provides: 4 Protein Exchanges; 1 Bread Exchange; 1 Vegetable Exchange
Per serving: 404 calories; 22 g protein; 19 g fat; 37 g carbohydrate; 941 mg sodium; 54 mg cholesterol

Fish Fillets "Out of Oven" ⏱

MAKES 2 SERVINGS

A fast, easy, and interesting entrée from the Netherlands.

8 ounces flounder fillets
1½ teaspoons lemon juice
2 teaspoons all-purpose flour
¼ teaspoon salt
Dash each ground nutmeg, dillseed, and pepper
1 tablespoon margarine, divided
1½ ounces Canadian-style bacon, cut into 2 equal pieces
2 tablespoons plain dried bread crumbs
½ ounce Gouda cheese, coarsely shredded
½ ounce blanched almonds, ground

In shallow bowl arrange fillets and sprinkle with lemon juice; let stand for 15 minutes. On sheet of wax paper or a paper plate combine flour, salt, nutmeg, dill, and pepper. Dredge fillets in flour mixture; set aside.

Preheat broiler. In 9-inch skillet that has a metal or removable handle heat 2 teaspoons margarine until bubbly and hot; add bacon and sauté until lightly browned. Using slotted spoon, remove bacon; set aside and keep warm. In same skillet cook fillets over medium heat, turning once, until lightly browned; top fish with bacon, sprinkle with bread crumbs, cheese, and almonds, then dot with remaining teaspoon margarine. Transfer skillet to broiler and broil until cheese is melted and topping is browned, about 3 minutes.

Each serving provides: 4 Protein Exchanges; 1½ Fat Exchanges; 80 calories Optional Exchange
Per serving: 277 calories; 28 g protein; 14 g fat; 9 g carbohydrate; 830 mg sodium; 76 mg cholesterol

Chicken Waterzooi

MAKES 2 SERVINGS

This chicken in creamed broth is our version of the classic Belgian stew.

1 pound 5 ounces chicken parts, skinned
¼ teaspoon salt
Dash white pepper
2 teaspoons margarine
1½ cups hot water
1 medium celery rib, cut into pieces
1 medium leek, trimmed, split in half, and well rinsed
½ medium carrot, cut into pieces
1 packet instant chicken broth and seasoning mix
2 parsley sprigs
3 peppercorns
Dash ground nutmeg
1 tablespoon lemon juice
1 egg, beaten
2 tablespoons evaporated skimmed milk
Garnish: 2 thin lemon slices

Sprinkle chicken with salt and pepper. In 3-quart saucepan heat margarine until bubbly and hot. Reduce heat to low and add chicken; cover and cook, turning chicken occasionally, for 10 minutes *(do not brown)*. Add water, celery, leek, carrot, broth mix, parsley, peppercorns, and nutmeg and bring to a boil. Reduce heat to low, cover, and let simmer until chicken is tender, 35 to 40 minutes.

Using slotted spoon, remove chicken to serving plate and keep warm. Set sieve over bowl and pour broth through sieve; discard solids and return broth to saucepan. Stir in lemon juice.

In small bowl combine egg and milk; gradually stir mixture into broth. Return chicken to pan and cook over low heat until sauce is slightly thickened. Serve garnished with lemon slices.

Each serving provides: 4 Protein Exchanges; 1 Fat Exchange; 15 calories Optional Exchange
Per serving: 257 calories; 32 g protein; 11 g fat; 6 g carbohydrate; 905 mg sodium; 227 mg cholesterol

Stuffed Endives au Gratin

**MAKES 2 SERVINGS,
2 STUFFED
ENDIVES EACH**

*A stylish,
elegant entrée.*

½ cup skim milk
¼ cup each evaporated skimmed milk and
   canned chicken broth
⅛ teaspoon salt
Dash white pepper
1 tablespoon plus 1 teaspoon reduced-calorie margarine
2 tablespoons finely chopped onion
½ teaspoon minced shallot
1 tablespoon all-purpose flour
4 medium Belgian endives (about 3 ounces each)
2 cups water
5 ounces diced cooked chicken
4 thin slices boiled ham (½ ounce each)
1 ounce Gruyère cheese, shredded

In 2-cup measure or small bowl combine skim milk, evaporated milk, broth, salt, and pepper; set aside.

In 1-quart saucepan heat margarine over medium-high heat until bubbly and hot; add onion and shallot and sauté until onion is translucent, 3 to 4 minutes. Sprinkle with flour and, using wire whisk, stir quickly to combine; gradually stir in milk mixture. Reduce heat to low and cook, stirring occasionally, until sauce is smooth and thickened, 15 to 20 minutes.

Carefully trim stem ends of endives (do not remove entire base or leaves will separate). In 9-inch skillet bring water to a boil; reduce heat to medium-low and add endives. Cover and cook until stem ends of endives are fork-tender, 8 to 10 minutes; drain and rinse with cold water.

Preheat oven to 400°F. In medium mixing bowl combine chicken with 2 tablespoons of the sauce and stir until combined. Cut each endive in half lengthwise to within 1 inch of stem end; spread endive open butterfly-fashion and fill each with ¼ of the chicken mixture. Wrap 1 ham slice around each endive and arrange seam-side down in

(CONTINUED)	8 x 8 x 2-inch flameproof baking dish; ladle remaining sauce over endives and sprinkle with cheese. Bake until sauce is bubbly, 10 to 15 minutes. Turn oven control to broil and broil until cheese is lightly browned, 2 to 3 minutes. Each serving provides: 4 Protein Exchanges; 2⅛ Vegetable Exchanges; 1 Fat Exchange; ½ Milk Exchange; 20 calories Optional Exchange Per serving: 363 calories; 38 g protein; 16 g fat; 17 g carbohydrate; 858 mg sodium; 96 mg cholesterol

Endive and Beet Salad

MAKES 2 SERVINGS *An interesting combination heightened by a sharp mustardy dressing.*	**2 medium Belgian endives (about 3 ounces each), trimmed** **½ cup julienne-cut peeled cooked beets (thin strips)** **2 teaspoons olive oil** **1½ teaspoons each white wine vinegar and water** **¼ teaspoon Dijon-style mustard** **⅛ teaspoon salt** **Dash white pepper** Cut endives crosswise into 1-inch pieces and transfer to salad bowl; add beets and toss to combine. In small bowl or a jar with tight-fitting cover combine oil, vinegar, water, mustard, salt, and pepper; mix or shake well. Pour over endives and beets and toss to combine; serve immediately. Each serving provides: 1½ Vegetable Exchanges; 1 Fat Exchange Per serving: 67 calories; 1 g protein; 5 g fat; 6 g carbohydrate; 184 mg sodium; 0 mg cholesterol

Rabbit Flemish Style

MAKES 2 SERVINGS

Fruit marries well with game in this delicious rabbit stew.

4 large pitted prunes
2 tablespoons each raisins and dry sherry
1 tablespoon margarine, divided
2 ounces Canadian-style bacon, diced
9 ounces rabbit, cut into small pieces
½ teaspoon salt
⅛ teaspoon pepper
1 cup small pearl onions
2 teaspoons all-purpose flour
1¼ cups plus 1 tablespoon water, divided
¼ teaspoon thyme leaves
1½ teaspoons granulated sugar
1 teaspoon red wine vinegar

In small bowl combine prunes, raisins, and sherry; set aside. In 3-quart saucepan heat 1 teaspoon margarine until bubbly and hot; add bacon and sauté until lightly browned. Using slotted spoon, remove bacon to plate; set aside.

Using paper towels, pat rabbit dry; sprinkle with salt and pepper. In same pan heat remaining 2 teaspoons margarine until bubbly; add rabbit and sauté, turning frequently, until well browned. Remove rabbit to plate and set aside. In same pan sauté onions until browned. Using slotted spoon, remove onions to a plate; set aside. Sprinkle flour in pan and stir; add 1¼ cups water and, stirring constantly and scraping in particles that cling to bottom and sides of pan, bring to a boil. Return bacon and rabbit to pan and sprinkle with thyme; turn rabbit pieces in liquid, cover, and let simmer until rabbit is almost tender, about 1 hour. Return onions to pan; stir in prune mixture, cover, and let simmer until rabbit is tender, 30 to 40 minutes longer.

Remove rabbit, onions, prunes, and raisins to serving plate; keep warm. Reserve broth. In small saucepan dissolve sugar in tablespoon water. Cook over high heat, stirring constantly, until sugar begins to turn golden; stir in vinegar and about ¼ cup rabbit broth and bring to a boil. Stir into saucepan containing remaining broth and let simmer for 2 minutes. Pour over rabbit and serve.

(CONTINUED)	Each serving provides: 4 Protein Exchanges; 1 Vegetable Exchange; 1½ Fat Exchanges; 1½ Fruit Exchanges; 40 calories Optional Exchange Per serving: 419 calories; 35 g protein; 14 g fat; 35 g carbohydrate; 1,080 mg sodium; 97 mg cholesterol

Flemish Carrots

MAKES 4 SERVINGS

Al dente carrots in a lemony sauce.

1 tablespoon plus 1 teaspoon margarine
3 cups carrot sticks (2-inch-long sticks)
½ teaspoon granulated sugar
¼ teaspoon salt
⅛ teaspoon white pepper
½ cup water
1 egg
¼ cup evaporated skimmed milk
1 teaspoon lemon juice

In 1½-quart saucepan heat margarine until bubbly and hot; add carrots and sauté over medium heat for 5 minutes. Add sugar, salt, and pepper and stir to combine; pour in water and bring to a boil. Reduce heat to low, cover, and let simmer until carrots are tender-crisp, 10 to 15 minutes. Remove saucepan from heat *(do not drain)*.

In small bowl beat together egg and milk; gradually add egg mixture and lemon juice to carrots, stirring to combine. Return to low heat and cook, stirring constantly, for 1 minute longer *(do not boil)*.

Each serving provides: 1½ Vegetable Exchanges; 1 Fat Exchange; 30 calories Optional Exchange
Per serving: 104 calories; 4 g protein; 5 g fat; 11 g carbohydrate; 244 mg sodium; 69 mg cholesterol

Carbonnades de Boeuf

MAKES 2 SERVINGS

Beer adds the special touch to this traditional Belgian beef casserole.

10 ounces boneless chuck, cut into 1-inch cubes
2 teaspoons vegetable oil
½ cup thinly sliced onion
½ garlic clove, minced
2 teaspoons all-purpose flour
½ cup each beer and water
1 parsley sprig
½ small bay leaf
½ packet (about ½ teaspoon) instant beef broth and seasoning mix
½ teaspoon red wine vinegar
⅛ teaspoon each thyme leaves, salt, and pepper
Dash ground nutmeg
1 slice white bread, lightly toasted
1 teaspoon Dijon-style mustard

On rack in broiling pan broil beef, turning once, until rare, 5 minutes on each side.

Preheat oven to 350°F. In 10-inch skillet heat oil over medium-high heat; add onion and garlic and sauté until onion is softened. Add beef, sprinkle with flour, and stir quickly to combine; cook, stirring constantly, for 2 minutes. Gradually stir in beer; add remaining ingredients except bread and mustard and, stirring, bring to a boil. Transfer to 1-quart casserole, cover, and bake until beef is tender, about 1½ hours.

Spread one side of toast evenly with mustard, then cut toast in half. Top beef mixture with toast halves, mustard-side up, and bake, uncovered, for 20 minutes longer. Remove and discard bay leaf and parsley sprig before serving.

Each serving provides: 4 Protein Exchanges; ½ Bread Exchange; ½ Vegetable Exchange; 1 Fat Exchange; 40 calories Optional Exchange
Per serving: 374 calories; 37 g protein; 16 g fat; 15 g carbohydrate; 529 mg sodium; 104 mg cholesterol

Brussels Sprouts-Potato Puree

MAKES 2 SERVINGS

Sour cream lends the tang to this puree.

1½ cups brussels sprouts
3 ounces pared potato, cut into cubes
3 cups water
½ teaspoon salt
2 tablespoons sour cream
2 teaspoons margarine
2 tablespoons minced onion
1 teaspoon all-purpose flour
Dash pepper

In 2-quart saucepan combine brussels sprouts and potato; add water and salt and bring to a boil. Cook until vegetables are fork-tender, about 20 minutes; drain well. Set saucepan with vegetables over low heat and shake pan until vegetables are dry. Transfer vegetables to work bowl of food processor and process just until pureed; transfer puree to bowl and stir in sour cream.

In same saucepan heat margarine until bubbly and hot; add onion and sauté until softened. Sprinkle with flour and stir quickly to combine; cook, stirring constantly, for 1 minute. Add vegetable puree and cook until thoroughly heated (*do not boil*); stir in pepper.

Each serving provides: ½ Bread Exchange; 1½ Vegetable Exchanges; 1 Fat Exchange; 40 calories Optional Exchange
Per serving: 136 calories; 4 g protein; 7 g fat; 16 g carbohydrate; 619 mg sodium; 6 mg cholesterol

Gaufres

**MAKES 4 SERVINGS,
2 WAFFLES EACH**

*For a special treat top
these waffles with
strawberries,
whipped topping,
reduced-calorie
fruit-flavored
spread, or
maple syrup.*

1 tablespoon granulated sugar, divided
½ packet fast-rising active dry yeast
2 tablespoons warm water (see yeast package directions
   for temperature)
1 cup plus 2 tablespoons all-purpose flour
¼ teaspoon salt
1 cup skim milk, heated to lukewarm
2 eggs, separated
2 tablespoons plus 2 teaspoons reduced-calorie
   margarine, melted
½ teaspoon vanilla extract

In small bowl sprinkle 1 teaspoon sugar and the yeast over water and stir to combine; let stand until foamy, about 5 minutes.

Into medium mixing bowl sift together flour, remaining 2 teaspoons sugar, and the salt; stir in yeast mixture, milk, egg yolks, margarine, and vanilla. Using electric mixer at medium speed, beat until smooth.

In separate mixing bowl, using clean beaters, beat egg whites at high speed until stiff peaks form; fold into batter. Let stand in warm draft-free area, stirring every 15 minutes, until mixture is doubled in volume, about 45 minutes.

Preheat nonstick waffle baker* according to manufacturer's directions. Following manufacturer's directions, prepare 8 waffles.

Each serving provides: ½ Protein Exchange; 1½ Bread Exchanges;
  1 Fat Exchange; ¼ Milk Exchange; 15 calories Optional Exchange
Per serving: 238 calories; 9 g protein; 7 g fat; 34 g carbohydrate;
  293 mg sodium; 138 mg cholesterol

Serving Suggestion: Top each portion of waffles with ½ cup ice milk. Increase Optional Exchange to 135 calories.

Per serving: 358 calories; 12 g protein; 10 g fat; 53 g carbohydrate;
  346 mg sodium (estimated); 147 mg cholesterol (estimated)

*If nonstick waffle baker is not available, spray waffle baker with nonstick cooking spray before preheating.

Plum Tart

MAKES 4 SERVINGS

Filling the unbaked tart shell with dry beans will prevent bubbling during baking; save the beans as they can be used over and over again for this purpose.

TART SHELL

¾ cup plus 1 tablespoon all-purpose flour
2 teaspoons granulated sugar
2 tablespoons plus 2 teaspoons reduced-calorie margarine
1 egg, lightly beaten
1 teaspoon grated lemon peel

FILLING

4 medium plums, pitted and cut into ¼-inch-thick
  wedges
2 tablespoons plus 2 teaspoons reduced-calorie
  strawberry spread (16 calories per 2 teaspoons)

To Prepare Tart Shell: In mixing bowl combine flour and sugar; with pastry blender, or 2 knives used scissors-fashion, cut in margarine until mixture resembles coarse meal. Add egg and lemon peel and mix until thoroughly combined. Form dough into a ball, wrap in plastic wrap, and refrigerate for about 2 hours.

Press dough into bottom and around rim of 7-inch tart pan that has a removable bottom; fill shell with uncooked dry beans. Cover and refrigerate for at least 1 hour.*

To Prepare Tart: Preheat oven to 375°F. Bake bean-filled tart shell for 8 minutes; remove beans. Arrange plum wedges cut-side up in concentric circles in pastry shell. Bake in middle of center oven rack until crust is browned and plums are soft, 40 to 45 minutes. Let cool for 10 minutes, then remove tart from pan. In small saucepan heat strawberry spread until melted; brush over warm tart and serve at room temperature.

Each serving provides: 1 Bread Exchange; 1 Fat Exchange; ½ Fruit
  Exchange; 50 calories Optional Exchange
Per serving: 205 calories; 5 g protein; 6 g fat; 34 g carbohydrate;
  109 mg sodium; 69 mg cholesterol

*If preferred, tart shell may be wrapped in plastic freezer wrap and frozen for future use; thaw before baking.

Saint Nicholas Spice Cookies

**MAKES 8 SERVINGS,
4 COOKIES EACH**

*Aniseed, nutmeg,
ginger, and cloves
work their flavor
magic in these
cookies.*

1½ cups all-purpose flour
2 teaspoons ground cinnamon
¼ teaspoon each crushed aniseed and double-acting
   baking powder
⅛ teaspoon each ground nutmeg, ground ginger,
   ground cloves, and salt
⅓ cup reduced-calorie margarine
¼ cup firmly packed light brown sugar
3 tablespoons evaporated skimmed milk
2 ounces shelled almonds, finely chopped

Onto sheet of wax paper or a paper plate sift together
flour, cinnamon, aniseed, baking powder, nutmeg, ginger,
cloves, and salt; set aside. In medium mixing bowl cream
margarine with sugar until fluffy; add dry ingredients
alternately with milk, mixing to form dough.

Preheat oven to 375°F. Spray baking sheet with nonstick
cooking spray. Divide dough in half; between 2 sheets of
wax paper roll 1 half into a 10 x 6-inch rectangle. Remove
paper and cut dough into 16 rectangles, 2½ x 1½ inches
each; transfer to sprayed baking sheet. Repeat procedure
with remaining dough, making 16 more rectangles.
Sprinkle cookies with almonds; bake until cookies are
lightly browned, 12 to 15 minutes. Using spatula, remove
cookies to wire rack; let cool.

Each serving provides: 1 Bread Exchange; 1 Fat Exchange; 75 calories
   Optional Exchange
Per serving: 192 calories; 4 g protein; 8 g fat; 27 g carbohydrate;
   147 mg sodium; 0.2 mg cholesterol

The British Isles

Toad-in-the-Hole, Rumbledethumps, Savouries....Don't be put off by the odd names for these specialties of the British Isles. Toad-in-the-Hole turns out to be a quite respectable egg-and-sausage dish served at high tea. Rumbledethumps may be simpler to cook than to pronounce, for it's a thrifty Scottish casserole of potatoes, cabbage, and cheese, while Savouries are usually the opposite of hors d'oeuvres: spicy *post-meal* bites. (Our recipe converts them into a tasty liver hors d'oeuvre.)

The names may be whimsical, but Britain's fare is usually plain and substantial, making good use of her superb beef, mutton, and dairy products. What could be more typical than Steak and Kidney Pie? Londoners picnic on them daily in the lush parks that dot the city. From scenic Cornwall, we've imported Cornish Pasties (in a version that helps make your mirror image scenic, too!).

Since the British Isles are surrounded by water, it's no surprise that fish is popular. It's the base of Scotland's national dish, Finnan Haddie, named for the fishing village of Findon where it originated and for the fish that's used—haddock. Scotch Broth offers a thrifty way to use up leftovers, as well as a good way to ward off chilly weather. Oatmeal is a legendary Scottish breakfast staple, but the Scots cannily double its usefulness by making Oatmeal Scones, their traditional teatime treat.

On Ireland's verdant shores, Tea Scones brighten the "misting" days, and Irish Stew makes nutritious use of Erin's staple, the potato. Irish cooks discovered long ago that making bread with baking soda instead of yeast is a time-saver, so don't forget to try our Irish Soda Bread. Sure 'n it won't only be Irish eyes that will be smilin'!

A Bit of British Bounty

Savouries*
(Liver Points)

Finnan Haddie with Mustard Sauce*

Rumbledethumps*
(Scottish Potato-and-Cabbage Casserole)

Boiled Sliced Carrots

Irish Soda Bread*

Tea

Scotch Broth

MAKES 2 SERVINGS

A hearty meal on a chilly night. Serve with a mixed green salad.

8 ounces boned lamb (leg or shoulder)
1 quart water, divided
1 teaspoon salt, divided
½ cup pared and diced rutabaga or turnips
¼ cup each diced leek (white portion only), carrot, celery, and onion
2 ounces uncooked pearl barley
3 tablespoons chopped fresh parsley, divided
½ teaspoon pepper

On rack in broiling pan broil lamb, turning once, until rare; let lamb cool slightly, then cut into bite-size pieces (about ½-inch cubes).

In 2-quart saucepan combine 2 cups water, the lamb, and ½ teaspoon salt; bring to a boil. Reduce heat, partially cover pan, and let simmer for 30 minutes. Add vegetables, barley, 2 tablespoons parsley, the pepper, and remaining 2 cups water and ½ teaspoon salt; increase heat and bring to a boil. Reduce heat, partially cover pan, and let simmer until lamb and vegetables are tender, about 45 minutes. Ladle into 2 soup bowls and sprinkle each portion with 1½ teaspoons parsley.

Each serving provides: 3 Protein Exchanges; 1 Bread Exchange;
   1½ Vegetable Exchanges
Per serving with rutabaga: 304 calories; 28 g protein; 6 g fat;
   33 g carbohydrate; 1,194 mg sodium; 85 mg cholesterol
Per serving with turnips: 298 calories; 28 g protein; 6 g fat;
   31 g carbohydrate; 1,208 mg sodium; 85 mg cholesterol

Cornish Pasties

MAKES 4 SERVINGS,
1 PASTY EACH

*Traditionally a
luncheon item,
these may be
served hot or
chilled. They
are usually
accompanied by
spicy-hot
mustard.*

PASTRY
¾ cup all-purpose flour
¼ teaspoon salt
2 tablespoons plus 2 teaspoons margarine
¼ cup plain low-fat yogurt

FILLING
10 ounces boneless beef sirloin or top round steak
2 teaspoons margarine
½ cup each cooked finely diced carrot and pared rutabaga
   or turnips
¼ cup each cooked finely diced onion and celery
1 tablespoon Worcestershire sauce

GLAZE
1 egg white, lightly beaten

To Prepare Pastry: In small bowl combine flour and salt; with
pastry blender, or 2 knives used scissors-fashion, cut in
margarine until mixture resembles coarse meal. Add
yogurt and mix to form soft dough; shape into a ball, wrap
in plastic wrap, and refrigerate for at least 1 hour.

To Prepare Filling: On rack in broiling pan broil steak,
turning once, until rare; set aside and let cool, then dice.
   In small nonstick skillet heat margarine until bubbly and
hot; add meat, vegetables, and Worcestershire sauce and
sauté for 1 minute. Remove meat mixture to a container
and let cool slightly; cover and refrigerate until chilled.

To Prepare Pasties: Preheat oven to 400°F. Cut chilled dough
into 4 equal pieces; roll each piece between 2 sheets of wax
paper, forming four 4-inch circles. Spoon ¼ of the chilled
filling onto each circle and flatten filling slightly; fold
dough in half, enclosing filling and forming 4 pasties. Using
tines of fork, seal edges of each; transfer to nonstick cookie
sheet and brush each with ⅛ of the egg white. Bake for

(CONTINUED)	15 minutes; brush pasties with remaining egg white and bake until golden brown, 10 to 15 minutes longer.

Each serving provides: 2 Protein Exchanges; 1 Bread Exchange; ¾ Vegetable Exchange; 2½ Fat Exchanges; 15 calories Optional Exchange
Per serving with sirloin steak and rutabaga: 323 calories; 23 g protein; 14 g fat; 24 g carbohydrate; 373 mg sodium; 52 mg cholesterol
With sirloin steak and turnips: 320 calories; 23 g protein; 14 g fat; 23 g carbohydrate; 380 mg sodium; 52 mg cholesterol
With round steak and rutabaga: 313 calories; 23 g protein; 13 g fat; 24 g carbohydrate; 372 mg sodium; 52 mg cholesterol
With round steak and turnips: 310 calories; 23 g protein; 13 g fat; 23 g carbohydrate; 379 mg sodium; 52 mg cholesterol

Toad-in-the-Hole ✕

MAKES 6 SERVINGS

Our British cousins serve this for high tea, but it also is a wonderful weekend brunch.

1½ cups skim milk
1 cup plus 2 tablespoons all-purpose flour
3 eggs
¼ teaspoon salt
2 tablespoons margarine
15 ounces cooked veal sausages, cut into 2-inch pieces

In blender container combine milk, flour, eggs, and salt, processing until smooth; refrigerate, covered, for 1 hour.

Preheat oven to 400°F. Spoon margarine into 10 x 6 x 1¾-inch baking dish; heat in oven until margarine is sizzling hot. Carefully remove baking dish from oven and brush margarine over bottom and up sides of dish. Arrange sausage pieces in 1 layer over bottom of baking dish; pour in egg mixture and bake until puffy and browned, 25 to 30 minutes.

Each serving provides: 3 Protein Exchanges; 1 Bread Exchange; 1 Fat Exchange; ¼ Milk Exchange
Per serving: 347 calories; 27 g protein; 16 g fat; 21 g carbohydrate; 1,119 mg sodium (estimated); 210 mg cholesterol

Finnan Haddie
with Mustard Sauce

MAKES 4 SERVINGS

A dinner entrée in true Scottish style. This is the national dish of Scotland.

FISH

1 pound boned smoked haddock, cut into 4 equal pieces
1 cup thinly sliced onions
1 tablespoon peppercorns
2 bay leaves
2 cups water

MUSTARD SAUCE

1 tablespoon plus 1 teaspoon margarine
1 tablespoon all-purpose flour
1 cup skim milk
1 tablespoon Dijon-style mustard
½ teaspoon each powdered mustard and white vinegar
4 to 6 drops hot sauce
Dash pepper

To Prepare Fish: In 10-inch skillet arrange fish; top with onions, peppercorns, and bay leaves. Add water and let soak for 30 minutes.

Bring water to a boil. Reduce heat to low, cover skillet, and let simmer until fish flakes easily at the touch of a fork, about 5 minutes.

To Prepare Sauce: In small saucepan heat margarine until bubbly and hot; add flour and stir quickly to combine. Cook, stirring, for 1 minute. Gradually add milk and, stirring constantly, bring to a boil; cook, stirring, until smooth and thickened. Reduce heat to low and add remaining ingredients; cook for 1 to 2 minutes.

To Serve: Using slotted spoon, transfer fish to serving platter and arrange onions around fish; discard peppercorns and bay leaves. Pour sauce over fish.

Each serving provides: 4 Protein Exchanges; ½ Vegetable Exchange; 1 Fat Exchange; ¼ Milk Exchange; 10 calories Optional Exchange
Per serving: 207 calories; 30 g protein; 5 g fat; 10 g carbohydrate; 7,266 mg sodium; 87 mg cholesterol

Irish Stew

MAKES 4 SERVINGS

A savory mix of carrots, potatoes, and onions with lamb.

1¼ pounds lamb for stew (1-inch cubes)
2 cups plus 2 tablespoons water, divided
½ teaspoon salt
¼ teaspoon pepper
6 ounces pared potatoes, cut into 1-inch cubes
1 cup each sliced carrots (½-inch-thick slices) and
　　onions (½-inch wedges)
¼ teaspoon thyme leaves
2 teaspoons all-purpose flour
1 tablespoon chopped fresh parsley

On rack in broiling pan broil lamb, turning once, until rare. In 3-quart saucepan combine lamb, 2 cups water, and the salt and pepper; bring to a boil. Reduce heat, cover, and let simmer for 1¼ hours. Add potatoes, carrots, onions, and thyme; cover and let simmer until vegetables are tender, about 30 minutes longer. Combine remaining 2 tablespoons water with the flour and stir to dissolve; add to stew and cook, stirring constantly, until liquid is thickened. Serve sprinkled with parsley.

Each serving provides: 4 Protein Exchanges; ½ Bread Exchange;
　1 Vegetable Exchange; 5 calories Optional Exchange
Per serving: 298 calories; 32 g protein; 11 g fat; 15 g carbohydrate;
　368 mg sodium; 113 mg cholesterol

Steak and Kidney Pie

MAKES 8 SERVINGS

This is a classic English favorite.

PASTRY DOUGH

¾ cup all-purpose flour
¼ teaspoon salt
2 tablespoons plus 2 teaspoons margarine
¼ cup plain low-fat yogurt

FILLING

2 teaspoons margarine
15 ounces trimmed beef or veal kidneys, cut into
    small pieces
12 ounces broiled boneless beef sirloin or top round steak
    (rare), cut into small cubes
2 cups each diced onions and sliced mushrooms
1 small garlic clove, minced
1 tablespoon all-purpose flour
1 cup water
1 packet instant beef broth and seasoning mix
1 tablespoon each chopped fresh parsley and red wine or
    dry sherry
1 teaspoon each thyme leaves, pepper, and Worcestershire
    sauce

To Prepare Pastry Dough: In small bowl combine flour and salt; with pastry blender, or 2 knives used scissors-fashion, cut in margarine until mixture resembles coarse meal. Add yogurt and mix thoroughly to form soft dough; shape into a ball, wrap in plastic wrap, and refrigerate for at least 1 hour (may be refrigerated overnight).

To Prepare Filling: In 10-inch nonstick skillet heat margarine until bubbly and hot; add kidneys and steak and sauté, stirring, until kidneys are browned. Remove from pan and set aside. To same skillet add vegetables and garlic; sauté until onions are translucent. Sprinkle flour over mixture and stir quickly to combine; cook, stirring, for 1 minute. Stirring constantly, gradually add water; add broth mix and, stirring, bring to a boil. Reduce heat and add kidneys, steak, and remaining ingredients; let simmer for 5 minutes.

(CONTINUED)

To Prepare Pie: Preheat oven to 400°F. Transfer filling to 8-inch glass pie plate. Between 2 sheets of wax paper roll dough, forming a circle about ⅛ inch thick; carefully lift dough onto pie plate. Trim off excess dough and reserve; crimp edge of dough to rim of pie plate. Make a slight cut in center of dough to allow steam to escape. Reroll reserved dough, form into decorative shapes, and arrange shapes around vent in dough. Bake until golden, about 45 minutes. Remove from oven and let stand 5 minutes before serving.

Each serving provides: 3 Protein Exchanges; ½ Bread Exchange;
  1 Vegetable Exchange; 1 Fat Exchange; 25 calories Optional Exchange
Per serving with sirloin: 276 calories; 25 g protein; 12 g fat;
  16 g carbohydrate; 363 mg sodium; 238 mg cholesterol
With top round steak: 269 calories; 25 g protein; 11 g fat;
  16 g carbohydrate; 362 mg sodium; 238 mg cholesterol

Horseradish Sauce

MAKES 4 SERVINGS

May be served chilled or at room temperature and is delicious as an accompaniment to roast beef or broiled fish.

2 teaspoons margarine
1 teaspoon all-purpose flour
1 cup evaporated skimmed milk
¼ teaspoon each powdered mustard, Worcestershire sauce, and salt
⅛ teaspoon white pepper
3 tablespoons prepared horseradish

In small saucepan heat margarine over medium heat until bubbly and hot; add flour and, using wooden spoon, stir well. Gradually stir in milk and, stirring constantly, cook until smooth. Add seasonings, reduce heat to low, and let simmer, stirring occasionally, until sauce has thickened, 15 to 20 minutes. Transfer to small bowl and let cool for at least 15 minutes. Add horseradish and mix well; cover with plastic wrap and refrigerate until ready to use.

Each serving provides: ½ Fat Exchange; ½ Milk Exchange; 3 calories Optional Exchange
Per serving: 74 calories; 5 g protein; 2 g fat; 9 g carbohydrate; 245 mg sodium; 3 mg cholesterol

Savouries

MAKES 8 SERVINGS,
2 LIVER POINTS
EACH

*The British serve
a savory light
course following a
formal dinner. These
liver points also
make excellent
hors d'oeuvres.*

10 ounces chicken livers
½ cup diced onion
1 tablespoon Worcestershire sauce
2 drained canned anchovy fillets, rinsed
8 thin slices rye bread (½ ounce each)
1 tablespoon plus 1 teaspoon margarine, melted
1 tablespoon grated Parmesan cheese

Spray 8-inch nonstick skillet with nonstick cooking spray
and heat over medium heat; add livers and onion, cover
skillet, and cook until livers are browned and onion is soft,
3 to 4 minutes. Let mixture cool slightly, then transfer to
work bowl of food processor; add Worcestershire sauce
and anchovies and, using an on-off motion, process just to
a smooth paste *(do not puree)*. Set aside.

Trim crusts from bread, reserving crusts; cut each bread
slice in half diagonally, forming 16 triangles. Arrange
triangles and crusts on nonstick cookie sheet and broil until
lightly browned; turn bread over and brown other side.

Turn oven control to 350°F. Transfer crusts to blender
container, setting aside triangles; process until fine crumbs
form. In small bowl combine crumbs, margarine, and
cheese. Spread each toasted triangle with an equal amount
of the liver paste (about 1 tablespoon) and return to cookie
sheet; sprinkle each with an equal amount of the crumb
mixture* and bake until hot, about 3 minutes.

Each serving provides: 1 Protein Exchange; ½ Bread Exchange;
⅛ Vegetable Exchange; ½ Fat Exchange; 5 calories Optional Exchange
Per serving: 112 calories; 9 g protein; 4 g fat; 10 g carbohydrate;
192 mg sodium; 157 mg cholesterol

*Savouries can be prepared in advance to this point, covered, and
refrigerated until ready to use; bake just before serving and serve hot.

Rumbledethumps ⏱

MAKES 4 SERVINGS

This Scottish potato-and-cabbage casserole is a hearty side dish.

12 ounces pared potatoes, boiled
1 tablespoon plus 1 teaspoon reduced-calorie margarine
⅔ cup skim milk
2½ cups shredded green cabbage, blanched
2 teaspoons minced fresh parsley
½ teaspoon salt
⅛ teaspoon white pepper
1 cup finely chopped onions
2 ounces sharp Cheddar cheese, shredded

In medium mixing bowl combine potatoes and margarine; using a potato masher or electric mixer and gradually adding milk, mash potatoes until smooth. Stir in cabbage, parsley, salt, and pepper and set aside.

Preheat oven to 350°F. Spray 8-inch nonstick skillet with nonstick cooking spray; add onions and cook over medium-high heat until translucent. Add onions to potato mixture and stir to combine.

Spray 2-quart casserole with nonstick cooking spray; spread potato mixture in even layer in casserole and sprinkle with cheese. Bake until potatoes are heated through and cheese is golden brown, 30 to 40 minutes.

Each serving provides: ½ Protein Exchange; 1 Bread Exchange; 1¾ Vegetable Exchanges; ½ Fat Exchange; 15 calories Optional Exchange
Per serving: 183 calories; 8 g protein; 7 g fat; 24 g carbohydrate; 446 mg sodium; 16 mg cholesterol

Stovies

MAKES 2 SERVINGS

This skillet potatoes 'n' onions dish is a Scottish treat, traditionally served at Sunday supper with cold meat and beer.

2 teaspoons vegetable oil
9 ounces small new or red potatoes, scrubbed and
    thinly sliced (⅛-inch-thick slices)
1 cup thinly sliced onions
2 tablespoons chopped fresh parsley
½ teaspoon salt
¼ teaspoon freshly ground pepper
¼ cup water

In small nonstick skillet heat oil, then remove from heat. Arrange half of the potatoes in a circular layer on bottom of skillet; top with ½ cup onions and sprinkle with 1 tablespoon parsley, ¼ teaspoon salt, and ⅛ teaspoon pepper. Repeat layers with remaining potatoes, onions, and seasonings; add water, drizzling it down sides of skillet. Return skillet to heat and bring liquid to a boil. Reduce heat and carefully cover skillet with foil or tight-fitting cover; let simmer until potatoes are tender and liquid is absorbed, 25 to 30 minutes.

Each serving provides: 1½ Bread Exchanges; 1 Vegetable Exchange;
    1 Fat Exchange
Per serving: 171 calories; 4 g protein; 5 g fat; 30 g carbohydrate;
    561 mg sodium; 0 mg cholesterol

Oatmeal Scones

MAKES 8 SERVINGS,
1 SCONE EACH

*A favorite in
Scotland. Delicious
with margarine or
reduced-calorie
fruit-flavored
spread.*

1¼ cups plus 1 tablespoon bread flour
1½ teaspoons cream of tartar
1 teaspoon baking soda
½ teaspoon salt
¾ ounce uncooked quick oats
¼ cup each reduced-calorie margarine and skim milk
2 teaspoons molasses

Into medium mixing bowl sift together first 4 ingredients; stir in oats. With pastry blender, or 2 knives used scissors-fashion, cut in margarine until mixture resembles coarse meal; add milk and molasses and stir to form dough.

Preheat oven to 425°F. Turn dough out onto work surface and knead lightly until smooth and elastic; between 2 sheets of wax paper roll dough to form 10-inch circle. Cut dough into 8 wedges. Spray baking sheet with nonstick cooking spray and arrange wedges on sheet; bake for 5 minutes. Using pancake turner, turn scones over and bake until golden brown, about 5 minutes longer.

Each serving provides: 1 Bread Exchange; ½ Fat Exchange; 20 calories Optional Exchange
Per serving: 124 calories; 3 g protein; 3 g fat; 20 g carbohydrate; 312 mg sodium; 0.2 mg cholesterol

Crumpets

MAKES 8 SERVINGS, 1 CRUMPET EACH

These are British cousins to our English muffins.

½ cup skim milk
2 tablespoons plus 2 teaspoons margarine, divided
1 packet fast-rising active dry yeast
¼ cup warm water (see yeast package directions for temperature)
1 tablespoon granulated sugar
1 egg
1½ cups all-purpose flour
½ teaspoon salt

In small saucepan combine milk and 1 tablespoon margarine; heat over medium heat until tiny bubbles form around edge *(do not boil)*. Remove from heat and set aside.

In mixing bowl sprinkle yeast over water; add sugar and stir until dissolved. Let stand until foamy, about 5 minutes. Add milk mixture and egg and beat to combine. Add flour and salt and beat until thoroughly blended; transfer to 1-quart measure (batter should measure about 2 cups). Cover with clean damp towel or plastic wrap and set in warm draft-free area; let stand until batter doubles in volume.

In small pan melt remaining 1 tablespoon plus 2 teaspoons margarine. Set 4 muffin or flan rings* into 10- or 12-inch nonstick skillet and brush inside of each with ⅛ of the melted margarine; spread margarine that drips into skillet over surface of skillet and heat over high heat until margarine is bubbly and hot. Pour ½ cup batter into each ring. Reduce heat to low and cook until bottom of crumpet is browned, about 10 minutes; using spatula, turn rings over and brown other side. Remove crumpets from skillet and repeat procedure, forming 4 more crumpets.

Each serving provides: 1 Bread Exchange; 1 Fat Exchange; 20 calories Optional Exchange
Per serving: 143 calories; 4 g protein; 5 g fat; 21 g carbohydrate; 199 mg sodium; 35 mg cholesterol

*If muffin or flan rings are unavailable, 8-ounce pineapple cans can be used; remove tops and bottoms of cans and thoroughly scrub out cans.

Dundee Cake

MAKES 8 SERVINGS

You can almost hear the Scottish bagpipes as you enjoy this delicacy.

2¼ cups cake flour
1¼ teaspoons double-acting baking powder
¼ teaspoon salt
⅓ cup each golden raisins, dark raisins, and dried currants
½ cup reduced-calorie margarine
¼ cup granulated sugar
4 eggs
1 tablespoon grated orange peel
1 teaspoon grated lemon peel
2 tablespoons lemon juice

Spray 9¼ x 5¼ x 3-inch loaf pan with nonstick cooking spray and set aside. Onto sheet of wax paper sift together flour, baking powder, and salt. In small bowl combine raisins, currants, and 1 tablespoon flour mixture, tossing to coat; set aside.

Preheat oven to 325°F. In large mixing bowl, using electric mixer at medium speed, cream margarine with sugar; add eggs, 1 at a time, beating after each addition. Continue beating until fluffy; beat in orange and lemon peel. Gradually beat in sifted dry ingredients alternately with lemon juice; fold in fruit. Pour batter into sprayed pan and bake for 1 hour to 70 minutes (until cake tester, inserted in center, comes out clean). Let cake cool in pan for 5 minutes, then invert onto wire rack to cool completely.

Each serving provides: ½ Protein Exchange; 1½ Bread Exchanges; 1½ Fat Exchanges; 1 Fruit Exchange; 30 calories Optional Exchange
Per serving: 266 calories; 6 g protein; 9 g fat; 42 g carbohydrate; 308 mg sodium; 137 mg cholesterol

English Cider Cake

MAKES 8 SERVINGS

A traditional English tea loaf.

1½ cups cake flour
1½ teaspoons double-acting baking powder
1 teaspoon ground cinnamon
¼ teaspoon salt
⅛ teaspoon ground nutmeg
2 tablespoons plus 2 teaspoons reduced-calorie margarine
1 tablespoon plus 2 teaspoons granulated sugar
2 eggs
⅔ cup unfermented apple cider (no sugar added)
1 small apple (McIntosh, Granny Smith, etc.), cored, pared, and grated
2 tablespoons golden raisins
1 teaspoon confectioners' sugar

Into medium mixing bowl sift together flour, baking powder, and seasonings; set aside.

Preheat oven to 375°F. In small mixing bowl, using electric mixer at medium speed, cream margarine with granulated sugar; add eggs, 1 at a time, beating well after each addition. Add egg mixture alternately with cider to flour mixture, stirring until batter is smooth; fold in fruit.

Line bottom of 7⅜ x 3⅝ x 2¼-inch loaf pan with wax paper; spray bottom and sides of pan with nonstick cooking spray. Pour batter into pan and bake for 40 to 50 minutes (until cake tester, inserted in center, comes out clean). Let cake cool in pan for 5 minutes, then remove to wire rack and let cool 10 minutes longer. Using a sieve or tea strainer, sift confectioners' sugar over loaf. To serve, cut into 8 equal slices.

Each serving provides: 1 Bread Exchange; ½ Fat Exchange; ½ Fruit Exchange; 35 calories Optional Exchange
Per serving: 153 calories; 3 g protein; 3 g fat; 27 g carbohydrate; 211 mg sodium; 69 mg cholesterol

Irish Kerry Cake

MAKES 6 SERVINGS

Serve lukewarm or at room temperature.

1½ cups cake flour
1½ teaspoons double-acting baking powder
⅛ teaspoon salt
⅓ cup plus 2 teaspoons reduced-calorie margarine
3 tablespoons granulated sugar
3 eggs
3 small tart apples, cored, pared, and diced
1 teaspoon grated lemon peel

Onto sheet of wax paper or a paper plate sift together flour, baking powder, and salt; set aside.

Preheat oven to 375°F. In mixing bowl, using electric mixer at medium speed, cream margarine with sugar; add eggs, 1 at a time, beating well after each addition. Stir in apples and lemon peel; gradually fold in flour mixture.

Spray 8 x 8 x 2-inch baking pan with nonstick cooking spray; pour batter into pan and bake for 25 to 30 minutes (until cake tester, inserted in center, comes out clean). Invert cake onto wire rack and let cool. To serve, cut into 6 equal slices.

Each serving provides: ½ Protein Exchange; 1 Bread Exchange; 1½ Fat Exchanges; ½ Fruit Exchange; 60 calories Optional Exchange
Per serving: 249 calories; 5 g protein; 9 g fat; 37 g carbohydrate; 324 mg sodium; 137 mg cholesterol

Irish Soda Bread

MAKES 20 SERVINGS

Serve with marmalade or margarine. This bread freezes well, either as a whole loaf or in individual slices; thaw at room temperature.

3¾ cups all-purpose flour, divided
¼ cup granulated sugar
1½ teaspoons double-acting baking powder
⅓ cup plus 2 tablespoons margarine, softened
1¼ cups raisins, soaked in warm water until plumped, then drained
1¼ cups buttermilk
1 egg
1 teaspoon baking soda

Spray 9- or 10-inch round baking pan with nonstick baking spray; set aside.

In large bowl combine dry ingredients, reserving 1 tablespoon flour; using pastry blender, or two knives used scissors-fashion, cut in margarine until mixture resembles coarse meal. Stir in raisins. In 2-cup measure or small mixing bowl combine milk, egg, and baking soda, beating until well mixed; pour into flour mixture and stir to combine.

Preheat oven to 350°F. Sprinkle reserved tablespoon flour onto work surface; turn dough out onto floured surface and knead until smooth and elastic. Shape into 8-inch round loaf and place in sprayed pan; cut a cross about ½ inch deep through surface of dough. Bake for about 1 hour (until golden and cake tester, inserted in center, comes out dry). Transfer bread to wire rack and let cool. To serve, cut into 20 equal slices.

Each serving provides: 1 Bread Exchange; 1 Fat Exchange; ½ Fruit Exchange; 25 calories Optional Exchange
Per serving: 169 calories; 4 g protein; 4 g fat; 28 g carbohydrate; 144 mg sodium; 14 mg cholesterol

Tea Scones

MAKES 8 SERVINGS, 1 SCONE EACH

Prepare ahead and freeze this Irish delight to serve when company comes to tea.

2 cups less 2 tablespoons all-purpose flour, divided
1 tablespoon each double-acting baking powder and
    granulated sugar
¼ cup margarine, softened
3 medium eggs
1 medium egg, separated
¼ cup skim milk
½ teaspoon grated orange peel
½ cup dried currants

In large mixing bowl combine 1¾ cups flour with the baking powder and sugar; using pastry blender, or 2 knives used scissors-fashion, cut in margarine until mixture resembles coarse meal.

In bowl, using electric mixer, beat 2 eggs with the egg white, milk, and orange peel just until combined. Make a well in center of flour mixture; pour in egg mixture and, with mixer, gradually blend into flour mixture, combining thoroughly. Add currants and beat at low speed just until combined.

Preheat oven to 400°F. Sprinkle 1 tablespoon flour on work surface and turn dough out onto floured surface; sprinkle remaining tablespoon flour over dough. Using hands, shape dough into an 8- or 9-inch circle; transfer circle to nonstick cookie sheet and cut into 8 wedges. In small cup beat together remaining egg and egg yolk; using half of mixture, brush each wedge with an equal amount of beaten eggs. Bake for 5 minutes; brush each wedge with ⅛ of remaining mixture and bake until golden brown, 8 to 10 minutes longer.

Each serving provides: ½ Protein Exchange; 1 Bread Exchange; 1½ Fat
    Exchanges; ½ Fruit Exchange; 30 calories Optional Exchange
Per serving: 232 calories; 7 g protein; 9 g fat; 32 g carbohydrate;
    266 mg sodium; 137 mg cholesterol

The Caribbean Islands

You can island-hop without leaving your dining table, via our Caribbean recipes. Each island has its native specialties as well as dishes derived from the European country that settled it, but certain foods are universal throughout the Caribbean. The heavy use of spices, such as hot red chili peppers, is a standard feature, and beans and rice (often combined) are daily fare. Pork is the favorite meat, followed by chicken, which appears frequently in the Spanish classic, Arroz con Pollo. For interesting variations, prepare arroz (rice) with fish—another favorite island entrée.

In Trinidad, shellfish is zestily prepared with ginger, garlic, and curry powder, as in our Trinidad Shrimp Stew. Jamaicans prefer codfish served as "Stamp and Go." The name arose when mothers making predawn lunches for children to take to school hastily slapped codfish cakes between slices of bread.

From the Dominican Republic, which mirrors Spanish tastes, comes Sancocho, a stew customarily made with seven types of meat. Our version is prudently limited to one—pork. Martinique and Guadaloupe were once known as the "fortunate islands"—perhaps because they have French cuisines! Martinique's cooks are reputedly the best in the Caribbean; their Eggplant Fritters is an exotic way to serve the vegetable known in France as *aubergine*.

The islands also boast a profusion of colorful fruits—guavas, papayas, mangoes, coconuts, as well as the bananas that flavor our Banana Bread and Frozen Tropical Banana-on-a-Stick. According to an old Caribbean custom, the pineapple has special meaning: it was hung on the door as a symbol of hospitality.

Island Treasures

Cuban Black Bean Soup[*]

Arroz con Pollo[*]
(Chicken with Rice)

Hearts of Palm Sauté[*]

Frozen Tropical Banana-on-a-Stick[*]

Cuban Black Bean Soup

MAKES 4 SERVINGS

A satisfying soup with a subtle mix of flavors.

1 tablespoon plus 1 teaspoon olive oil
½ cup each chopped onion and green bell pepper
1 ounce Canadian-style bacon, diced
1 tablespoon minced fresh cilantro (Chinese parsley)
4 garlic cloves, minced
1 tablespoon red wine vinegar
1½ quarts water
5¼ ounces sorted uncooked black turtle beans (frijoles negros), rinsed
2 packets instant chicken broth and seasoning mix
½ teaspoon each salt, oregano leaves, and ground cumin
1 teaspoon ground red pepper
Garnish: cilantro leaves (Chinese parsley)

In 3-quart saucepan heat oil over medium-high heat; add onion, bell pepper, bacon, minced cilantro, and garlic and sauté until vegetables are softened, 4 to 6 minutes. Add vinegar and sauté for 1 minute longer; add remaining ingredients and bring to a boil. Reduce heat to low and let simmer until beans are tender, 50 to 60 minutes. Let soup cool slightly.

In blender container at low speed, in batches (about 2 cups at a time), process half of soup until pureed; return to saucepan containing remaining soup and cook, stirring occasionally, until thoroughly combined and heated. Serve garnished with cilantro leaves.

Each serving provides: 2 Protein Exchanges; ½ Vegetable Exchange; 1 Fat Exchange; 5 calories Optional Exchange
Per serving: 202 calories; 11 g protein; 6 g fat; 28 g carbohydrate; 806 mg sodium; 4 mg cholesterol

Serving Suggestion: Top each portion of soup with 1 tablespoon sour cream. Increase Optional Exchange to 40 calories.

Per serving: 233 calories; 12 g protein; 9 g fat; 29 g carbohydrate; 813 mg sodium; 10 mg cholesterol

Stamp and Go ⏱

**MAKES 4 SERVINGS,
2 FISH CAKES EACH**

*These fish cakes
come to us
from the island
of Jamaica.*

½ cup chopped onion
8 ounces cooked cod fillets, flaked
¾ cup all-purpose flour
1 teaspoon each double-acting baking powder and salt
¼ teaspoon ground red pepper
½ cup skim milk
1 egg, beaten
1 tablespoon plus 1 teaspoon vegetable oil
Garnish: 4 lemon wedges

Spray 8-inch nonstick skillet with nonstick cooking spray and heat over medium heat; add onion and cook, stirring frequently, until onion is softened, about 1 minute. Transfer onion to medium bowl and add cod, flour, baking powder, salt, and pepper, mixing well to combine; stir in milk and egg.

In 12-inch nonstick skillet heat oil over medium heat; drop fish mixture by heaping tablespoonfuls into skillet, making 8 equal fish cakes. Using back of spoon, press top of each to flatten slightly; cook until golden brown on bottom, 4 to 5 minutes. Using pancake turner, turn cakes over and cook until browned on other side, 4 to 5 minutes longer. Transfer to serving plate and garnish with lemon wedges.

Each serving provides: 2 Protein Exchanges; 1 Bread Exchange; ¼ Vegetable Exchange; 1 Fat Exchange; 30 calories Optional Exchange
Per serving: 220 calories; 18 g protein; 6 g fat; 22 g carbohydrate; 742 mg sodium; 105 mg cholesterol

Trinidad Shrimp Stew
with Gingered Rice

MAKES 2 SERVINGS

A zesty marinade flavors the shrimp, and ginger highlights the rice.

10 ounces shelled and deveined large shrimp
1 medium tomato, blanched, peeled, seeded, and chopped
½ cup thinly sliced onion
1 tablespoon each chopped chives and lime juice
 (no sugar added)
1 green chili pepper, seeded and chopped
1 garlic clove, minced
¼ teaspoon salt, divided
⅛ teaspoon ground thyme
Dash pepper
2 ounces uncooked regular long-grain rice
½ cup water
¼ teaspoon ground ginger
⅛ teaspoon curry powder
1 teaspoon each vegetable oil and margarine

In medium glass or stainless-steel bowl combine shrimp, tomato, onion, chives, lime juice, chili pepper, garlic, ⅛ teaspoon salt, and the thyme and pepper; stir to combine and let marinate at room temperature for 30 minutes.

In small saucepan combine rice, water, ginger, curry powder, and remaining ⅛ teaspoon salt and bring to a boil. Reduce heat to low, cover, and let simmer until rice is tender, 15 to 20 minutes.

In 10-inch nonstick skillet combine oil and margarine and heat until margarine is bubbly and hot; pour shrimp and marinade mixture into pan, cover, and let cook over high heat until shrimp turn pink, about 2 minutes. To serve, arrange gingered rice on serving plate and top with shrimp.

Each serving provides: 4 Protein Exchanges; 1 Bread Exchange;
 1¾ Vegetable Exchanges; 1 Fat Exchange
Per serving: 313 calories; 29 g protein; 6 g fat; 35 g carbohydrate;
 501 mg sodium; 213 mg cholesterol

Arroz con Pollo

MAKES 2 SERVINGS

This chicken with rice entrée is popular fare throughout the Caribbean.

1 tablespoon red wine vinegar
2 garlic cloves, minced
¼ teaspoon oregano leaves
Pepper
1½ pounds chicken parts, skinned
2 teaspoons olive oil
½ cup diced drained canned Italian tomatoes
¼ cup each chopped onion and green bell pepper
1 cup water
3 ounces uncooked regular long-grain rice
4 pimiento-stuffed green olives
1½ teaspoons each drained capers and chopped fresh cilantro (Chinese parsley)
1 packet instant chicken broth and seasoning mix
½ teaspoon salt

In small cup or bowl combine vinegar, garlic, oregano, and ⅛ teaspoon pepper; using pastry brush, lightly brush mixture over chicken. Place chicken on plate, cover with plastic wrap, and refrigerate for at least 1 hour.

In 3-quart saucepan heat oil over medium heat; add chicken and cook, turning occasionally, until chicken is browned on all sides, 6 to 8 minutes. Transfer chicken to plate and set aside.

To same saucepan add tomatoes, onion, and bell pepper and cook over medium-high heat, stirring occasionally, until onions are softened, 3 to 4 minutes; add water, rice, olives, capers, cilantro, broth mix, salt, and ¼ teaspoon pepper and stir to combine. Reduce heat to low and return chicken to pan; cover and let simmer until liquid is absorbed and rice is tender, 25 to 30 minutes.

Each serving provides: 4 Protein Exchanges; 1½ Bread Exchanges; 1 Vegetable Exchange; 1 Fat Exchange; 15 calories Optional Exchange
Per serving: 409 calories; 35 g protein; 10 g fat; 42 g carbohydrate; 1,407 mg sodium; 99 mg cholesterol

Calypso Chicken

MAKES 2 SERVINGS

A heady mix of flavors, from hot chilies to sweet fruit juices.

10 ounces chicken cutlets
2 tablespoons plus ¾ teaspoon all-purpose flour
1 teaspoon each olive oil and margarine
¼ cup chopped scallions (green onions)
2 garlic cloves, minced
¼ cup light rum
½ cup diced fresh or drained canned pineapple chunks
  (no sugar added)
½ cup Chinese snow peas (stem ends and strings removed)
⅓ cup plus 2 teaspoons canned chicken broth
¼ cup each seeded and julienne-cut drained canned Italian
  tomatoes (thin strips) and orange juice (no sugar added)
2 tablespoons plus 2 teaspoons pineapple juice
  (no sugar added)
¾ ounce sliced drained canned water chestnuts
1 strip green chili pepper (½ x ⅛ inch), seeded
Dash finely chopped dried red chili pepper or crushed
  red pepper

Pat chicken dry and cut into 3 x 1-inch strips. On sheet of wax paper or a paper plate sprinkle chicken evenly with flour to coat. In 12-inch skillet combine oil and margarine and heat until margarine is bubbly; add chicken and sauté until lightly browned on all sides. Remove from pan.

In same skillet combine scallions and garlic and sauté briefly (until garlic is lightly browned); carefully pour in rum. Bring mixture to a boil; stir in remaining ingredients except chicken and cook until mixture returns to a boil, about 5 minutes. Return chicken to skillet and cook until liquid has thickened and chicken is heated through, about 10 minutes. Remove and discard fresh chili pepper.

Each serving provides: 4 Protein Exchanges; ½ Bread Exchange;
  1 Vegetable Exchange; 1 Fat Exchange; 1 Fruit Exchange; 80 calories
  Optional Exchange
Per serving with fresh pineapple: 386 calories; 36 g protein; 6 g fat;
  27 g carbohydrate; 361 mg sodium; 82 mg cholesterol
With canned pineapple: 404 calories; 36 g protein; 5 g fat;
  32 g carbohydrate; 362 mg sodium; 82 mg cholesterol

Puerto Rican Lamb
with Orange-Raisin Sauce

MAKES 2 SERVINGS

Tender chunks of lamb are enhanced by this very special sauce.

10 ounces boneless lamb shoulder, cut into 2-inch cubes
1 garlic clove, minced
¼ cup each orange juice (no sugar added) and dry white wine
1 tablespoon each lime juice (no sugar added) and raisins
¾ teaspoon chopped drained capers
½ bay leaf
¼ teaspoon salt
Dash crushed red pepper
2 pimiento-stuffed green olives, sliced

On rack in broiling pan broil lamb 6 inches from heat source, turning once, until rare; set aside.

Spray 2-quart saucepan with nonstick cooking spray and heat over medium heat; add garlic and cook, stirring constantly, until lightly browned, about 1 minute. Add orange juice, wine, lime juice, raisins, capers, and seasonings and stir to combine; bring to a boil, then stir in lamb. Reduce heat to low, cover, and let simmer, stirring occasionally, until meat is fork-tender, about 1½ hours. Add olives and cook until olives are heated through, about 5 minutes longer. Remove and discard bay leaf before serving.

Each serving provides: 4 Protein Exchanges; ½ Fruit Exchange; 35 calories Optional Exchange
Per serving: 294 calories; 31 g protein; 12 g fat; 9 g carbohydrate; 473 mg sodium; 113 mg cholesterol

Eggplant Fritters
à la Martinique

MAKES 2 SERVINGS, 3 FRITTERS EACH

Eggplant a new way, courtesy of the island of Martinique.

1 cup diced pared eggplant (1-inch dice)
¼ cup each finely chopped onion and red bell pepper
1 garlic clove, minced
½ teaspoon each minced green chili pepper and chopped fresh cilantro (Chinese parsley)
⅓ cup plus 2 teaspoons all-purpose flour
½ teaspoon double-acting baking powder
¼ teaspoon salt
⅛ teaspoon pepper
1 egg, beaten
2 teaspoons vegetable oil

Preheat oven to 425°F. Spray nonstick baking sheet with nonstick cooking spray; spread eggplant in an even layer on sprayed sheet and bake until tender, 10 to 15 minutes. Transfer to work bowl of food processor and process until smooth; pour into medium bowl and set aside.

Spray 8-inch nonstick skillet with nonstick cooking spray and heat over medium heat; add onion, bell pepper, garlic, chili pepper, and cilantro and cook, stirring frequently, until vegetables are softened, 2 to 3 minutes. Add onion mixture and remaining ingredients except oil to eggplant mixture and stir to combine.

In 10-inch nonstick skillet heat oil over medium heat; drop batter by heaping tablespoonfuls into skillet, forming 6 equal fritters; using the back of a spoon, press top of each fritter to flatten slightly. Cook until golden brown on bottom, 4 to 5 minutes. Using pancake turner, turn fritters over; cook until browned on other side, 4 to 5 minutes longer.

Each serving provides: ½ Protein Exchange; 1 Bread Exchange; 1½ Vegetable Exchanges; 1 Fat Exchange
Per serving: 194 calories; 7 g protein; 8 g fat; 25 g carbohydrate; 417 mg sodium; 137 mg cholesterol

Haitian Pumpkin Pancakes

MAKES 4 SERVINGS, 6 PANCAKES EACH

A novel pancake that can be served as a side dish or for breakfast.

¾ cup all-purpose flour
1 teaspoon double-acting baking powder
¾ teaspoon baking soda
½ teaspoon each salt and ground cinnamon
¼ teaspoon each ground allspice and ground ginger
1 cup evaporated skimmed milk
½ cup canned or cooked and pureed pumpkin
1 egg
½ teaspoon vanilla extract

Into medium mixing bowl sift together flour, baking powder, baking soda, and seasonings. In separate medium bowl combine remaining ingredients; add to dry ingredients and mix until thoroughly combined.

Spray 9-inch nonstick skillet with nonstick cooking spray and heat over medium heat. Drop batter by rounded tablespoonfuls into skillet, making 6 equal pancakes; cook until underside is browned. Using pancake turner, turn pancakes over and cook until browned on other side. Transfer pancakes to warmed plate and keep warm. Repeat procedure 3 more times, using remaining batter and making 18 more pancakes.

Each serving provides: 1 Bread Exchange; ¼ Vegetable Exchange; ½ Milk Exchange; 20 calories Optional Exchange
Per serving with canned pumpkin: 169 calories; 9 g protein; 2 g fat; 28 g carbohydrate; 627 mg sodium; 71 mg cholesterol
With cooked pumpkin: 165 calories; 9 g protein; 2 g fat; 27 g carbohydrate; 626 mg sodium; 71 mg cholesterol

Serving Suggestion: Top each portion of pancakes with 2 teaspoons reduced-calorie margarine and 1 tablespoon reduced-calorie maple syrup (60 calories per fluid ounce). Add 1 Fat Exchange to Exchange Information and increase Optional Exchange to 50 calories.

Per serving with canned pumpkin: 232 calories; 9 g protein; 6 g fat; 36 g carbohydrate; 718 mg sodium; 71 mg cholesterol
With cooked pumpkin: 227 calories; 9 g protein; 6 g fat; 35 g carbohydrate; 717 mg sodium; 71 mg cholesterol

Haitian Rice and Beans

MAKES 2 SERVINGS

Pink beans, hot pepper, garlic, and bacon make this version of rice and beans special.

1 teaspoon olive oil
¼ cup chopped onion
½ ounce Canadian-style bacon, diced
1½ teaspoons seeded and chopped red chili pepper or dash crushed red pepper
2 garlic cloves, minced
½ cup water
2 ounces drained canned pink beans (reserve 2 tablespoons liquid)
1½ ounces uncooked regular long-grain rice
½ teaspoon each salt and chopped fresh cilantro (Chinese parsley)
⅛ teaspoon pepper

In 1-quart saucepan heat oil over medium heat; add onion, bacon, chili pepper (or crushed pepper), and garlic and sauté, stirring occasionally, until onion is softened, 1 to 2 minutes. Add water, cover, and bring to a boil; stir in beans, reserved liquid, and remaining ingredients. Reduce heat to low and let simmer until rice is tender and liquid is absorbed, about 20 minutes.

Each serving provides: ½ Protein Exchange; 1 Bread Exchange; ¼ Vegetable Exchange; ½ Fat Exchange
Per serving: 159 calories; 6 g protein; 3 g fat; 27 g carbohydrate; 791 mg sodium (estimated); 4 mg cholesterol

Surullitos

These Puerto Rican corn sticks are the perfect accompaniment for chicken or fish.

1 teaspoon salt
Dash white pepper
1½ cups water
3¾ ounces (½ cup plus 2 tablespoons) uncooked yellow cornmeal
2½ ounces Edam cheese, shredded
1 tablespoon plus 2 teaspoons vegetable oil

In 1-quart saucepan combine salt and pepper; pour in water and bring to a boil. Stirring constantly, add cornmeal in a slow stream to boiling water and cook until mixture is smooth and thickened, 2 to 3 minutes; remove saucepan from heat and vigorously stir in cheese. Let stand at room temperature until mixture is cool enough to handle, about 5 minutes; using heaping tablespoonfuls of mixture, shape into ten 3 x 1-inch-long sticks.

In 10-inch nonstick skillet heat oil over medium heat; add corn sticks and cook, turning occasionally, until golden brown on all sides, about 2 minutes on each side. Serve hot or at room temperature.

Each serving provides: ½ Protein Exchange; 1 Bread Exchange; 1 Fat Exchange
Per serving: 153 calories; 5 g protein; 9 g fat; 14 g carbohydrate; 577 mg sodium; 13 mg cholesterol

Hearts of Palm Sauté ⏱

MAKES 2 SERVINGS

An interesting side dish from the Dominican Republic.

1 teaspoon olive oil
2 garlic cloves, minced
½ cup canned Italian tomatoes (with liquid), drain, seed, and chop tomatoes, reserving liquid
2 tablespoons canned chicken broth
1½ teaspoons each chopped fresh parsley and white vinegar
¾ cup drained canned hearts of palm (palmettos), cut into 1-inch pieces
2 pimiento-stuffed green olives, sliced crosswise
1½ teaspoons drained capers
¼ teaspoon salt
⅛ teaspoon pepper
Dash crushed red pepper, or to taste

In 9-inch nonstick skillet heat oil over medium heat; add garlic and sauté for 1 minute. Add tomatoes with reserved liquid, broth, parsley, and vinegar and cook until sauce begins to thicken, 3 to 4 minutes. Reduce heat to low and add remaining ingredients; cook, stirring occasionally, until palm hearts are heated through, 3 to 5 minutes.

Each serving provides: 1¼ Vegetable Exchanges; ½ Fat Exchange; 10 calories Optional Exchange
Per serving: 55 calories; 2 g protein; 3 g fat; 6 g carbohydrate; 525 mg sodium; 0 mg cholesterol

Sancocho de Frijoles

MAKES 4 SERVINGS

A spicy bean stew from the Dominican Republic.

8 ounces boneless pork shoulder, cut into 1-inch cubes
½ cup each chopped onion and green bell pepper
1 tablespoon seeded and minced jalapeño pepper
4 garlic cloves, minced
1 cup canned Italian tomatoes (with liquid), drain, seed, and chop tomatoes, reserving liquid
2 tablespoons white vinegar
1 tablespoon lime juice (no sugar added)
1 quart water
¾ ounce each sorted uncooked pigeon peas and pink beans, rinsed
3 packets instant chicken broth and seasoning mix
1 tablespoon each minced fresh parsley and minced fresh cilantro (Chinese parsley)
1 bay leaf
½ teaspoon oregano leaves
¼ teaspoon each salt and pepper
6 ounces pared sweet potato, cut into ¼-inch-thick slices

 On rack in broiling pan broil pork 6 inches from heat source, turning once, until pork is rare; set aside.

 Spray 3-quart saucepan with nonstick cooking spray and heat over medium heat; add onion, bell pepper, jalapeño pepper, and garlic and cook, stirring frequently, until vegetables are softened, 2 to 3 minutes. Add tomatoes with reserved liquid, vinegar, and lime juice and, stirring constantly, cook for 1 minute. Add water, cooked pork, peas, beans, broth mix, parsley, cilantro, and seasonings; stir to combine. Reduce heat to low, cover pan, and let simmer, stirring occasionally, for 30 to 35 minutes. Stir in sweet potato slices, cover, and continue cooking until potato, beans, and pork are tender, 20 to 25 minutes longer. Remove and discard bay leaf before serving.

Each serving provides: 2 Protein Exchanges; ½ Bread Exchange;
  1 Vegetable Exchange; 10 calories Optional Exchange
Per serving: 235 calories; 16 g protein; 8 g fat; 27 g carbohydrate;
  882 mg sodium; 42 mg cholesterol

Hidden Sushi
Vegetarian Sushi Rolls

Cuban Black Bean Soup
Orange Soup
Soup au Pistou

Minestra di Pasta e Ceci
Misoshiru with Shrimp,
  Tofu, and Radish Sprouts
Boerenkass Soup

Irish Soda Bread

Melon and Asparagus Valenciana

Swedish Hasselback Potatoes

Pork Chops with
Apple and Sauerkraut

Kiwi Vacherin

Cuban Sweet Pepper Sauce

MAKES 4 SERVINGS

Traditionally this sauce is served with Cuban black beans, but it's equally delicious with beef, chicken, or fish.

4 medium red bell peppers
2 teaspoons olive oil
2 garlic cloves, minced
½ cup seeded and chopped drained canned Italian tomatoes
¼ cup tomato puree
¼ teaspoon each granulated sugar and salt
⅛ teaspoon each pepper, ground red pepper, and oregano leaves
1 tablespoon red wine vinegar

On baking sheet broil peppers 3 inches from heat source, turning frequently, until charred on all sides; transfer peppers to brown paper bag and let stand until cool enough to handle, 15 to 20 minutes.

Fit strainer into small bowl and peel peppers over strainer; remove and discard stem ends and seeds, allowing juice from peppers to drip through strainer into bowl. Chop peppers and set aside peppers and juice.

In 1-quart saucepan heat oil over medium heat; add garlic and sauté for 1 minute. Add chopped peppers, juice from peppers, tomatoes, puree, sugar, and seasonings. Reduce heat to low and cook, stirring frequently with wooden spoon, until sauce is thickened, 20 to 25 minutes. Remove from heat and stir in vinegar; transfer to serving bowl and serve warm or at room temperature.

Each serving provides: 2½ Vegetable Exchanges; ½ Fat Exchange;
  1 calorie Optional Exchange
Per serving: 67 calories; 2 g protein; 3 g fat; 11 g carbohydrate;
  250 mg sodium; 0 mg cholesterol

Trinidad Creole Sauce

MAKES 2 SERVINGS

Serve this sauce with pork, beef, chicken, or fish, either hot or at room temperature. For an extra-spicy sauce, add a few more drops hot sauce.

2 teaspoons olive oil
¼ cup each finely chopped onion and green bell pepper
1½ teaspoons all-purpose flour
⅓ cup plus 2 teaspoons canned chicken broth
2 tablespoons dry white wine
1 medium tomato, blanched, peeled, seeded, and chopped
½ teaspoon each lime juice (no sugar added) and white vinegar
⅛ teaspoon each salt and hot sauce

In small saucepan heat oil over medium heat; add onion and bell pepper and sauté, stirring occasionally, until vegetables are softened, 2 to 3 minutes. Sprinkle flour over vegetables and cook, stirring constantly, until mixture is lightly browned, 2 to 3 minutes. Gradually stir in broth; add wine and, stirring constantly, cook until sauce is smooth, about 2 minutes. Reduce heat to low and add remaining ingredients; let simmer until sauce is thickened, 15 to 20 minutes.

Each serving provides: 1½ Vegetable Exchanges; 1 Fat Exchange; 30 calories Optional Exchange
Per serving: 92 calories; 2 g protein; 5 g fat; 8 g carbohydrate; 349 mg sodium; 0 mg cholesterol

Frozen Tropical Banana-on-a-Stick ⊙

MAKES 2 SERVINGS

A favorite with children of all ages.

2 tablespoons plus 2 teaspoons thawed frozen dairy whipped topping
½ ounce shelled peanuts, chopped (about 2 tablespoons)
1 tablespoon chunky-style peanut butter
1 medium banana, peeled
2 teaspoons shredded coconut, toasted and finely chopped

In small bowl, using small wire whisk or fork, combine topping, peanuts, and peanut butter; set aside.

Cut banana in half crosswise. Insert a wooden ice cream bar stick about 2 inches into cut side of each half. Using butter knife or small spatula, spread half of peanut butter mixture over surface of each banana half; sprinkle each with half of the coconut.

Line freezer-safe plate with sheet of wax paper and place banana halves on plate; cover with wax paper and freeze until coating has hardened and bananas are frozen, about 30 minutes.

Each serving provides: ½ Protein Exchange; ½ Fat Exchange; 1 Fruit Exchange; 70 calories Optional Exchange
Per serving: 149 calories; 4 g protein; 8 g fat; 18 g carbohydrate; 50 mg sodium; 0 mg cholesterol

West Indies Banana Bread

**MAKES 12 SERVINGS,
1 SLICE EACH**

*Slices of this bread
can be individually
wrapped in freezer
wrap and frozen for
future use; thaw at
room temperature.*

2¼ cups all-purpose flour
1 tablespoon double-acting baking powder
½ teaspoon each salt and ground cinnamon
¼ teaspoon ground nutmeg
½ cup each granulated sugar and unsalted margarine
1 egg
1 teaspoon vanilla extract
3 very ripe medium bananas, peeled and mashed
¾ cup raisins
2 ounces chopped walnuts
2 tablespoons shredded coconut

Into medium bowl sift together flour, baking powder, salt, cinnamon, and nutmeg; set aside.

Preheat oven to 350°F. In separate medium mixing bowl, using electric mixer, beat together sugar and margarine until light and fluffy; add egg and vanilla and continue beating until mixture is thoroughly combined. Add sifted ingredients alternately with bananas, beating slightly after each addition until mixture is well combined (do not overbeat, as this will cause loaf to become tough). Stir in raisins, nuts, and coconut.

Spray 9 x 5 x 3-inch nonstick loaf pan with nonstick cooking spray and pour batter into pan; bake for about 50 minutes (until loaf is browned and cake tester, inserted in center, comes out clean). Remove loaf from pan to wire rack and let cool. To serve, cut cooled loaf into 12 equal slices.

Each serving provides: 1 Bread Exchange; 2 Fat Exchanges; 1 Fruit
  Exchange; 85 calories Optional Exchange
Per serving: 282 calories; 4 g protein; 12 g fat; 42 g carbohydrate;
  206 mg sodium; 23 mg cholesterol

Central and Eastern Europe

The art of baking thrives throughout central Europe—a lure for sweet-toothed tourists. In fact, the city of Budapest is so pastry-loving that it holds a jubilee to celebrate the anniversary of a torte! However, you won't need a passport to sample our versions of such specialties as Bublanina, Czechoslovakia's renowned cherry cake.

Central and eastern European nations have a lot in common, for they form a union of cuisines. Germany's staples—ham, pork, and noodles—are popular everywhere, while Poland shares the Russian taste for sour cream, reflected in dishes like our Warsaw Salad. From the Baltic has come the abundant use of poppy seeds as well as the caraway that dots an array of foods, including our Liptauer Cheese, a dish popular in both Hungary and Austria.

Hungary is famed for its paprika (the Hungarian word for sweet pepper). Actually, the native spice ranges from mild to tongue-burning, and is used in every imaginable dish—including our versions of the characteristic Stuffed Cabbage and Broiled Chicken Paprika.

Schinkenfleckerln, a ham-and-noodle casserole, is a traditional Austrian dish, as is Viennese Coffee, which has crossed the Atlantic and is now popular in both the New World and the Old.

Switzerland blends the cuisine of its neighbors France, Germany, and Italy. Perhaps the foods most synonymous with this dairy-rich country are its cheeses—Emmentaler, known in the United States as "Swiss cheese," and Gruyère. Use them the way the Swiss do—in Cheese Soup and Rosti Potatoes as well as Swiss Fondue, into which your guests can dip convivially.

A Sampling from the Heart of Europe

Cheese Soup[*]

Hungarian Stuffed Cabbage[*]

Swiss Rosti Potatoes[*]

Warsaw Salad[*]

Bublanina[*]
(Cherry Cake)

Viennese Coffee[*]

Liptauer Cheese

MAKES 4 SERVINGS

This flavorful spread is even better prepared a day in advance. For a traditional snack, serve it with black bread and crisp raw vegetables.

1⅓ cups cottage cheese
3 tablespoons sour cream
2 tablespoons minced onion
1 tablespoon sweet Hungarian paprika
2 teaspoons chopped rinsed capers
1 drained canned anchovy fillet, mashed
1 teaspoon each caraway seed and Dijon-style mustard
¼ teaspoon salt
⅛ teaspoon white pepper

Force cottage cheese through a sieve into a small bowl; add remaining ingredients and stir until thoroughly combined. Cover with plastic wrap and refrigerate for at least 1 hour before serving.

Each serving provides: 1 Protein Exchange; 30 calories Optional Exchange
Per serving: 107 calories; 10 g protein; 6 g fat; 4 g carbohydrate;
    507 mg sodium; 16 mg cholesterol

Cheese Soup

MAKES 2 SERVINGS, ABOUT ¾ CUP EACH

Emmentaler, a native Swiss cheese, gives this satisfying soup its authentic flavor.

2 teaspoons margarine
½ cup diced onion
1 small garlic clove, minced
1 cup water
1 packet instant chicken broth and seasoning mix
⅛ teaspoon caraway seed
Dash ground nutmeg
½ cup skim milk
2 teaspoons all-purpose flour
2 ounces Emmentaler cheese, shredded
Dash white pepper

In 1-quart saucepan heat margarine until bubbly and hot; add onion and garlic and sauté until onion is tender, 2 to 3 minutes. Add water, broth mix, caraway seed, and nutmeg and stir to combine; bring to a boil. Reduce heat to low; let simmer 10 minutes.

In small bowl thoroughly combine milk with flour, making certain that no lumps remain; gradually stir into broth mixture and cook, stirring constantly, until mixture is thickened and bubbly. Add cheese and cook over low heat, stirring constantly, until cheese is partially melted; sprinkle with pepper and serve immediately.

Each serving provides: 1 Protein Exchange; ½ Vegetable Exchange; 1 Fat Exchange; ¼ Milk Exchange; 15 calories Optional Exchange
Per serving: 195 calories; 12 g protein; 12 g fat; 11 g carbohydrate; 571 mg sodium; 27 mg cholesterol

Warsaw Salad

MAKES 2 SERVINGS

Apple is the unexpected ingredient in this Polish salad.

1 medium cucumber, scored and thinly sliced (⅛-inch-thick slices)
4 white radishes, trimmed and thinly sliced (⅛-inch-thick slices)
½ teaspoon salt
1 small Red or Golden Delicious apple, cored and thinly sliced (⅛-inch-thick slices)
1½ teaspoons lemon juice
1 tablespoon sour cream
2 teaspoons mayonnaise
1½ teaspoons minced fresh parsley
¼ teaspoon freshly ground pepper

Set colander into sink or a 2-quart mixing bowl; add cucumber and radishes to colander. Sprinkle vegetables with salt and toss to combine; let stand about 1 hour to drain, discarding accumulated liquid.

In medium mixing bowl combine apple and lemon juice; toss to coat. In small bowl combine remaining ingredients; add drained vegetables and sour cream mixture to apple mixture and toss to combine thoroughly. Serve immediately or cover and refrigerate until chilled; toss again before serving.

Each serving provides: 1¼ Vegetable Exchanges; 1 Fat Exchange; ½ Fruit Exchange; 15 calories Optional Exchange
Per serving: 96 calories; 1 g protein; 5 g fat; 12 g carbohydrate; 185 mg sodium; 6 mg cholesterol

Broiled Chicken Paprika

MAKES 4 SERVINGS

Serve this Hungarian specialty with noodles and a tossed green salad.

2 tablespoons margarine, divided
2 tablespoons lemon juice
1 tablespoon sweet Hungarian paprika, divided
1 small garlic clove, minced
1 whole chicken (3 pounds), skinned and cut into 12 pieces
½ cup diced onion
¼ cup each diced green bell pepper and sliced mushrooms
1 tablespoon all-purpose flour
1 packet instant chicken broth and seasoning mix, dissolved in 1 cup hot water
½ cup tomato sauce
2 teaspoons dry sherry

In small saucepan melt 1 tablespoon margarine; transfer to large glass or stainless-steel bowl. Add lemon juice, 1 teaspoon paprika, and the garlic to melted margarine and stir to combine. Rinse chicken and pat dry with paper towels; add to margarine mixture, turning to coat with marinade. Cover and refrigerate overnight.

Remove chicken from marinade, reserving marinade. Set chicken in broiling pan, skin-side down; broil 20 minutes, basting occasionally with half of the reserved marinade. Turn chicken pieces over; broil, basting occasionally with remaining marinade, until chicken is cooked throughout, 15 to 20 minutes longer. Transfer chicken to serving platter and keep warm; reserve any pan juices.

In 1-quart saucepan heat remaining tablespoon margarine until bubbly and hot; add onion and sauté until translucent. Add green pepper and mushrooms; cook, stirring occasionally, until tender. Sprinkle vegetables with flour and stir quickly to combine; cook, stirring constantly, for 1 minute. Gradually stir in dissolved broth mix; add tomato sauce, sherry, and remaining 2 teaspoons paprika, stir to combine, and bring to a boil. Reduce heat to low and

(CONTINUED) simmer, stirring occasionally, until sauce thickens; stir in reserved pan juices. Serve sauce with chicken.

Each serving provides: 4 Protein Exchanges; 1 Vegetable Exchange; 1½ Fat Exchanges; 15 calories Optional Exchange
Per serving: 261 calories; 32 g protein; 10 g fat; 8 g carbohydrate; 540 mg sodium; 99 mg cholesterol

Schinkenfleckerln

MAKES 2 SERVINGS

In Austria, this ham 'n' noodle casserole sometimes includes caraway seed, and noodles in the shape of little squares are used.

¼ cup skim milk
1 egg, separated
1 tablespoon margarine, melted, divided
⅛ teaspoon pepper
5 ounces boiled ham, cut into ½-inch cubes
1 cup cooked noodles (medium width)
Dash salt

Preheat oven to 375°F. In small mixing bowl combine milk, egg yolk, 2½ teaspoons margarine, and the pepper, mixing thoroughly; add ham and noodles and stir well to combine thoroughly. In separate bowl beat egg white with salt until stiff but not dry; gently fold into noodle mixture.

Grease 2-cup casserole with remaining margarine and spoon noodle mixture into casserole; bake until browned on top, 45 to 50 minutes.

Each serving provides: 3 Protein Exchanges; 1 Bread Exchange; 1½ Fat Exchanges; 10 calories Optional Exchange
Per serving: 304 calories; 22 g protein; 14 g fat; 22 g carbohydrate; 1,037 mg sodium; 200 mg cholesterol

Swiss Fondue ⏱

MAKES 4 SERVINGS

A Swiss classic, popular round the world.

6 ounces Brie cheese, cut into cubes
6 ounces Gruyère cheese, shredded
2 teaspoons cornstarch
1 garlic clove, cut in half
½ cup dry white wine
2 tablespoons dry sherry
½ cup skim milk
⅛ teaspoon white pepper
4 ounces French bread, cut into ½-inch cubes and toasted

In large bowl combine cheeses with cornstarch and toss lightly to coat; set aside.

Rub the inside of top half of double boiler with cut sides of garlic; discard garlic. Add wine and sherry and cook over hot water until mixture begins to steam, 5 to 7 minutes. Gradually stir in cheese-cornstarch mixture, about ¼ cup at a time, and cook over medium heat, stirring constantly with a wooden spoon, until cheese is melted. Stir in milk and pepper and cook, stirring occasionally, until mixture is smooth. Reduce heat to low and keep warm.*

To serve, let each person spear 1 ounce bread, 1 cube at a time, on a long-handled fondue fork and dip into cheese mixture.

Each serving provides: 3 Protein Exchanges; 1 Bread Exchange; 55 calories Optional Exchange
Per serving: 453 calories; 25 g protein; 26 g fat; 21 g carbohydrate; 593 mg sodium; 91 mg cholesterol

*To serve fondue in an authentic fashion, pour cheese mixture into fondue pot. Keep hot over low heat on fondue stand.

Hungarian Sauerkraut

MAKES 2 SERVINGS

Paprika, relish, and a touch of sour cream make this sauerkraut deliciously different.

2 teaspoons margarine
½ cup diced onion
2 ounces each diced cooked Canadian-style bacon and sliced "precooked" smoked beef sausage
2 cups drained sauerkraut,* rinsed
2 tablespoons pickle relish
1 teaspoon sweet Hungarian paprika
½ teaspoon caraway seed
2 tablespoons sour cream

In 9-inch skillet heat margarine over medium heat until bubbly and hot; add onion and sauté until golden. Stir in bacon and sausage; cook, stirring constantly, for 1 minute. Add remaining ingredients except sour cream; stir to combine. Reduce heat, cover, and let simmer until thoroughly heated, about 10 minutes. Divide into 2 portions; top each portion with 1 tablespoon sour cream.

Each serving provides: 2 Protein Exchanges; 2½ Vegetable Exchanges; 1 Fat Exchange; 70 calories Optional Exchange
Per serving: 265 calories; 12 g protein; 18 g fat; 15 g carbohydrate; 1,462 mg sodium (estimated); 36 mg cholesterol

*Use the sauerkraut that is packaged in plastic bags and stored in the refrigerator section of the supermarket; it is usually crisper and less salty than the canned.

Hungarian Stuffed Cabbage

MAKES 4 SERVINGS, 2 STUFFED CABBAGE LEAVES EACH

Cabbage rolls on a bed of sauerkraut make a hearty main dish.

6 ounces broiled ground pork, crumbled (rare)
5 ounces broiled ground beef (preferably ground round or sirloin), crumbled (rare)
1 cup cooked long-grain rice
½ cup finely chopped onion
1 egg, slightly beaten
2 tablespoons minced fresh parsley
1 tablespoon sweet Hungarian paprika, divided
2 garlic cloves, minced
1 teaspoon salt
½ teaspoon each white pepper, divided, and marjoram leaves
8 medium or large green cabbage leaves, blanched
1½ cups drained sauerkraut,* rinsed
1 cup canned Italian tomatoes (with liquid); seed and chop tomatoes, reserving liquid
½ cup canned chicken broth

In medium mixing bowl combine pork, beef, rice, onion, egg, parsley, 2 teaspoons paprika, garlic, salt, ¼ teaspoon pepper, and the marjoram leaves, mixing well. Spoon ⅛ of mixture onto center of each cabbage leaf; fold stem end of leaf over filling, then fold sides over to enclose. Starting from stem end, roll each leaf tightly, tucking in ends as you roll, making 8 stuffed cabbage rolls.

Preheat oven to 350°F. In 10 x 9 x 2-inch baking pan combine sauerkraut, tomatoes with reserved liquid, broth, and remaining teaspoon paprika and ¼ teaspoon pepper, spreading mixture in an even layer over bottom of pan; top with cabbage rolls, seam-side down. Cover pan and bake until cabbage is tender and filling is cooked through, 50 to 60 minutes.

Each serving provides: 3 Protein Exchanges; ½ Bread Exchange; 2½ Vegetable Exchanges; 5 calories Optional Exchange
Per serving with ground round: 327 calories; 28 g protein; 11 g fat; 28 g carbohydrate; 1,310 mg sodium (estimated); 142 mg cholesterol

With ground sirloin: 334 calories; 28 g protein; 12 g fat;
28 g carbohydrate; 1,311 mg sodium (estimated); 142 mg cholesterol

*Use the sauerkraut that is packaged in plastic bags and stored in the refrigerator section of the supermarket; it is usually crisper and less salty than the canned.

Dilled Yellow Squash

MAKES 2 SERVINGS

Sour cream and dill combine in this easy-to-prepare side dish from Hungary.

2 medium yellow straightneck squash, pared, seeded, and cut into 3 x 1-inch strips
½ teaspoon salt
1 teaspoon margarine
¼ cup diced onion
2 teaspoons lemon juice
1½ teaspoons chopped fresh dill, divided
½ teaspoon granulated sugar
⅛ teaspoon sweet Hungarian paprika
1 teaspoon all-purpose flour
1 tablespoon water
3 tablespoons sour cream

In medium bowl toss squash with salt; set a small plate on top of squash and let stand for 1 hour.

Pat squash dry with paper towels. In 9-inch skillet heat margarine until bubbly and hot; add onion and sauté until softened. Add squash, lemon juice, 1 teaspoon dill, and the sugar and paprika; cover and cook over medium heat for 10 minutes, stirring occasionally. Sprinkle flour over squash mixture and stir to combine; add water and bring to a boil. Stir in sour cream and heat *(do not boil)*. Serve hot or chilled, sprinkled with remaining ½ teaspoon dill.

Each serving provides: 2¼ Vegetable Exchanges; ½ Fat Exchange;
60 calories Optional Exchange
Per serving: 110 calories; 3 g protein; 7 g fat; 11 g carbohydrate;
586 mg sodium; 9 mg cholesterol

Green Beans Paprika

MAKES 4 SERVINGS

Hungarian paprika and sour cream add a festive touch to this fast and easy side dish.

2 teaspoons margarine
½ cup sliced onion
1 tablespoon sweet Hungarian paprika
2 teaspoons all-purpose flour
¾ cup canned chicken broth
2 cups trimmed and halved green beans, cooked
1 small tomato, blanched, peeled, seeded, and chopped
⅛ teaspoon each salt and pepper
3 tablespoons sour cream

In 10-inch skillet heat margarine over medium heat until bubbly and hot; add onion and sauté until golden. Add paprika and flour; stir well to combine. Using a wooden spoon, gradually stir in chicken broth; continue to stir until sauce is smooth. Add green beans, tomato, salt, and pepper; stir to combine. Cook until green beans are heated through; stir in sour cream and cook, stirring constantly, until heated throughout *(do not boil)*.

Each serving provides: 1½ Vegetable Exchanges; ½ Fat Exchange;
    40 calories Optional Exchange
Per serving: 86 calories; 3 g protein; 5 g fat; 9 g carbohydrate;
    305 mg sodium; 5 mg cholesterol

Swiss Rosti Potatoes

MAKES 2 SERVINGS

Try this as a side dish with roast beef or chicken, or as a hearty breakfast topped with poached eggs.

6 ounces pared potatoes
1 ounce Swiss cheese, shredded
¼ cup thinly sliced onion
⅛ teaspoon each salt and paprika
Dash pepper

In 1-quart saucepan add potatoes to 2 cups boiling water and cook until potatoes begin to soften but are still firm, about 10 minutes *(do not overcook)*. Drain potatoes and rinse under running cold water; set aside to cool.

In work bowl of food processor, or using a sharp knife, shred potatoes as fine as possible. Transfer to small mixing bowl; add cheese, onion, salt, paprika, and pepper and mix well.

Spray 8-inch nonstick skillet with nonstick cooking spray and heat over medium heat. Spoon half of the potato mixture into pan; using the back of spoon or a pancake turner, press top of mixture to flatten and shape into a circle. Cook until crisp and browned on bottom, about 5 minutes; turn over and cook 5 minutes longer. Remove to plate and keep warm. Repeat procedure, using remaining potato mixture.

Each serving provides: ½ Protein Exchange; 1 Bread Exchange; ¼ Vegetable Exchange
Per serving: 127 calories; 6 g protein; 4 g fat; 17 g carbohydrate; 180 mg sodium; 13 mg cholesterol

Raisin Pie

*Raisins and spice
in a creamy
filling, nestled
in pastry.*

CRUST
½ cup plus 2 tablespoons all-purpose flour
¼ teaspoon salt
3 tablespoons margarine
¼ cup plain low-fat yogurt

FILLING
3 eggs, separated
3 tablespoons granulated sugar
1 teaspoon grated lemon peel
½ teaspoon ground cinnamon
⅛ teaspoon ground cloves
½ cup sour cream
½ cup raisins, chopped
1 tablespoon all-purpose flour

To Prepare Crust: In mixing bowl combine flour and salt; with pastry blender, or 2 knives used scissors-fashion, cut in margarine until mixture resembles coarse meal. Add yogurt and mix thoroughly; form dough into a ball.

Preheat oven to 400°F. Between 2 sheets of wax paper roll dough, forming a 9-inch circle about ⅛ inch thick. Fit dough into an 8-inch pie plate and flute or crimp edge. Using a fork, prick bottom and sides of pie shell; bake until lightly browned, about 10 minutes. Remove crust from oven and let cool while preparing filling; reduce oven temperature to 350°F.

To Prepare Filling: In medium mixing bowl, using electric mixer, beat egg yolks until thick and lemon-colored, about 5 minutes. Add sugar, lemon peel, cinnamon, and cloves and beat 3 minutes longer; add sour cream and stir to combine. In small bowl toss raisins with flour; stir into batter.

In separate medium mixing bowl, using clean beaters, beat egg whites until stiff peaks form; gently fold into

(CONTINUED) batter. Spoon mixture into prepared crust and bake for 25 to 30 minutes (until thin-bladed knife, inserted in center, comes out clean). Transfer to wire rack and let cool; serve warm or at room temperature.

Each serving provides: ½ Protein Exchange; ½ Bread Exchange; 1½ Fat Exchanges; ½ Fruit Exchange; 100 calories Optional Exchange
Per serving: 251 calories; 6 g protein; 13 g fat; 29 g carbohydrate; 210 mg sodium; 146 mg cholesterol

Viennese Coffee

MAKES 2 SERVINGS

This should be served in heated mugs. To heat, pour boiling water into 2 mugs and let stand for a few seconds, then pour out water.

½ cup skim milk
¼ cup evaporated skimmed milk
1¼ cups coffee (hot)
¼ cup thawed frozen dairy whipped topping
¼ ounce semisweet or milk chocolate, shaved or grated
½ teaspoon confectioners' sugar

In small saucepan combine milks and heat over medium heat until tiny bubbles form around edge *(do not boil)*. Divide milk into 2 heated mugs, then pour half of the hot coffee into each mug; top each portion with 2 tablespoons whipped topping and half of the chocolate. Sift an equal amount of sugar over each; serve immediately.

Each serving provides: ½ Milk Exchange; 50 calories Optional Exchange
Per serving: 92 calories; 5 g protein; 3 g fat; 11 g carbohydrate; 70 mg sodium; 2 mg cholesterol

Variation: Before adding whipped topping, add a 3-ounce scoop vanilla dietary frozen dessert to each portion; proceed as directed. Add 1 Fruit Exchange to Exchange Information and increase Milk Exchange to 1 Exchange.

Per serving: 193 calories; 9 g protein; 4 g fat; 31 g carbohydrate; 140 mg sodium; 4 mg cholesterol

Bablanina

MAKES 8 SERVINGS

From Czechoslovakia, a cherry cake that's a delicious end to any dinner.

⅓ cup reduced-calorie margarine
3 tablespoons granulated sugar
1 teaspoon grated lemon peel
½ teaspoon vanilla extract
4 eggs, separated
¾ cup cake flour, sifted
40 large cherries, pitted*

Preheat oven to 350°F. Spray 9-inch round cake pan that has a removable bottom with nonstick cooking spray; set aside.

In large mixing bowl, using electric mixer, beat together margarine, sugar, lemon peel, and vanilla until fluffy; beat in egg yolks, 1 at a time, beating until thick and lemon-colored, about 5 minutes. Continuing to beat, gradually add cake flour.

In separate bowl, using clean beaters, beat egg whites until stiff peaks form; gently fold whites into yolk mixture. Pour batter into prepared pan; using a spatula, smooth top. Arrange cherries on top of batter, spacing them evenly. Bake until lightly browned, 25 to 30 minutes (until cake tester, inserted in center, comes out clean). Transfer pan to wire rack and let cool 10 minutes; remove cake from pan and let cool completely on wire rack.

Each serving provides: ½ Protein Exchange; ½ Bread Exchange; 1 Fat Exchange; ½ Fruit Exchange; 25 calories Optional Exchange
Per serving: 156 calories; 4 g protein; 7 g fat; 20 g carbohydrate; 125 mg sodium; 137 mg cholesterol

*If fresh cherries are not available, 2 cups drained canned cherries (no sugar added) or frozen cherries (no sugar added), thawed and drained, may be substituted.
Per serving: 160 calories; 4 g protein; 7 g fat; 21 g carbohydrate; 125 mg sodium; 137 mg cholesterol

Chocolate-Raspberry Fondue

MAKES 8 SERVINGS

Raspberries and apples are also delicious when dipped into this wonderful dessert.

12 ounces milk chocolate, broken into small pieces
¼ cup each whole milk and raspberry liqueur
2 medium bananas, peeled and cut into ½-inch-thick slices
2 cups strawberries, hulled
2 medium kiwi fruit, pared and cut into eight wedges each
2 small pears, halved, cored, and cut into eight
   wedges each
2 small oranges, peeled and sectioned

In double boiler heat chocolate over hot *(not boiling)* water until chocolate is melted, 3 to 5 minutes; using wire whisk, stir to remove any remaining lumps. Add milk and liqueur and stir until thoroughly combined; continue cooking, stirring frequently, until fondue is heated through, 2 to 3 minutes. Pour into small fondue pot and keep warm over low heat. On serving platter decoratively arrange fruit; to serve, let each person spear fruit on long-handled fondue fork and dip into fondue.

Each serving provides: 1½ Fruit Exchanges; 255 calories Optional
   Exchange
Per serving: 329 calories; 5 g protein; 15 g fat; 47 g carbohydrate;
   45 mg sodium; 10 mg cholesterol

Variation: Chocolate-Orange Fondue—Substitute ¼ cup orange liqueur for the raspberry liqueur.

China

In China, many foods are emblems, so meals often have a message. For example, if you want to wish your dinner companions good health, serve them bamboo shoots. Rice, the number one accompaniment, symbolizes fertility! Noodles symbolize longevity, so it's considered bad luck to break them. Because lions are believed to ward off evil spirits, the Mandarin dish called Lion's Head (pork rolled into a ball resembling the head of the king of the beasts) is very popular. Our meatless version turns that "head" into more convenient patties and also helps ward off sad spirits at the scale!

Chinese cuisine, the world's oldest (5,000 years) and rated the finest along with French, varies from one province to another. The best-known style, both in China and abroad, is Cantonese, which often uses shellfish. Our traditional Cantonese Shrimp with Lobster Sauce is actually lobster-*less*. (The sauce is similar to one that is sometimes used for cooking lobster—hence the name.)

Despite provincial variations, most Chinese dishes share certain ingredients, among them fresh ginger, scallions, dried mushrooms, cornstarch, miso (bean paste), and sesame and peanut oils, while soy sauce is to China what salt is to the West.

The Chinese juggle five basic flavors—salty, sweet, sour, bitter, and pungent, so that no one flavor dominates. An exception is the highly spiced Szechuan cooking of the north, as typified by our Szechuan Squid. The most common cooking methods are steaming— especially in the Shanghai region—and stir-frying, which depends on advance slicing and dicing of foods into bite-size pieces, followed by swift cooking so that vegetables retain their crunchy texture.

Dessert is usually fruit, invariably followed by *cha* (tea), sipped plain. For an authentic touch, wish guests *"ho yum ho sic"* (good drinking, good eating).

Flavors from the Provinces of China

Wonton Soup[*]

Bean Curd Appetizer[*]

Shrimp with Lobster Sauce[*]

Steamed Chinese Snow Peas

Mandarin Almond Jelly[*]

Tea

Bean Curd Appetizer

MAKES 2 SERVINGS

Versatile tofu absorbs the flavors of the dipping sauce.

6 ounces drained firm-style tofu (soybean curd), cut into 1-inch cubes
1 tablespoon cornstarch
1½ teaspoons peanut oil
2 tablespoons soy sauce
1 tablespoon rice vinegar
1½ teaspoons each chopped scallion (green onion) and honey
½ teaspoon chili oil*

Using paper towels, pat tofu dry. On paper plate dredge tofu in cornstarch. In 9-inch skillet or a wok heat peanut oil; add tofu and cook, stirring quickly and frequently, until browned on all sides. Remove to serving plate and keep warm.

In small bowl combine remaining ingredients; serve as a dipping sauce with tofu.

Each serving provides: 1 Protein Exchange; 1 Fat Exchange; 30 calories Optional Exchange
Per serving: 145 calories; 8 g protein; 8 g fat; 12 g carbohydrate; 1,334 mg sodium; 0 mg cholesterol

*Chili oil is a vegetable oil that can be found in Oriental food shops and in the section of the supermarket that carries Oriental products. If not available, substitute any vegetable oil and add ¼ fresh red chili pepper, seeded and chopped, or ⅛ teaspoon chopped dried red chili pepper.

Wonton Soup

MAKES 4 SERVINGS, ABOUT ¾ CUP SOUP AND 5 WONTONS EACH

A classic Chinese soup.

WONTONS
2 ounces cooked ground pork
¼ cup chopped scallions (green onions)
2 teaspoons teriyaki sauce
½ teaspoon cornstarch
¼ teaspoon ground ginger
20 wonton wrappers (3 x 3-inch squares)

SOUP
2¾ quarts water, divided
3 packets instant chicken broth and seasoning mix
1 cup shredded spinach
¼ cup thinly sliced mushrooms

To Prepare Wontons: In small bowl combine pork, scallions, teriyaki sauce, cornstarch, and ginger, mixing well. Spoon an equal amount of pork mixture (about ½ teaspoon) onto center of each wonton wrapper; moisten edges of wrappers with water and fold wrappers in half, triangle-fashion, enclosing filling and forming 20 wontons. Press edges together to seal; bring base corners of each triangle together, overlapping corners, and press to seal. Cover and refrigerate until ready to use.

To Prepare Soup: In 3-quart saucepan bring 2 quarts water to a boil. Add wontons and, when wontons rise to surface, cook for 1 minute longer. Using slotted spoon, remove wontons to plate; set aside. Discard cooking liquid.

In 1-quart saucepan bring remaining 3 cups water to a boil; add broth mix and stir to dissolve. Add spinach and mushrooms and cook for 1 minute; add wontons and cook until heated through.

Each serving provides: ½ Protein Exchange; 1 Bread Exchange; ¾ Vegetable Exchange; 10 calories Optional Exchange
Per serving: 166 calories; 9 g protein; 4 g fat; 24 g carbohydrate; 747 mg sodium; 41 mg cholesterol

Szechuan Squid

MAKES 4 SERVINGS

A squid dish with the hot touch of the province of Szechuan.

1¼ pounds cleaned squid (discard head, tentacles, and ink sac)
1 quart water
1 tablespoon peanut oil
1 teaspoon chili oil*
½ cup each diagonally sliced scallions (green onions) and celery (thin slices)
1 garlic clove, minced
1 tablespoon miso (fermented soybean paste)
2 tablespoons each canned chicken broth, reduced-sodium soy sauce, and dry sherry
2 teaspoons cornstarch

Using a scissors, cut squid open. Lay flat and, using a sharp knife, score inside of squid in a diamond pattern; cut into 1½-inch pieces. In 2-quart saucepan bring water to a boil; add squid and blanch for 30 seconds. Drain and set aside.

In 10-inch skillet or a wok combine oils and heat over medium heat; add scallions, celery, and garlic and sauté for 1 minute. Stir in miso and cook for 30 seconds longer. In small bowl combine broth, soy sauce, sherry, and cornstarch, stirring to dissolve cornstarch; add to vegetable mixture and, stirring constantly, bring to a boil. Add squid and cook until heated through.

Each serving provides: 4 Protein Exchanges; ½ Vegetable Exchange; 1 Fat Exchange; 20 calories Optional Exchange
Per serving: 191 calories; 24 g protein; 6 g fat; 7 g carbohydrate; 159 mg sodium; 78 mg cholesterol

*If chili oil is not available, substitute any vegetable oil and add ½ fresh red chili pepper, seeded and chopped, or ¼ teaspoon chopped dried red chili pepper.

Shrimp with Lobster Sauce

MAKES 4 SERVINGS

Garlic- and ginger-flavored shrimp in a rich sauce.

1 pound 1 ounce large shrimp
2 tablespoons cornstarch, divided
1 tablespoon each dry sherry and water
½ teaspoon salt
2 tablespoons peanut or vegetable oil, divided
2 garlic cloves, minced
1 teaspoon minced pared ginger root
3 ounces cooked ground pork, crumbled
1 cup diagonally sliced scallions (green onions), divided
2 packets instant chicken broth and seasoning mix,
    dissolved in 1½ cups hot water, divided
1 tablespoon each granulated sugar and black bean sauce
    or oyster sauce
2 eggs, lightly beaten
2 cups cooked long-grain rice (hot)

Shell and devein shrimp, leaving tail "feathers" on. In large glass or stainless-steel bowl combine 1 tablespoon cornstarch with the sherry, water, and salt, mixing to dissolve cornstarch; add shrimp and toss to coat. Let stand at room temperature for 20 minutes.

In 12-inch nonstick skillet or a wok heat 1 tablespoon oil over high heat; add shrimp and sherry mixture and cook, stirring quickly and frequently, until shrimp barely turn pink. Remove shrimp from pan and set aside.

In same pan heat remaining tablespoon oil; add garlic and ginger and stir-fry briefly *(be careful not to burn)*. Add pork and stir to combine; add ¾ cup scallions, all but 2 tablespoons dissolved broth mix, and the sugar and black bean (or oyster) sauce and bring to a boil. Reduce heat to low and return shrimp to pan.

In cup or small bowl dissolve remaining tablespoon cornstarch in remaining 2 tablespoons dissolved broth mix; add to shrimp mixture and, stirring constantly, return mixture to a boil. Reduce heat and let simmer for 1 minute.

(CONTINUED)	Gradually stir in eggs, stirring just until eggs have set; remove from heat. Arrange rice on serving plate, spoon shrimp mixture onto rice, and sprinkle with remaining ¼ cup scallions.

Each serving provides: 4 Protein Exchanges; 1 Bread Exchange;
  ½ Vegetable Exchange; 1½ Fat Exchanges; 45 calories Optional
  Exchange
Per serving: 411 calories; 30 g protein; 14 g fat; 37 g carbohydrate;
  1,029 mg sodium; 275 mg cholesterol

Stir-Fried Oysters ○

MAKES 2 SERVINGS

Oysters quick-cooked the Oriental way.

1 teaspoon peanut oil
1½ teaspoons each minced pared ginger root and hoisin
  sauce
1 garlic clove, minced
18 small oysters, shucked
1½ teaspoons soy sauce
1 teaspoon dry sherry
½ teaspoon cornstarch, dissolved in 1½ teaspoons water
¼ cup diagonally sliced scallions (green onions)

In 10-inch nonstick skillet heat oil over medium heat; add ginger, hoisin sauce, and garlic and cook, stirring quickly and frequently, for 15 seconds *(be careful not to burn)*. Add oysters to skillet in a single layer, sprinkle with soy sauce and sherry, and let cook for 1 minute *(do not stir)*; stir in dissolved cornstarch and cook, stirring constantly, until mixture thickens. Transfer to serving plate and sprinkle with scallions.

Each serving provides: 3 Protein Exchanges; ¼ Vegetable Exchange;
  ½ Fat Exchange; 15 calories Optional Exchange
Per serving: 99 calories; 8 g protein; 4 g fat; 7 g carbohydrate;
  523 mg sodium; 43 mg cholesterol

Chicken and Chestnuts

MAKES 2 SERVINGS

Chestnuts lend an unusual taste to this entrée.

10 ounces skinned and boned chicken, cut into 1½-inch pieces
1 tablespoon reduced-sodium soy sauce
1½ teaspoons peanut oil
¼ cup diced red bell pepper
2 tablespoons chopped scallion (green onion)
½ garlic clove, minced
¼ teaspoon minced pared ginger root
6 small chestnuts, boiled and peeled
¾ cup water
1 tablespoon dry sherry
½ packet (about ½ teaspoon) instant chicken broth and seasoning mix
1 teaspoon cornstarch
½ teaspoon each granulated sugar and Chinese sesame oil
Dash pepper

In medium bowl combine chicken and soy sauce; cover with plastic wrap and let stand at room temperature for 30 minutes.

In 9-inch skillet or a wok heat peanut oil over medium heat; add bell pepper, scallion, garlic, and ginger and sauté until vegetables are tender, about 2 minutes.

Drain chicken, reserving marinade. Add chicken, a few pieces at a time, to vegetable mixture, stirring after each addition. Add chestnuts, increase heat to high, and cook, stirring constantly, until chicken begins to brown, about 2 minutes; stir in water, sherry, and broth mix and bring to a boil. Reduce heat to low and let simmer for 1 minute. To reserved marinade add cornstarch, sugar, sesame oil, and pepper and stir to dissolve cornstarch; pour over chicken mixture and, stirring constantly, bring to a boil and cook until thickened.

Each serving provides: 4 Protein Exchanges; ½ Bread Exchange; ¼ Vegetable Exchange; 1 Fat Exchange; 20 calories Optional Exchange
Per serving: 328 calories; 33 g protein; 10 g fat; 24 g carbohydrate; 627 mg sodium; 99 mg cholesterol

Orange Chicken ⏱

MAKES 4 SERVINGS

*Orange zest gives
this dish color
and piquancy.*

1¼ pounds skinned and boned chicken, cut into
   1½-inch pieces
⅓ cup plus 2 teaspoons dry sherry, divided
¼ teaspoon salt
1 tablespoon plus 1 teaspoon peanut oil
½ cup julienne-cut red bell pepper
¼ cup diagonally sliced scallions (green onions)
Zest of ½ small orange,* cut into 2 x ⅛-inch strips
   and blanched
1 garlic clove, minced
1 tablespoon each reduced-sodium soy sauce and water
1 teaspoon each cornstarch, granulated sugar, and
   rice vinegar
Garnish: 4 trimmed scallions (about 4 inches long each)

In glass or stainless-steel medium bowl combine chicken, 3 tablespoons sherry, and the salt and let stand at room temperature for 30 minutes.

In 9-inch skillet or a wok heat oil over medium-high heat; add bell pepper, scallions, orange zest, and garlic and cook, stirring quickly and frequently, until vegetables are tender-crisp, about 3 minutes. Using slotted spoon remove chicken from marinade, reserving marinade; add chicken to skillet (or wok), increase heat, and continue stir-frying until browned, about 5 minutes.

To reserved marinade add remaining 3 tablespoons sherry and the soy sauce, water, cornstarch, sugar, and vinegar and stir to dissolve cornstarch. Pour over chicken mixture and cook, stirring constantly, until mixture thickens. Serve garnished with scallions.

Each serving provides: 4 Protein Exchanges; ½ Vegetable Exchange;
  1 Fat Exchange; 30 calories Optional Exchange
Per serving: 260 calories; 31 g protein; 9 g fat; 6 g carbohydrate;
  400 mg sodium; 99 mg cholesterol

*The zest of the orange is the peel without any of the pith (white membrane). To remove zest from orange, use a zester or vegetable peeler; wrap orange in plastic wrap and refrigerate for use at another time.

Lion's Head Casserole ⏱

MAKES 4 SERVINGS

Spiced tofu on a bed of Chinese cabbage, a specialty of eastern China.

1 tablespoon peanut oil
1 teaspoon Chinese sesame oil
1 cup chopped scallions (green onions)
2 garlic cloves, minced
1 teaspoon minced pared ginger root
15 ounces drained tofu (soybean curd), mashed
3 eggs
1 tablespoon each cornstarch and reduced-sodium
  soy sauce
2 packets instant chicken broth and seasoning mix
4 cups shredded Chinese cabbage, divided
1 cup hot water
2 tablespoons dry sherry

In 8-inch skillet combine oils and heat; add scallions, garlic, and ginger and sauté until scallions are softened, about 1 minute. Transfer half of scallion mixture to medium mixing bowl, reserving remaining mixture; add tofu, eggs, cornstarch, soy sauce, and 1 packet broth mix and, using wooden spoon, combine thoroughly.

In bottom of 3-quart flameproof casserole spread 2 cups cabbage. In small bowl combine remaining packet broth mix with hot water and stir to dissolve; pour over cabbage in casserole. Using a tablespoon or your hands, shape tofu mixture into 8 equal patties and arrange patties over cabbage in casserole; top with remaining 2 cups cabbage and the sautéed scallions. Add sherry, cover casserole, and cook over low heat until patties are firm, about 40 minutes (check occasionally to be sure liquid does not evaporate; if necessary add some water).

Each serving provides: 2 Protein Exchanges; 2½ Vegetable Exchanges; 1 Fat Exchange; 20 calories Optional Exchange
Per serving: 225 calories; 15 g protein; 13 g fat; 12 g carbohydrate; 647 mg sodium; 206 mg cholesterol

Turkish
Sis Kebab

Empanaditas

Tostadas

Steak and Kidney Pie

Boston
Brown Bread

Caldo Gallego
Portuguese Clams
Gambas con Salsa Verde

Panettone

Chinese Cold Noodles in Sesame Sauce

MAKES 2 SERVINGS

Delicious peanutty-flavored noodles.

3 tablespoons canned chicken broth
2 tablespoons smooth peanut butter
1 tablespoon soy sauce
¼ teaspoon minced pared ginger root
⅛ teaspoon minced fresh garlic
½ teaspoon Chinese sesame oil
Dash ground red pepper, or to taste
1 cup cooked thin spaghetti, chilled
¼ cup chopped scallions (green onions)
½ ounce shelled roasted peanuts, chopped

In small saucepan combine broth, peanut butter, soy sauce, ginger, and garlic and cook over medium heat, stirring frequently, until mixture comes to a boil; remove from heat and stir in oil and pepper. Transfer to small bowl, cover with plastic wrap, and refrigerate for at least 30 minutes.

In serving bowl combine spaghetti with sauce and toss to combine; sprinkle with scallions and peanuts.

Each serving provides: 1 Protein Exchange; 1 Bread Exchange;
¼ Vegetable Exchange; 1 Fat Exchange; 55 calories Optional Exchange
Per serving: 222 calories; 9 g protein; 12 g fat; 22 g carbohydrate;
863 mg sodium; 0 mg cholesterol

"Fried" Wontons
with Orange Dipping Sauce

The sweet-sour dipping sauce makes these special.

WONTONS

1 ounce each cooked ground pork and chopped cooked shrimp
¼ cup each finely chopped scallions (green onions) and finely shredded Chinese cabbage
2 teaspoons reduced-sodium soy sauce
½ teaspoon cornstarch
¼ teaspoon ground ginger
20 wonton wrappers (3 x 3-inch squares)
1 tablespoon peanut oil
2 teaspoons reduced-calorie margarine
2 tablespoons teriyaki sauce

DIPPING SAUCE

1 tablespoon plus 1 teaspoon reduced-calorie orange marmalade (16 calories per 2 teaspoons)
2 teaspoons each hoisin sauce and rice vinegar

To Prepare Wontons: In medium bowl combine pork, shrimp, scallions, cabbage, soy sauce, cornstarch, and ginger, mixing well. Spoon an equal amount of pork mixture (about 1 teaspoon) onto center of each wonton wrapper; moisten edges of wrappers with water and fold wrappers in half, triangle-fashion, enclosing filling and forming 20 wontons. Press edges together to seal; bring base corners of each triangle together, overlapping corners, and press to seal.

In 12-inch nonstick skillet or a wok combine oil and margarine and heat, over high heat, until margarine is bubbly and hot; add wontons and cook, turning frequently, until browned on all sides. Add teriyaki sauce and bring to a boil, stirring to coat wontons; using slotted spoon, remove wontons to serving plate, reserving pan drippings. Set wontons aside and keep warm.

(CONTINUED)	*To Prepare Dipping Sauce:* To same skillet (or wok) add ingredients for dipping sauce and stir to combine with pan drippings; pour into small bowl and serve with wontons.
	Each serving provides: ½ Protein Exchange; 1 Bread Exchange; ¼ Vegetable Exchange; 1 Fat Exchange; 15 calories Optional Exchange Per serving: 200 calories; 8 g protein; 7 g fat; 26 g carbohydrate; 527 mg sodium; 44 mg cholesterol

Hot and Sour Cabbage

MAKES 2 SERVINGS

Chinese cabbage in a flavorful, spicy marinade.

2 cups coarsely shredded Chinese cabbage
½ teaspoon salt
½ small red chili pepper, seeded and thinly sliced
½ teaspoon minced pared ginger root
2 teaspoons Chinese sesame oil
1 tablespoon rice vinegar
½ teaspoon granulated sugar
Dash pepper

In 1-quart glass or stainless-steel bowl combine cabbage and salt and toss lightly to combine; cover with plastic wrap and let stand at room temperature for 2 hours. Add chili pepper and ginger to cabbage and toss to combine.

In small saucepan heat oil; remove from heat and add vinegar, sugar, and pepper, stirring to dissolve sugar. Pour over cabbage and toss to coat; cover with plastic wrap and let stand for about 1 hour to allow flavors to blend.

Each serving provides: 2⅛ Vegetable Exchanges; 1 Fat Exchange; 5 calories Optional Exchange
Per serving: 60 calories; 1 g protein; 5 g fat; 5 g carbohydrate; 564 mg sodium; 0 mg cholesterol

Sautéed Eggplant with Bean Paste

MAKES 2 SERVINGS

Enjoy this dish as an appetizer or as an accompaniment to your entrée; serve warm or chilled.

1 cup cubed pared eggplant
½ teaspoon salt
1½ teaspoons peanut or vegetable oil
½ teaspoon Chinese sesame oil
2 tablespoons chopped scallion (green onion)
1 garlic clove, minced
½ teaspoon minced pared ginger root
1 tablespoon each canned chicken broth and dry sherry
1½ teaspoons reduced-sodium soy sauce
½ teaspoon miso (fermented soybean paste)
¼ teaspoon granulated sugar

In colander set in sink combine eggplant and salt, tossing thoroughly; place a plate on top of eggplant and set a can onto plate to weigh it down. Let eggplant drain for about 1 hour. Rinse eggplant under running cold water and, using paper towels, dry gently but thoroughly.

In 9-inch skillet or a wok combine oils and heat over medium heat; add scallion, garlic, and ginger and sauté for 1 minute. Add eggplant and cook, stirring occasionally, until eggplant is fork-tender and begins to brown, about 5 minutes; add remaining ingredients and stir to combine. Reduce heat to low and cook for about 2 minutes longer to blend flavors.

Each serving provides: 1⅛ Vegetable Exchanges; 1 Fat Exchange;
    15 calories Optional Exchange
Per serving: 75 calories; 1 g protein; 5 g fat; 5 g carbohydrate;
    325 mg sodium; 0 mg cholesterol

Sesame Spinach

MAKES 2 SERVINGS

Fresh spinach enhanced with ginger, sesame oil, and sesame seed.

1½ teaspoons peanut oil
½ garlic clove, minced
½ teaspoon minced pared ginger root
2 cups firmly packed spinach leaves, washed well and drained
¼ teaspoon salt
⅛ teaspoon granulated sugar
½ teaspoon each Chinese sesame oil and toasted sesame seed

In 10-inch skillet or a wok heat peanut oil; add garlic and ginger and sauté briefly, about 30 seconds. Add spinach; sprinkle with salt and sugar, cover, and cook over medium heat until spinach is wilted, about 3 minutes. Sprinkle sesame oil around sides of pan and stir to combine. Transfer to serving bowl and sprinkle with sesame seed.

Each serving provides: 2 Vegetable Exchanges; 1 Fat Exchange; 5 calories Optional Exchange
Per serving: 60 calories; 2 g protein; 5 g fat; 3 g carbohydrate; 310 mg sodium; 0 mg cholesterol

Mandarin Almond Jelly

MAKES 4 SERVINGS

A light and delicious dessert.

1 envelope unflavored gelatin
2 cups skim milk, divided
1 tablespoon plus 1 teaspoon granulated sugar, divided
1 tablespoon almond extract
1 cup canned mandarin orange sections (no sugar added), drain and reserve juice (about ¼ cup)
½ teaspoon cornstarch

In 1-quart saucepan sprinkle gelatin over ½ cup milk and let stand to soften; cook over medium heat, stirring constantly, until gelatin is completely dissolved. Remove from heat and add remaining 1½ cups milk, 1 tablespoon sugar, and the almond extract. Pour mixture into four ½-cup dessert dishes, cover, and refrigerate until set, about 1½ hours.

In small saucepan blend reserved juice from orange sections with remaining teaspoon sugar and the cornstarch, stirring until cornstarch is dissolved; cook over medium heat, stirring constantly, until thickened. Remove from heat; add orange sections and stir to coat. Cover and refrigerate until chilled, about 30 minutes.

To serve, top each portion of almond jelly with ¼ of the orange topping.

Each serving provides: ½ Fruit Exchange; ½ Milk Exchange; 20 calories Optional Exchange
Per serving: 99 calories; 6 g protein; 0.2 g fat; 16 g carbohydrate; 68 mg sodium; 2 mg cholesterol

France

The world's most lauded cuisine doesn't have to be fattening, for the savvy French have streamlined their sauces, and today their *nouvelle cuisine* is in tune with sound nutritional thinking.

So come with us to France on a cook's tour (literally!). Although the dishes vary from one province to another, certain culinary arts are national hallmarks. One is the respect for fresh vegetables, which are artfully arranged in salads or combined in delicious soups like our Soup au Pistou from Provence—where dishes tend to be spiciest.

French cooks are also renowned for their skillful use of seasonings, which they believe should *enhance* the food's natural flavor, not overwhelm it. It's this skill that turns fish into delicacies like Salmon en Papillote, and that transforms ordinary steak into the gourmet favorite, Steak au Poivre (pepper steak).

Typical of French regional cookery is Cassoulet, a thrifty dried bean-and-meat stew that originated in the area around Toulouse; you'll find our recipe, which uses chicken and sausages, a convenient do-ahead dish. Another favorite French stew is Veal Marengo, a dish created by Napoleon's chef in honor of the Emperor's victory at the Battle of Marengo.

Where battles are concerned, you won't have to meet your Waterloo at dessert time, for you can enjoy our variations on some of France's most famed temptations, including a Vacherin (meringue) exotically flavored with kiwi. The French traditionally use sherbets to refresh the palate during banquets. Refresh yours safely with our Pear Sorbet.

No French meal is considered complete without wine, but here's an international tip. Your wine portion will go twice as far when mixed with seltzer to concoct a spritzer. *A votre santé!*

A French Provincial Fête

Soup au Pistou*
(Vegetable Soup with Garlic and Basil)

Cassoulet*

Braised Lettuce with Vegetables*

Brioche*

Red Wine Spritzer
(2 fluid ounces red wine with club soda)

Black Cherry Clafouti*
(French Fruit Pudding)

Coffee or Tea

Soup au Pistou

MAKES 8 SERVINGS, ABOUT 1 CUP EACH

A hearty vegetable soup laced with fresh basil, garlic, and robust Parmesan cheese.

SOUP

1¼ ounces sorted uncooked red kidney beans, rinsed
1 ounce sorted uncooked great northern beans, rinsed
2 quarts water
½ cup each diced onion and sliced celery
6 ounces pared potato, cut into ¼-inch cubes
4 small plum tomatoes, blanched, peeled, seeded, and diced
¾ cup each sliced carrots and zucchini
½ cup diagonally sliced green beans
2 tablespoons tomato paste
2 bay leaves
Dash pepper
3 ounces uncooked small macaroni (e.g., ditalini, elbows)

PISTOU

1 cup fresh basil leaves
2 tablespoons hot water
1 tablespoon plus 1 teaspoon olive oil
2 garlic cloves, minced
1 ounce grated Parmesan cheese

To Prepare Soup: In 4-quart saucepan combine beans; add water and bring to a boil. Reduce heat to low, add onion and celery, and simmer for 30 minutes. Add remaining ingredients for soup except macaroni and simmer until vegetables and beans are tender, 45 minutes to 1 hour. Add macaroni, stir, and cook for about 5 minutes.

To Prepare Pistou: While macaroni is cooking, in blender container combine all ingredients for pistou except cheese; process until smooth, scraping down sides of container as necessary. Transfer to small bowl and stir in cheese.

To Serve: Remove and discard bay leaves from soup. Into each of 8 soup bowls spoon ⅛ of the pistou, then ladle ⅛ of the soup over pistou; serve immediately.

Each serving provides: ½ Protein Exchange; ½ Bread Exchange;
1 Vegetable Exchange; ½ Fat Exchange; 25 calories Optional Exchange
Per serving: 148 calories; 6 g protein; 4 g fat; 23 g carbohydrate;
116 mg sodium; 3 mg cholesterol

Salmon en Papillote

MAKES 2 SERVINGS

This foil-baked salmon is an interesting blend of colors, flavors, and textures.

2 teaspoons olive oil, divided
1 medium carrot (about 4 ounces), cut into long matchstick pieces
1 medium zucchini (about 5 ounces), cut into long matchstick pieces
1 medium leek, cut into long matchstick pieces
1 tablespoon minced shallots
¼ cup water
1 tablespoon plus 1 teaspoon dry vermouth
1 tablespoon each minced fresh parsley and lemon juice
1 teaspoon each grated lemon peel and Dijon-style mustard
¼ teaspoon salt
⅛ teaspoon white pepper
2 salmon steaks (6 ounces each)

In 10-inch skillet heat 1 teaspoon oil over medium-high heat; add carrot, zucchini, leek, and shallots and sauté until slightly tender, 3 to 4 minutes. Stir in remaining ingredients except fish and cook, stirring occasionally, for 2 minutes.

Preheat oven to 375°F. Using pastry brush, grease centers of two 15-inch-long sheets of foil with ½ teaspoon oil each; place a salmon steak on center of each sheet. Spoon half of vegetable mixture and liquid over each steak; fold foil over steaks to enclose, crimping edges to seal. Place foil packets on baking sheet and bake 15 to 20 minutes (until salmon flakes easily when tested with a fork and vegetables are tender). Carefully remove salmon and vegetables to serving plate.

Each serving provides: 4 Protein Exchanges; 2½ Vegetable Exchanges; 1 Fat Exchange; 10 calories Optional Exchange
Per serving: 415 calories; 34 g protein; 24 g fat; 13 g carbohydrate; 474 mg sodium; 55 mg cholesterol

Veal Marengo

MAKES 2 SERVINGS

Traditionally, this delicious stew is served over noodles.

10 ounces boneless veal shoulder, cut into 1-inch cubes
2 teaspoons margarine
¼ cup chopped onion
1 garlic clove, minced
1 tablespoon all-purpose flour
¾ cup water
½ packet (about ½ teaspoon) each instant chicken and instant beef broth and seasoning mixes
½ cup seeded and chopped drained canned Italian tomatoes
2 tablespoons dry white wine
¼ teaspoon grated lemon peel
½ bay leaf
¼ teaspoon thyme leaves
½ cup quartered mushrooms
1½ teaspoons minced fresh parsley
⅛ teaspoon pepper, or to taste

On rack in broiling pan broil veal 5 to 6 inches from heat source until meat is browned on all sides, 4 to 5 minutes; set aside.

In 2-quart saucepan heat margarine over medium-high heat until bubbly and hot; add onion and garlic and sauté, stirring occasionally, until onion is translucent, 1 to 2 minutes. Add flour and stir quickly to combine; stirring constantly, gradually add water. Add broth mixes and, stirring constantly, cook until sauce is smooth. Reduce heat to low and add tomatoes, wine, lemon peel, bay leaf, thyme, and veal; cover pan and let simmer, stirring occasionally, until meat is tender, about 1 hour. Stir in mushrooms, parsley, and pepper and cook until mushrooms are tender, about 5 minutes longer. Remove bay leaf before serving.

Each serving provides: 4 Protein Exchanges; 1¼ Vegetable Exchanges; 1 Fat Exchange; 35 calories Optional Exchange
Per serving: 362 calories; 34 g protein; 19 g fat; 11 g carbohydrate; 580 mg sodium; 115 mg cholesterol

Steak au Poivre

MAKES 2 SERVINGS

No repertoire of French cooking would be complete without a traditional pepper steak.

1½ teaspoons coarsely ground peppercorns
10 ounces boneless beef sirloin or top or bottom round
   steak
2 teaspoons margarine
½ teaspoon salt
1 cup sliced mushrooms
1 tablespoon minced shallots
2 tablespoons dry red wine
Garnish: watercress or parsley sprigs

Firmly press ¾ teaspoon pepper into each side of meat; let stand 10 to 15 minutes. Preheat broiler for 5 minutes. Place meat on rack in broiling pan and broil 3 inches from heat source until rare, about 2 minutes on each side.

In 9-inch nonstick skillet heat margarine over high heat until bubbly and hot. Using tongs,* transfer meat to skillet and quickly sear on both sides; sprinkle each side with ¼ teaspoon salt. Remove meat to warmed serving platter; set aside and keep warm.

In same skillet combine mushrooms and shallots and sauté until mushrooms are golden, about 1 minute; add wine and cook, stirring constantly, until liquid is slightly reduced, about 3 minutes. Pour sauce over meat and serve garnished with watercress or parsley.

Each serving provides: 4 Protein Exchanges; 1 Vegetable Exchange;
   1 Fat Exchange; 15 calories Optional Exchange
Per serving with sirloin steak: 298 calories; 38 g protein; 13 g fat;
   4 g carbohydrate; 688 mg sodium; 103 mg cholesterol
With round steak: 278 calories; 37 g protein; 11 g fat; 4 g carbohydrate;
   686 mg sodium; 103 mg cholesterol

*If tongs are not available, use 2 wooden spoons; the objective is to avoid piercing the meat so that juices will not flow and meat will remain as rare as possible.

Pan Bagna

MAKES 2 SERVINGS

*This sandwich
Niçoise is sold
everywhere on the
streets and beaches
of Nice.*

1 drained canned anchovy fillet
1 teaspoon drained capers
¼ teaspoon thyme leaves
Dash pepper
1 tablespoon olive oil
2 teaspoons water
1 teaspoon red wine vinegar
2 round French-bread rolls (1½ ounces each)*
1 garlic clove, slightly crushed
4 large fresh basil or mint leaves
½ medium tomato, thinly sliced
¼ cup thinly sliced red onion
2 ounces drained canned chunk white tuna, flaked

Using a mortar and pestle, or in a small bowl using back of
spoon, mash together anchovy, capers, thyme, and pepper,
forming a smooth paste; add oil, water, and vinegar and
mix well. Set aside.

Cut rolls into halves horizontally and rub cut sides with
garlic clove; discard garlic. Brush bottom half of each roll
with 1 teaspoon anchovy mixture, then top each with
2 basil (or mint) leaves, half of the tomato slices, half of the
onion slices, 1 ounce tuna, and half of the remaining
anchovy mixture. Replace top halves of rolls and place a
heavy plate on top of each sandwich; let stand for 3 to 4
minutes to press filling together and blend flavors.

Each serving provides: 1 Protein Exchange; 1½ Bread Exchanges;
 ¾ Vegetable Exchange; 1½ Fat Exchanges; 3 calories Optional
 Exchange
Per serving: 242 calories; 13 g protein; 9 g fat; 29 g carbohydrate;
 419 mg sodium; 19 mg cholesterol

*If 1½-ounce rolls are not available, substitute two 2-ounce soft rolls;
increase Bread Exchange to 2 Exchanges.
Per serving: 295 calories; 14 g protein; 10 g fat; 37 g carbohydrate;
 490 mg sodium; 21 mg cholesterol

Cassoulet

MAKES 4 SERVINGS

Prepare this stew in steps. Soak the beans on Saturday, cook the Cassoulet on Sunday, and refrigerate it to serve on Monday. Time will improve its flavor.

3 ounces sorted uncooked white kidney (cannellini) beans, rinsed
2 cups water, divided
1 teaspoon each vegetable oil and margarine, divided
12 ounces chicken thighs, skinned, boned, and cut into 2-inch pieces
3 whole cloves
1 cup each carrot chunks (2-inch-thick pieces) and thickly sliced Spanish onion
¼ cup chopped Italian (flat-leaf) parsley, divided
2 garlic cloves, minced
2 packets instant chicken broth and seasoning mix
⅛ teaspoon each marjoram leaves and sage leaves, crumbled
Dash pepper
1 cup canned Italian tomatoes (with liquid), drain and chop tomatoes, reserving liquid
1 bay leaf
4 ounces "precooked" smoked beef sausage

In large bowl combine beans and 1 cup water; cover and let stand overnight.

In 9-inch nonstick skillet combine ½ teaspoon each oil and margarine and heat until margarine is bubbly and hot; add chicken and sauté until browned on all sides. Transfer to shallow 2-quart casserole and set aside.

Preheat oven to 350°F. Press cloves into carrot slices (this will make it easy to remove cloves after cooking). In same skillet combine remaining ½ teaspoon each oil and margarine and heat over medium-high heat until margarine is bubbly and hot; add carrots, onion, 2 tablespoons parsley, and the garlic, broth mix, marjoram, sage, and pepper and cook, stirring occasionally, until onion slices are translucent. Cover skillet and cook for 5 minutes longer. Transfer vegetable mixture to casserole containing chicken; add beans, soaking liquid, tomatoes

(CONTINUED) with reserved liquid, bay leaf, and remaining 1 cup water and stir to combine. Cover casserole tightly and bake for 1 hour.

Using sharp knife, cut slashes in sausage at ½-inch intervals; top mixture in casserole with sausage and bake, uncovered, until sausage is heated through, about 20 minutes. Remove and discard cloves and bay leaf. Serve sprinkled with remaining 2 tablespoons parsley.

Each serving provides: 3 Protein Exchanges; 1½ Vegetable Exchanges; ½ Fat Exchange; 5 calories Optional Exchange
Per serving: 312 calories; 28 g protein; 12 g fat; 24 g carbohydrate; 923 mg sodium; 88 mg cholesterol

Leeks and
Mushrooms Provençal ⏲

MAKES 2 SERVINGS

This is excellent as an appetizer or as a side dish with poultry or fish; it's delicious served hot or at room temperature and adds a dash of color to any meal.

2 teaspoons olive oil
2 medium leeks, washed thoroughly and cut lengthwise into halves, then cut into 1½-inch-long pieces (about 1 cup)
1 garlic clove, minced
½ cup each quartered mushrooms and seeded and diced drained canned Italian tomatoes
2 large pitted black olives, thinly sliced
1 tablespoon dry white wine
1½ teaspoons lemon juice
½ teaspoon Dijon-style mustard
¼ teaspoon mashed drained canned anchovy fillets (about ½ fillet)
⅛ teaspoon pepper

In 8-inch skillet heat oil over medium-high heat; add leeks and garlic and sauté, stirring occasionally, until leeks begin to wilt, 3 to 4 minutes. Add mushrooms and continue sautéing until mushrooms begin to soften, 2 to 3 minutes. Stir in remaining ingredients and cook until tomatoes and olives are heated through, 2 to 3 minutes longer.

Each serving provides: 2 Vegetable Exchanges; 1 Fat Exchange; 15 calories Optional Exchange
Per serving: 121 calories; 3 g protein; 6 g fat; 14 g carbohydrate; 162 mg sodium; 0.6 mg cholesterol

Braised Lettuce with Vegetables

MAKES 2 SERVINGS

A dish that proves that lettuce need not be limited to salads.

1 head Boston lettuce (about 8 ounces)
1 quart water
½ cup thinly sliced onion
¼ cup julienne-cut carrot (thin strips)
1 ounce julienne-cut Canadian-style bacon (thin strips)
½ cup canned chicken broth
½ bay leaf
⅛ teaspoon pepper
1 teaspoon each all-purpose flour and margarine, softened

Remove and discard outer leaves from lettuce and trim stem; rinse lettuce several times under running cold water, gently separating leaves to remove any sand but keeping head intact. In 1½-quart saucepan bring water to a boil; plunge lettuce into water and cook for 1 minute. Transfer to colander and immediately rinse with cold water; set aside.

Spray 9-inch skillet with nonstick cooking spray and heat over medium heat; add onion, carrot, and bacon and cook, stirring frequently, until vegetables are tender, 4 to 5 minutes *(do not brown)*. Reduce heat to low and add broth and seasonings; cover skillet and let simmer for 15 minutes. Add lettuce, cover, and cook for 10 minutes longer.

In small bowl mix together flour and margarine until well combined; add to skillet and stir until flour is dissolved. Cook, stirring constantly, until sauce is thickened, about 5 minutes. To serve, cut head of lettuce in half lengthwise; transfer to serving platter, surround with vegetable mixture, and top with sauce.

Each serving provides: ½ Protein Exchange; 2 Vegetable Exchanges; ½ Fat Exchange; 15 calories Optional Exchange
Per serving: 93 calories; 6 g protein; 4 g fat; 10 g carbohydrate; 435 mg sodium; 7 mg cholesterol

Brioche

MAKES 12 SERVINGS,
1 ROLL EACH

*Enjoy a continental
breakfast of Brioche
spread with
marmalade and
served with coffee or
tea. These delicious
French rolls can be
frozen, individually
wrapped; just
reheat when
ready to use.*

1 packet fast-rising active dry yeast
2 tablespoons each warm water (see yeast package
   directions for temperature) and granulated sugar
6 large eggs
⅓ cup plus 2 teaspoons margarine, softened
Dash salt
2¼ cups plus 2 tablespoons all-purpose flour, divided
1 cup cake flour

Spray twelve 2½-inch-diameter muffin pan cups or 12
individual brioche pans with nonstick cooking spray; set
aside.

In mixing bowl sprinkle yeast over water; add sugar and
stir to dissolve. Let stand until mixture becomes foamy,
about 5 minutes. Using electric mixer at medium speed,
beat in 5 eggs, 1 at a time; add margarine and salt and beat
until well combined. Beat in 2¼ cups all-purpose flour and
the cake flour, beating until dough becomes smooth and
sticky, about 3 minutes. Scrape down sides of bowl; cover
bowl with a clean damp towel or plastic wrap and let stand
in warm draft-free area until dough doubles in volume,
about 45 minutes.

Sprinkle work surface with remaining 2 tablespoons
flour and turn dough out onto floured surface; gently
shape into 12-inch-long loaf. Cut off ¼ of dough and set
aside; cut remaining loaf into 12 equal portions and shape
each into a smooth ball, tucking all ends under. Place
dough balls, seam-side down, in sprayed pan. Cut
remaining dough into 12 equal portions and shape each
into a small ball. Using finger, press down center of each
large dough ball, making an indentation; dip bottom of
each small ball into water, then, pressing gently but firmly,
press a small ball into each indentation.

Lightly beat remaining egg and, using pastry brush,
brush an equal amount over surface of each roll; let stand
in warm draft-free area until rolls double in volume.

(CONTINUED)

Preheat oven to 375°F. Bake rolls for 15 minutes (until golden brown). Remove rolls from pan to wire rack and let cool.

Each serving provides: ½ Protein Exchange; 1½ Bread Exchanges; 1½ Fat Exchanges; 10 calories Optional Exchange

Per serving: 226 calories; 7 g protein; 9 g fat; 29 g carbohydrate; 113 mg sodium; 137 mg cholesterol

Black Cherry Clafouti

MAKES 6 SERVINGS

A French fruit pudding that is a classic.

30 large dark sweet cherries, pitted
1½ cups evaporated skimmed milk
3 eggs
1 teaspoon vanilla extract
⅛ teaspoon each ground cinnamon and salt
Dash ground nutmeg
½ cup plus 1 tablespoon self-rising flour

Preheat oven to 375°F. Spray 9-inch pie plate with nonstick cooking spray; spread cherries over bottom and set aside.

In medium mixing bowl, using electric mixer at medium speed, beat together milk, eggs, vanilla, cinnamon, salt, and nutmeg until combined, about 1 minute; add flour and stir until smooth. Pour batter over fruit and bake for 35 to 40 minutes (until a knife, inserted in center, comes out clean). Serve warm or at room temperature.

Each serving provides: ½ Protein Exchange; ½ Bread Exchange; ½ Fruit Exchange; ½ Milk Exchange
Per serving: 158 calories; 9 g protein; 3 g fat; 22 g carbohydrate; 280 mg sodium; 140 mg cholesterol

Variation: For an added treat, top each serving with 1 tablespoon thawed frozen whipped topping. Add 15 calories Optional Exchange to Exchange Information.

Per serving: 173 calories; 9 g protein; 4 g fat; 23 g carbohydrate; 280 mg sodium; 140 mg cholesterol

Kiwi Vacherin

**MAKES 4 SERVINGS,
1 VACHERIN EACH**

*Delicately light
kiwi-topped
meringues.*

2 egg whites
1 tablespoon superfine sugar*
⅛ teaspoon each cream of tartar and orange extract
½ cup thawed frozen dairy whipped topping
2 medium kiwi fruit, pared and thinly sliced

Line baking sheet with parchment paper; set aside. In medium mixing bowl, using electric mixer at medium speed, beat egg whites until foamy; add sugar, cream of tartar, and extract and continue beating until stiff peaks form.

Preheat oven to 200°F. Using a pastry bag fitted with star tip, fill bag with egg white mixture and pipe some of mixture onto lined baking sheet, forming four 5 x 3-inch ovals (if pastry bag is not available, spoon mixture onto baking sheet); fill center of each oval with an equal amount of remaining mixture. Bake until golden and crisp, 45 minutes to 1 hour. Carefully remove meringues from paper to wire rack and let cool.

To serve, spread 2 tablespoons whipped topping over each meringue and decoratively top each portion with ¼ of the kiwi fruit slices; serve immediately.

Each serving provides: ½ Fruit Exchange; 50 calories Optional Exchange
Per serving: 68 calories; 2 g protein; 2 g fat; 11 g carbohydrate;
    27 mg sodium; 0 mg cholesterol

*If superfine sugar is not available, process granulated sugar in blender container until superfine.

Peach Crêpe Torte

MAKES 4 SERVINGS

A wonderful tart made from fruit and crêpes.

CRÊPES

1 cup skim milk
¾ cup all-purpose flour
2 eggs

FILLING

2 ounces sliced almonds, toasted
3 tablespoons dark brown sugar
⅛ teaspoon ground cinnamon
2 tablespoons plus 2 teaspoons reduced-calorie margarine
1 tablespoon light rum
½ teaspoon vanilla extract
8 medium peaches, blanched, peeled, pitted, and
    thinly sliced

To Prepare Crêpes: In blender container combine milk, flour, and eggs and process until smooth; let stand for 15 to 20 minutes.

Lightly spray 8-inch nonstick skillet or crêpe pan with nonstick cooking spray and heat (to test, sprinkle pan with drop of water; if water sizzles, pan is hot enough). Pour ¼ cup of batter into pan and quickly swirl batter so that it covers entire bottom of pan; cook over medium-high heat until edges and underside are dry. Using pancake turner, carefully turn crêpe over; cook other side briefly just to dry, about 30 seconds. Slide crêpe onto plate. Repeat procedure 7 more times, making 7 more crêpes and stacking crêpes on plate, using a sheet of wax paper between each to separate; cover to prevent drying.

To Prepare Filling: In work bowl of food processor combine almonds, sugar, and cinnamon; process until almonds are finely ground. Add margarine, rum, and vanilla; process until thoroughly combined. Transfer to small mixing bowl.

To Prepare Torte: Preheat oven to 350°F. Lightly spray a 10-inch ovenproof serving plate with nonstick cooking spray. Place 1 crêpe on plate; spread 1 tablespoon of almond mixture over crêpe and top evenly with ⅛ of the peach slices. Repeat procedure, making 7 layers and topping final

(CONTINUED) layer with the eighth crêpe; spread remaining almond mixture over crêpe. Decoratively arrange remaining peach slices on top of torte; bake until peaches are fork-tender and top is browned, about 20 minutes.

Each serving provides: ½ Protein Exchange; 1 Bread Exchange;
 1 Fat Exchange; 2 Fruit Exchanges; ¼ Milk Exchange; 140 calories
 Optional Exchange
Per serving: 388 calories; 11 g protein; 15 g fat; 53 g carbohydrate;
 161 mg sodium; 138 mg cholesterol

Pots de Crème au Chocolat

MAKES 2 SERVINGS

This delicious chocolate custard with cream is the French version of chocolate pudding.

½ cup skim milk
¼ cup whole milk
1¾ ounces semisweet chocolate pieces
1 egg, lightly beaten
½ teaspoon vanilla extract
2 tablespoons thawed frozen dairy whipped topping
¼ ounce shaved semisweet chocolate (curls)

Preheat oven to 350°F. In double boiler combine milks and chocolate pieces; cook over hot water until chocolate is melted *(do not boil)*. Add small amount of chocolate mixture to egg and stir to combine; add egg mixture to remaining chocolate mixture and stir to blend. Stir in extract.

Spray two 10-ounce custard cups with nonstick cooking spray and pour half of chocolate mixture into each cup; set cups in 8 x 8 x 2-inch baking pan and pour boiling water into pan to a depth of about ½ inch. Bake for 20 minutes (until custard begins to set). Remove baking pan from oven and cups from water bath; set cups on wire rack and let cool. Cover with plastic wrap and refrigerate for at least 4 hours. To serve, top each portion with 1 tablespoon whipped topping and half the chocolate curls.

Each serving provides: ½ Protein Exchange; ¼ Milk Exchange;
 190 calories Optional Exchange
Per serving: 239 calories; 7 g protein; 15 g fat; 22 g carbohydrate;
 82 mg sodium; 142 mg cholesterol

Pear Sorbet

MAKES 4 SERVINGS, ABOUT ½ CUP EACH

A dessert that refreshes the palate.

4 small pears, cored, pared, and sliced
1 tablespoon lemon juice
1½ teaspoons light corn syrup
Dash ground ginger
Garnish: 4 mint sprigs

In medium bowl combine pear slices and lemon juice, tossing slices with juice to prevent browning; add syrup and ginger and stir to combine.

In work bowl of food processor or in blender container process pear mixture until pureed; transfer to 8 x 8 x 2-inch freezer-safe pan, cover with plastic freezer wrap, and freeze until edges of mixture are firm, about 3 hours.

Scrape mixture into large mixing bowl and, using electric mixer at high speed, beat until smooth but not melted; turn into resealable plastic container (or cover bowl with plastic freezer wrap) and freeze until firm. To serve, scoop into 4 dessert glasses and garnish each with a mint sprig.

Each serving provides: 1 Fruit Exchange; 10 calories Optional Exchange
Per serving: 85 calories; 0.5 g protein; 0.5 fat; 22 g carbohydrate;
    3 mg sodium; 0 mg cholesterol

Variation: Substitute ½ medium pineapple, pared, cored, and sliced, for the pears.

Per serving: 41 calories; 0.3 g protein; 0.3 g fat; 10 g carbohydrate;
    3 mg sodium; 0 mg cholesterol

Germany

If you look at a German menu, you may be startled to see that heaven and earth (Himmel und Erde) is being served. That's what the appreciative Germans labeled the dish that combines two of their favorite foods: potatoes and apples. Potatoes are daily fare, often served as Kartoffelklösse (dumplings), while apples show up as a surprising flavoring in dishes like Sauerkraut Salad and a Berlin version of calf's liver.

A robust people, the Germans opt for substantial meals. Pork in some form is on almost every menu, invariably paired with sauerkraut. Sausages are immensely popular; frankfurters were named for Frankfurt (as were hamburgers for Hamburg's touted steak). Beef is more commonly served stewed or potted, as in the national dish Sauerbraten, which varies from one region to another. In the Rhineland, it is prepared with a thick, sweet sauce, while in Munich the sauce is thin and made with wine. Veal generally appears as a cutlet, as in our Paprika Schnitzel.

The Germans have a predilection for sweet-and-sour dishes like Rotkohl, red cabbage with vinegar and brown sugar. Onions appear in almost every dish, and sweet paprika and poppy seeds are basic seasonings. To savor the Germanic spirit, choose one of the country's internationally famed beers or a wine from the Rhine Valley.

In the area of desserts, the Germans produce spectacular effects, like glazed Baumkuchen or fruit tarts. Our adaptations are your "permits" for safe-eating conduct!

A German Gala

Birnensuppe*
(Pear Soup)

Sauerbraten*

Kartoffelklösse*
(Potato Dumplings)

Rotkohl*
(Red Cabbage)

Baumkuchen*
(Tree Cake)

Birnensuppe

MAKES 2 SERVINGS

Pear soup, flavored with cinnamon and served chilled.

2 tablespoons raisins
1 tablespoon dry sherry
2 small pears, cored, pared, and sliced
1½ cups water
1-inch cinnamon stick
Dash crushed aniseed
2 teaspoons granulated sugar
½ teaspoon lemon juice

In small bowl combine raisins and sherry; set aside.

In 1-quart saucepan combine pears, water, cinnamon stick, and aniseed; bring to a boil and cook until pears are very soft, about 15 minutes. Remove cinnamon stick and let mixture cool. Transfer to blender container and process until smooth; pour into bowl or container and stir in raisin mixture, sugar, and lemon juice. Cover and refrigerate until well chilled.

Each serving provides: 1½ Fruit Exchanges; 30 calories Optional
    Exchange
Per serving: 147 calories; 0.9 g protein; 0.7 fat; 36 g carbohydrate;
    2 mg sodium; 0 mg cholesterol

Sauerkraut Salad

MAKES 4 SERVINGS

A cold version of a favorite combination: sauerkraut, apples, and onion.

2¼ cups drained sauerkraut*
2 small Golden Delicious apples, cored, pared, and
   shredded
¾ cup diced red onion
1 tablespoon plus 1 teaspoon vegetable oil
Dash pepper, or to taste

Rinse sauerkraut several times in cold water and drain. In bowl combine all ingredients; cover and refrigerate for at least 2 hours. Toss before serving.

Each serving provides: 1½ Vegetable Exchanges; 1 Fat Exchange;
   ½ Fruit Exchange
Per serving: 104 calories; 2 g protein; 5 g fat; 15 g carbohydrate;
   738 mg sodium (estimated); 0 mg cholesterol

*Use the sauerkraut that is packaged in plastic bags and stored in the refrigerator section of the supermarket; it is usually crisper and less salty than the canned.

Gebratene Kalbsleber auf Berliner Art

MAKES 2 SERVINGS

Apple and onion rings dress up this calf liver Berlin style.

1 tablespoon plus 1 teaspoon reduced-calorie margarine, divided
½ cup thinly sliced onion (separated into rings)
1 small apple, cored, pared, and cut into ¼-inch-thick rings
1 tablespoon all-purpose flour
¼ teaspoon salt
⅛ teaspoon pepper
2 slices calf liver (5 ounces each)

In 10-inch skillet heat 1 teaspoon margarine until bubbly and hot; add onion rings and sauté until lightly browned. Using slotted spoon, remove rings to warmed plate; keep warm. In same skillet heat another teaspoon margarine until bubbly and hot; add apple rings and sauté until golden on both sides. Remove to plate with onion rings.

On sheet of wax paper or a paper plate combine flour, salt, and pepper; dredge liver in seasoned flour, turning to coat all sides. In same skillet heat remaining 2 teaspoons margarine until bubbly and hot; add liver and cook, turning once, until done to taste *(do not overcook)*. Remove to serving plate and top with onion and apple rings.

Each serving provides: 4 Protein Exchanges; ½ Vegetable Exchange; 1 Fat Exchange; ½ Fruit Exchange; 15 calories Optional Exchange
Per serving: 290 calories; 28 g protein; 11 g fat; 20 g carbohydrate; 469 mg sodium; 425 mg cholesterol

Paprika Schnitzel

MAKES 2 SERVINGS

A national favorite in Germany.

1 tablespoon reduced-calorie margarine
¼ cup finely chopped onion
1 teaspoon minced shallots
1 tablespoon plus 1 teaspoon all-purpose flour, divided
2 teaspoons sweet Hungarian paprika
½ cup canned chicken broth
3 tablespoons sour cream
⅛ teaspoon each salt and white pepper
10 ounces veal cutlets, pounded to ¼-inch thickness
1½ teaspoons vegetable oil

In 1-quart saucepan heat margarine over medium-high heat until bubbly and hot; add onion and shallots and sauté until onion is translucent, 1 to 2 minutes. Add 2 teaspoons flour and the paprika and, using wire whisk, stir quickly to combine; gradually stir in broth. Stirring constantly with whisk, bring to a boil. Reduce heat and let simmer, stirring occasionally, until sauce is smooth and thickened, 5 to 10 minutes; add sour cream, salt, and pepper and stir to combine. Set aside.

On sheet of wax paper or a paper plate sprinkle veal evenly with remaining 2 teaspoons flour. In 10-inch skillet heat oil over medium-high heat; add veal and cook, turning once, until browned on both sides, about 1 minute each side. Transfer to warmed serving platter and keep warm. Add reserved sauce to skillet and heat through *(do not boil)*; pour sauce over veal and serve immediately.

Each serving provides: 4 Protein Exchanges; ¼ Vegetable Exchange; 1½ Fat Exchanges; 80 calories Optional Exchange
Per serving: 375 calories; 30 g protein; 24 g fat; 8 g carbohydrate; 586 mg sodium; 110 mg cholesterol

Pork Chops with Apples and Sauerkraut

MAKES 2 SERVINGS

In true German fashion, accompany this dish with a mug of chilled beer.

1 tablespoon plus 1 teaspoon reduced-calorie margarine
1 small apple, cored and sliced
¼ cup sliced onion
¾ cup drained sauerkraut*
¼ cup canned chicken broth
1 tablespoon plus 1 teaspoon dry white wine
2 teaspoons country Dijon-style mustard
½ teaspoon caraway seed
⅛ teaspoon coarsely ground pepper
2 pork loin chops (6 ounces and about ½ inch thick each)

In 10-inch skillet heat margarine over high heat until bubbly and hot; add apple and onion and sauté until apple is lightly browned and onion is translucent, 2 to 3 minutes. Remove mixture from skillet and set aside.

To same skillet add sauerkraut and sauté, stirring occasionally, until liquid is evaporated, 4 to 5 minutes; add broth, wine, mustard, caraway seed, and pepper and stir well. Reduce heat to low, cover, and let simmer, stirring occasionally, for 8 to 10 minutes.

While mixture is simmering, on rack in broiling pan broil pork chops 4 to 6 inches from heat source, turning once, for 4 to 5 minutes on each side. Add chops and reserved apple mixture to skillet and let simmer until apple slices are cooked through but still retain their shape, about 2 minutes. Remove chops to serving plate and surround with sauerkraut mixture.

Each serving provides: 4 Protein Exchanges; 1 Vegetable Exchange; 1 Fat Exchange; ½ Fruit Exchange; 20 calories Optional Exchange
Per serving: 379 calories; 34 g protein; 19 g fat; 15 g carbohydrate; 940 mg sodium (estimated); 103 mg cholesterol

*Use the sauerkraut that is packaged in plastic bags and stored in the refrigerator section of the supermarket; it is usually crisper and less salty than the canned.

Sauerbraten

MAKES 12 SERVINGS

In truly traditional style, this dish is marinated for at least 3 days. So—plan ahead! In Germany, gingersnaps are used in the gravy; we have substituted fresh ginger and brown sugar. For a real German repast, serve with Kartoffelklösse (see page 152) and Rotkohl (see page 154) and top the meal off with a glass of dark beer.

4 cups onions (2 cups cut-up and 2 cups diced), divided
2½ cups water, divided
1 cup each cut-up celery and carrots
1 small lemon, sliced
2 tablespoons chopped pared ginger root or 1 teaspoon ground ginger
12 peppercorns
6 whole cloves
1 bay leaf
3¾ pounds boneless beef chuck, rump, or bottom round roast
2 tablespoons vegetable oil
1 tablespoon all-purpose flour
2 tablespoons firmly packed brown sugar or dark corn syrup
2 packets instant beef broth and seasoning mix

In 1-quart saucepan combine cut-up onions, 1 cup water, and the celery, carrots, lemon, and seasonings; bring marinade to a boil. In 4-quart stainless-steel or glass bowl pour marinade over beef; cover with plastic wrap and refrigerate for 3 to 4 days, turning meat over once every day.

Preheat oven to 350°F. Drain meat, reserving marinade, and transfer meat to rack in roasting pan; strain marinade, discarding solids and reserving liquid. Roast meat until rare, about 45 minutes.

In 4-quart saucepan or a Dutch oven heat oil; add meat and cook until well browned on all sides. Remove meat from pan and set aside. In same pan sauté diced onions until browned; sprinkle with flour and cook, stirring constantly, for 1 minute. Gradually stir in reserved marinade; add remaining 1½ cups water and the sugar (or syrup) and broth mix and, stirring constantly, bring to a boil. Return meat to pan and reduce heat to a simmer; cover and let simmer until meat is tender, about 45 minutes,

(CONTINUED) turning meat several times during cooking. Serve each portion with an equal amount of gravy.

Each serving provides: 4 Protein Exchanges; ¼ Vegetable Exchange; ½ Fat Exchange; 15 calories Optional Exchange
Per serving with chuck: 297 calories; 35 g protein; 13 g fat; 8 g carbohydrate; 197 mg sodium; 103 mg cholesterol
With rump: 290 calories; 34 g protein; 13 g fat; 8 g carbohydrate; 218 mg sodium; 103 mg cholesterol
With round: 268 calories; 37 g protein; 9 g fat; 8 g carbohydrate; 225 mg sodium; 103 mg cholesterol

Grüne Bohnen mit Zwiebel und Speck

MAKES 2 SERVINGS

Green beans with onion and bacon, a fast and easy, delicious side dish.

1 teaspoon margarine
¼ cup sliced onion
2 ounces Canadian-style bacon, diced
2 cups cut green beans, cooked until tender-crisp
1 to 2 tablespoons white vinegar

In small skillet heat margarine until bubbly and hot; add onion and sauté until softened. Add bacon and sauté until lightly browned. In serving bowl toss beans with vinegar, then top with bacon mixture.

Each serving provides: 1 Protein Exchange; 2¼ Vegetable Exchanges; ½ Fat Exchange
Per serving: 105 calories; 8 g protein; 4 g fat; 11 g carbohydrate; 431 mg sodium; 14 mg cholesterol

Königsberger Klopse

Meatballs Königsberg style, a blend of beef and pork given added interest by the flavor of capers.

12 ounces ground beef
6 ounces ground pork
1 slice white bread, made into crumbs, then soaked in
   2 tablespoons water
¼ cup minced onion, divided
2 eggs
1½ teaspoons caper juice (from bottled capers)
1 teaspoon lemon juice
½ teaspoon salt
¼ teaspoon each pepper and grated lemon peel
3 cups water
2 packets instant chicken broth and seasoning mix
1 tablespoon plus 1 teaspoon margarine
3 tablespoons all-purpose flour
¼ cup dry white wine
2 teaspoons chopped or small drained capers

In medium bowl combine beef, pork, crumbs, 2 tablespoons onion, 1 egg, and the caper juice, lemon juice, salt, pepper, and lemon peel; shape into 12 equal meatballs. On rack in broiling pan broil meatballs 6 inches from heat source, turning once, until browned and cooked throughout.

In 3-quart saucepan combine water and broth mix and bring to a boil; add meatballs and cook for 12 minutes or until done to taste. Using slotted spoon, remove meatballs to warmed deep serving dish; keep warm. Reserve cooking liquid.

In 1-quart saucepan heat margarine until bubbly and hot; add remaining 2 tablespoons onion and sauté until softened. Add flour and cook, stirring constantly, for 3 minutes. Gradually stir in wine; add reserved cooking liquid and let simmer, stirring occasionally, until sauce is thick and smooth. Stir in capers; remove from heat. In small bowl beat remaining egg; stir about ½ cup sauce into beaten egg, then slowly pour egg mixture into remaining sauce, stirring rapidly to prevent lumping. Cook, stirring

(CONTINUED)	constantly, until heated throughout *(do not boil)*. Pour sauce over meatballs and serve hot.
	
	Each serving provides: 4 Protein Exchanges; ½ Bread Exchange;
	  ⅛ Vegetable Exchange; 1 Fat Exchange; 20 calories Optional Exchange
	Per serving: 430 calories; 31 g protein; 27 g fat; 10 g carbohydrate;
	  925 mg sodium; 232 mg cholesterol

Himmel und Erde

MAKES 2 SERVINGS

This delicious mixture of potatoes, apple, and bacon is a typically German side dish. The name means "heaven and earth."

6 ounces pared potatoes, cut into cubes
¼ cup boiling water
¼ teaspoon salt
1 small apple, cored, pared, and sliced
2 teaspoons reduced-calorie margarine
¼ cup diced onion
2 ounces Canadian-style bacon, cut into cubes

In 1-quart saucepan combine potatoes, water, and salt and cook until potatoes are almost tender, about 15 minutes; stir in apple and cook over low heat, stirring occasionally, until apple slices are tender-crisp.

While potatoes are cooking, in small saucepan heat margarine until bubbly; add onion and sauté until softened. Add bacon and sauté until onion is lightly browned.

Using a large spoon or fork, mash potato mixture until blended but still lumpy. Stir in some of the bacon mixture; spoon potato-bacon mixture into a serving bowl and top with remaining bacon mixture.

Each serving provides: 1 Protein Exchange; 1 Bread Exchange;
  ¼ Vegetable Exchange; ½ Fat Exchange; ½ Fruit Exchange
Per serving: 161 calories; 8 g protein; 4 g fat; 24 g carbohydrate;
  720 mg sodium; 14 mg cholesterol

Kartoffelklösse

MAKES 12 SERVINGS,
2 DUMPLINGS EACH

Potato dumplings that are a wonderful accompaniment to Sauerbraten (see page 148).

2 tablespoons margarine
1 slice white bread, cut into 72 equal pieces
1⅓ cups less 1 teaspoon all-purpose flour, divided
1 pound 14 ounces peeled cooked boiling potatoes, riced
1 egg
1 teaspoon salt
⅛ teaspoon each ground nutmeg and white pepper
1 gallon water

In small skillet heat margarine until bubbly and hot; add bread and sauté, stirring constantly, until bread has absorbed margarine and is browned. Set aside.

Measure out and reserve 2 tablespoons flour. In mixing bowl combine remaining flour with the potatoes, egg, and seasonings, mixing well; portion dough into 24 equal mounds. Flour hands with reserved flour and shape mounds into balls; press 3 bread cubes into each ball and seal closed, forming dumplings.

In 5-quart saucepot or Dutch oven bring water to a boil; using slotted spoon, gently lower several dumplings into water (they will sink to bottom); when dumplings rise to surface, cook for 3 to 5 minutes longer. With slotted spoon, remove dumplings to warmed serving platter; repeat procedure with remaining dumplings.

Each serving provides: 1½ Bread Exchanges; ½ Fat Exchange; 5 calories Optional Exchange
Per serving: 125 calories; 3 g protein; 3 g fat; 22 g carbohydrate; 223 mg sodium; 23 mg cholesterol

Potato-Sauerkraut Casserole

MAKES 4 SERVINGS

A hearty dish for a winter's night.

12 ounces peeled cooked potatoes
¼ cup skim milk
2 tablespoons plus 2 teaspoons reduced-calorie margarine, divided
¼ teaspoon salt
½ cup diced onion
2 cups rinsed sauerkraut*
½ cup water
1 slice (1 ounce) reduced-calorie Swiss process cheese slices (up to 50 calories per ounce), coarsely shredded

In bowl combine potatoes, milk, 2 teaspoons margarine, and the salt and mash until smooth; set aside.

In 1-quart saucepan heat 2 teaspoons margarine until bubbly and hot; add onion and sauté until soft. Add sauerkraut and water, cover pan, and let simmer for 20 minutes.

Preheat oven to 350°F. Spray 1-quart casserole with nonstick cooking spray; spread half of potato mixture in bottom of casserole. Spoon sauerkraut mixture over potatoes and top with remaining potato mixture; sprinkle with cheese and dot with remaining 1 tablespoon plus 1 teaspoon margarine. Cover and bake for 20 minutes; uncover and bake for 10 minutes longer. If crisper topping is desired, broil for 3 minutes.†

Each serving provides: 1 Bread Exchange; 1¼ Vegetable Exchanges; 1 Fat Exchange; 15 calories Optional Exchange
Per serving: 129 calories; 5 g protein; 5 g fat; 18 g carbohydrate; 997 mg sodium (estimated); 2 mg cholesterol

*Use the sauerkraut that is packaged in plastic bags and stored in the refrigerator section of the supermarket; it is usually crisper and less salty than the canned.

†If casserole is to be broiled, be sure to use a flameproof casserole.

Rotkohl

**MAKES 12 SERVINGS,
ABOUT 1 CUP EACH**

*Our version of red
cabbage, a classic
German favorite.
Serve with
Sauerbraten
(see page 148).*

3½- to 4-pound head red cabbage, trimmed, cored, and
  finely shredded
½ cup red wine vinegar
2 tablespoons vegetable oil
2 cups diced onions
3 small tart apples, cored, pared, and thinly sliced
2 tablespoons firmly packed brown sugar
2 teaspoons salt
2 bay leaves
½ teaspoon pepper
6 whole cloves
¼ cup dry red wine

In large bowl combine cabbage and vinegar and toss;
set aside.

In 12-inch nonstick skillet heat oil over medium-high
heat; add onions and sauté until translucent. Add cabbage
mixture and remaining ingredients except wine and stir to
combine. Reduce heat to low, cover skillet tightly, and let
steam for about 15 minutes or until cabbage is done to
taste; stir in wine and cook, uncovered, for about
5 minutes longer. Remove bay leaves and cloves before
serving.

Each serving provides: 2 Vegetable Exchanges; ½ Fat Exchange;
  30 calories Optional Exchange
Per serving: 87 calories; 2 g protein; 3 g fat; 15 g carbohydrate;
  393 mg sodium; 0 mg cholesterol

Baumkuchen

MAKES 10 SERVINGS

Fresh cherries or frozen (no sugar added) may be used in this German delicacy. The name means "tree cake."

CAKE
50 large cherries
⅓ cup less 1 teaspoon unsalted margarine, softened
2 tablespoons granulated sugar
5 large eggs, separated
2 teaspoons vanilla extract
½ cup plus 1 tablespoon cake flour, sifted

GLAZE
3 tablespoons confectioners' sugar, sifted
1 to 2 tablespoons boiling water

To Prepare Cake: Reserve 10 cherries; pit and chop remaining 40 cherries and set aside. Spray 7- or 8-inch round springform pan with nonstick baker's spray; set aside.

In mixing bowl, using electric mixer, cream margarine with sugar until light and fluffy; gradually beat in egg yolks and vanilla, beating until blended. Blend in flour. In another bowl, using clean beaters, beat egg whites until stiff but not dry; fold small amount of yolk mixture into whites, then fold beaten whites into yolk mixture. Pour a thin layer (about ¼ cup) batter into sprayed pan, tilting pan and using rubber scraper to spread batter so that entire bottom of pan is covered. Broil just until batter is lightly browned, no more than 1 minute *(be careful not to overbrown or burn).* Pour another thin layer of batter over first layer and sprinkle with some of the chopped cherries; broil until lightly browned. Repeat procedure until all batter and cherries have been used and ending with a layer of batter. Let cake cool in pan for 5 minutes, then carefully loosen cake and remove sides of pan; let cake cool completely.

To Prepare Glaze: In small bowl combine sugar and water, stirring well to dissolve sugar; drizzle glaze over top of cooled cake. Immediately (before glaze sets) garnish cake with reserved whole cherries.

Each serving provides: ½ Protein Exchange; 1½ Fat Exchanges; ½ Fruit Exchange; 55 calories Optional Exchange
Per serving: 160 calories; 4 g protein; 9 g fat; 16 g carbohydrate; 35 mg sodium; 137 mg cholesterol

Cheese-Filled Fruit Tart

MAKES 8 SERVINGS

A mouth-watering dessert that's as decorative as it is delicious.

CRUST

2¼ cups all-purpose flour
2 teaspoons double-acting baking powder
½ teaspoon each baking soda and ground cinnamon
¼ teaspoon salt
⅛ teaspoon ground nutmeg
2 tablespoons plus 2 teaspoons margarine
2 eggs
¼ cup plain low-fat yogurt
2 tablespoons granulated sugar
1 teaspoon vanilla extract

FILLING

1 cup pot-style cottage cheese
¾ cup part-skim ricotta cheese
2 tablespoons sour cream
¼ teaspoon each grated lemon peel, sifted confectioners' sugar, and vanilla extract

TOPPING

8 medium peaches or small nectarines, pitted and thinly sliced
2 tablespoons granulated sugar, mixed with ¼ teaspoon ground cinnamon

To Prepare Crust: Into large mixing bowl sift together flour, baking powder, baking soda, cinnamon, salt, and nutmeg; with pastry blender, or two knives used scissors-fashion, cut in margarine until mixture resembles coarse meal.

In medium mixing bowl beat together remaining ingredients for crust until thoroughly combined; pour into flour mixture and stir to form smooth dough, kneading lightly if necessary. Cover with plastic wrap and refrigerate for 20 to 30 minutes; while dough is chilling, prepare filling.

(CONTINUED)

To Prepare Filling: Set fine sieve over small mixing bowl and force cottage cheese through sieve into bowl; stir in remaining ingredients for filling, combining thoroughly.

To Prepare Tart: Preheat oven to 350°F. Spray 12-inch pizza pan with nonstick cooking spray. Between 2 sheets of wax paper roll dough to form circle, 12 inches in diameter; gently fit dough onto sprayed pan. Spread filling evenly over dough to within ½ inch from edge and arrange peach (or nectarine) slices decoratively over filling; sprinkle with cinnamon sugar and bake until crust is golden brown, 40 to 45 minutes. Turn oven control to broil and broil tart until fruit is golden brown, 3 to 5 minutes.

Each serving provides: 1 Protein Exchange; 1½ Bread Exchanges; 1 Fat
    Exchange; 1 Fruit Exchange; 45 calories Optional Exchange
Per serving with peaches: 307 calories; 12 g protein; 8 g fat;
    46 g carbohydrate; 326 mg sodium; 79 mg cholesterol
With nectarines: 357 calories; 12 g protein; 8 g fat; 60 g carbohydrate;
    333 mg sodium; 79 mg cholesterol

Greece and the
Other Balkan States

The cuisine that inspired a poet: that's the story behind the world's first cookbook. It was written by the Athenian poet Archestratus nearly 2,400 years ago, and people have been lyrical about Greek cookery ever since.

The countryside of Europe's oldest civilization blooms with the fragrant lemons so widely used for flavoring, and with vegetables like the popular eggplant. As in ancient times, the landscape is dotted with olive trees, source of the world-famed olives and the oil that's so integral a part of Greek cooking. (The culinary term "à la Grecque" means prepared with olive oil.)

Feta, the national cheese, shows up in an array of dishes; we've included it in recipes for shrimp, flounder, beef, and vegetables. Seafood is another specialty of this seacoast land. (The Greeks were said to be the first to discover that oysters are edible.) Although lamb is usually associated with Greek cuisine, beef is becoming increasingly popular. We've provided a classic beef-and-custard casserole — Sfougato — from the Isle of Rhodes. And from neighboring Yugoslavia comes a hearty casserole made of pork and vegetables.

A spillover of national dishes is typical of the Balkan countries, which share similar culinary heritages. Dolmathes — meats or other fillings with rice, enticingly wrapped in grape leaves — are popular throughout the region.

When it comes to the Balkans' traditional honey-glazed pastries, the Greeks have the edge. Since time immemorial, Greece's Mount Hymettus has won the vote for producing the world's best honey (proving that "It's Greek to me" can make sweet menu reading).

A Balkan Banquet

Greek Marinated Vegetable Salad*

Shrimp with Tomatoes and Feta Cheese*

Pita Bread

Greek Honey Twists*

Sparkling Mineral Water with Lime Wedge

Srpski Aijvar

MAKES 4 SERVINGS

Serve this Yugoslavian vegetable caviar as an hors d'oeuvre with saltines or crispbread, or as a side dish.

1 small eggplant (about 12 ounces)
2 medium green bell peppers
2 tablespoons lemon juice
2 teaspoons olive oil
¼ teaspoon each salt and pepper

Preheat oven to 475°F. Using the tines of a fork, pierce eggplant. Place eggplant and peppers on rack in 8 x 8 x 2-inch baking pan and bake, turning once, until vegetables are tender, about 25 minutes. Remove from oven, cover, and let cool.

Using paring knife, peel eggplant and peppers; remove and discard seeds from peppers. Finely chop vegetables and transfer to small bowl; add remaining ingredients and mix well to combine. Cover and refrigerate until chilled.

Each serving provides: 2 Vegetable Exchanges; ½ Fat Exchange
Per serving: 54 calories; 2 g protein; 3 g fat; 8 g carbohydrate;
  145 mg sodium; 0 mg cholesterol

Greek Marinated Vegetable Salad

MAKES 4 SERVINGS

Eggplant, red pepper, artichoke hearts, and mushrooms in an herbed marinade.

1 very small eggplant (about 6 ounces)
1 medium red bell pepper
1 cup drained thawed frozen artichoke hearts
1 cup small mushroom caps, cut into quarters
¼ cup water
1 tablespoon plus 1 teaspoon olive oil
1 tablespoon lemon juice
2 garlic cloves, minced
1 teaspoon each oregano leaves and red wine vinegar
¼ teaspoon each marjoram leaves, thyme leaves, basil leaves, and pepper

On baking sheet broil eggplant and bell pepper 3 inches from heat source, turning frequently, until charred on all sides; transfer to brown paper bag and let stand until cool enough to handle, 15 to 20 minutes. Peel and dice eggplant; transfer to medium bowl. Peel pepper; remove and discard stem end and seeds. Cut pepper into thin strips and add to eggplant; add artichoke hearts to bowl and set aside.

Spray 9-inch skillet with nonstick cooking spray and heat over medium-high heat; add mushrooms and cook, stirring occasionally, until just cooked through, 1 to 2 minutes. Add to eggplant mixture.

In small bowl combine remaining ingredients, mixing well; pour over vegetable mixture and toss to coat. Cover with plastic wrap and let marinate for at least 30 minutes.

Each serving provides: 2 Vegetable Exchanges; 1 Fat Exchange
Per serving: 84 calories; 3 g protein; 5 g fat; 9 g carbohydrate;
  28 mg sodium; 0 mg cholesterol

Shrimp with Tomatoes and Feta Cheese

MAKES 2 SERVINGS

A colorful main dish.

2 teaspoons olive oil
1 cup diced eggplant
¼ cup each diced yellow bell pepper and sliced scallions (green onions)
2 garlic cloves, minced
8 small plum tomatoes, blanched, peeled, seeded, and diced
2 tablespoons each dry white wine and water
1 tablespoon each minced fresh parsley and grated lemon peel
1 teaspoon oregano leaves
¼ teaspoon pepper
9 ounces shelled and deveined large shrimp
1 ounce feta cheese, crumbled

In 12-inch skillet heat oil over high heat; add eggplant and cook, stirring frequently, until browned on all sides, about 2 minutes. Add bell pepper, scallions, and garlic and sauté until vegetables are softened, about 1 minute; add remaining ingredients except shrimp and cheese and stir to combine. Reduce heat to medium and cook, stirring occasionally, for 3 to 5 minutes; add shrimp to skillet and sauté, turning occasionally, until shrimp turn pink, 1 to 2 minutes. Add cheese, stir to combine, and cook until cheese is heated through, about 1 minute *(do not overcook)*. Serve immediately.

Each serving provides: 4 Protein Exchanges; 3½ Vegetable Exchanges; 1 Fat Exchange; 15 calories Optional Exchange
Per serving: 273 calories; 28 g protein; 9 g fat; 18 g carbohydrate; 348 mg sodium; 204 mg cholesterol

Stuffed Mussels

**MAKES 4 SERVINGS,
8 MUSSELS EACH**

*When cooking
mussels, discard
any that do
not open.*

½ cup each bottled clam juice and water
32 small mussels, well scrubbed, beards removed
1 tablespoon plus 1 teaspoon olive oil
½ cup minced onion
1 ounce uncooked regular long-grain rice
¼ cup raisins
1 tablespoon chopped fresh parsley
2 teaspoons dry white wine
¼ teaspoon each salt and pepper
1 ounce pignolias (pine nuts), lightly toasted
Garnish: lemon wedges

In 4-quart saucepan or Dutch oven bring clam juice and water to a boil; add mussels, cover, and steam until mussels open, 2 to 3 minutes. Using slotted spoon, remove mussels from cooking liquid, reserving liquid. Remove mussels from shells, reserving 32 shell halves and discarding remaining shells; set 1 mussel on each shell half and set aside. Line sieve with cheesecloth and strain cooking liquid into bowl; set aside.

In 8-inch nonstick skillet heat oil over medium-high heat; add onion and sauté until golden. Stir in rice and cook for 1 minute. Measure 1¼ cups of strained cooking liquid; stir into skillet and bring to a boil. Reduce heat to low and stir in remaining ingredients except nuts and garnish; cover and let simmer until liquid is absorbed and rice is tender, about 20 minutes. Stir in nuts.

Preheat oven to 400°F. Spoon an equal amount of rice mixture onto each mussel. In 13 x 9 x 2-inch baking pan arrange stuffed mussels and bake until heated through, about 10 minutes; serve garnished with lemon wedges.

Each serving provides: 2 Protein Exchanges; ¼ Vegetable Exchange; 1 Fat Exchange; ½ Fruit Exchange; 70 calories Optional Exchange
Per serving: 220 calories; 15 g protein; 10 g fat; 19 g carbohydrate; 478 mg sodium; 40 mg cholesterol

Stuffed Flounder Athenian

MAKES 2 SERVINGS

Spinach and feta cheese combine well in the filling of this typically Greek dish.

1 cup well-drained cooked chopped spinach
2 ounces feta cheese, crumbled
1 tablespoon plus 1 teaspoon lemon juice, divided
¼ teaspoon each dillweed and pepper
2 flounder fillets (4 ounces each)*
¼ cup water
2 tablespoons dry white wine
1 tablespoon chopped fresh parsley
⅛ teaspoon paprika

Preheat oven to 375°F. In medium bowl combine spinach, cheese, 2 teaspoons lemon juice, and the dill and pepper, mixing well. Spoon half of cheese mixture onto the center of each fillet and roll fish lengthwise to enclose; transfer fish rolls, seam-side down, to 8 x 8 x 2-inch baking dish.

In small bowl combine water, wine, parsley, paprika, and remaining 2 teaspoons lemon juice; pour over fillets and bake until fish flakes easily when tested with a fork, 15 to 20 minutes.

Each serving provides: 4 Protein Exchanges; 1 Vegetable Exchange; 15 calories Optional Exchange
Per serving: 202 calories; 26 g protein; 7 g fat; 6 g carbohydrate; 454 mg sodium; 82 mg cholesterol

*Grey sole, lemon sole, or scrod may be substituted for the flounder.
Per serving with scrod: 201 calories; 27 g protein; 7 g fat; 6 g carbohydrate; 445 mg sodium; 82 mg cholesterol

Lemon-Chicken Oregano

MAKES 2 SERVINGS

In Greece, lemon is highly favored as a seasoning and is frequently used with poultry as well as fish.

1½ teaspoons margarine
1 tablespoon lemon juice
1½ teaspoons olive oil
1 small garlic clove, mashed
½ teaspoon oregano leaves
¼ teaspoon each salt and pepper
2 chicken cutlets (5 ounces each)
Garnish: 2 lemon slices and 1 teaspoon chopped
    fresh parsley

In small saucepan melt margarine; add lemon juice, oil, garlic, oregano, salt, and pepper and bring to a boil. Reduce heat to low and let simmer for 1 minute. Transfer to shallow glass or stainless-steel bowl; let cool slightly. Add chicken and turn to coat with marinade. Cover and refrigerate overnight or for at least 1 hour.

Transfer chicken to shallow baking pan that is large enough to hold chicken in a single layer; brush with half of the marinade and broil for 4 minutes. Turn chicken over, brush with remaining marinade, and broil until browned, about 4 minutes longer. To serve, transfer chicken to serving platter, top with any pan juices, and garnish with lemon and parsley.

Each serving provides: 4 Protein Exchanges; 1½ Fat Exchanges
Per serving: 216 calories; 33 g protein; 8 g fat; 1 g carbohydrate;
    398 mg sodium; 82 mg cholesterol

Sfougato

MAKES 2 SERVINGS

Zucchini and onion add flavor and texture to this delicious Greek beef custard.

1 teaspoon each olive oil and margarine
½ cup each diced onion and shredded zucchini
5 ounces cooked ground beef, crumbled
1 cup skim milk
3 eggs, beaten
2 teaspoons minced fresh parsley
½ teaspoon salt
Dash white pepper, or to taste

Spray 1½-quart casserole with nonstick cooking spray; set aside.

Preheat oven to 350°F. In small nonstick skillet combine oil and margarine and heat until margarine is bubbly and hot; add onion and zucchini and cook, stirring occasionally, until vegetables are softened, 3 to 4 minutes. Transfer to medium bowl and add remaining ingredients; stir to combine. Pour into sprayed casserole and bake in middle of center oven rack until firm, 45 to 55 minutes.

Each serving provides: 4 Protein Exchanges; 1 Vegetable Exchange; 1 Fat Exchange; ½ Milk Exchange
Per serving: 448 calories; 34 g protein; 29 g fat; 12 g carbohydrate; 789 mg sodium; 480 mg cholesterol

Stefado

MAKES 4 SERVINGS

Greek-style oven beef stew, flavored with cinnamon and cumin and topped with feta cheese.

15 ounces boneless chuck steak
2 teaspoons olive oil
2 cups water
¼ cup tomato paste
2 tablespoons red wine vinegar
2-inch cinnamon stick
½ teaspoon salt
¼ teaspoon each cumin seed and pepper
1 cup pearl onions, parboiled
2 ounces feta cheese, crumbled

On rack in broiling pan broil chuck, turning once, until rare, about 5 minutes on each side; cut into 1-inch cubes.

In 10-inch skillet heat oil over medium-high heat; add chuck and sauté for 5 minutes. Using slotted spoon, transfer meat to 1½-quart casserole, reserving pan drippings.

Preheat oven to 350°F. In same skillet stir water, tomato paste, vinegar, and seasonings into pan drippings; bring to a boil, stirring to scrape up any browned particles clinging to skillet. Pour over meat in casserole; cover and bake for 1½ hours. Add onions, cover, and bake until meat is tender, about 30 minutes longer. Remove and discard cinnamon stick. Top with feta cheese and bake, uncovered, until cheese is softened and heated through, about 5 minutes.

Each serving provides: 3½ Protein Exchanges; ¾ Vegetable Exchange; ½ Fat Exchange
Per serving: 302 calories; 28 g protein; 17 g fat; 8 g carbohydrate; 610 mg sodium; 90 mg cholesterol

Yugoslavian Meat 'n' Vegetable Casserole

MAKES 2 SERVINGS

Pork and eggplant add variety to this entrée.

10 ounces boneless pork shoulder
2 teaspoons olive oil, divided
¾ cup thinly sliced onions
1 medium tomato, cut into ¼-inch-thick slices
¾ teaspoon salt, mixed with ⅛ teaspoon pepper
1 cup cubed pared eggplant (½-inch cubes)
½ cup each diced green bell pepper and
  chopped green beans
¼ cup thinly sliced carrot
2 ounces uncooked regular long-grain rice
½ cup water

On rack in broiling pan broil pork, turning once, until rare, 2 to 3 minutes on each side. Cut pork into 1-inch pieces and set aside.

Preheat oven to 350°F. In 9-inch skillet heat 1 teaspoon oil over medium-high heat; add onions and sauté until softened. In shallow 2-quart casserole spread half of the sautéed onions; top with half of the tomato slices and sprinkle about ¼ of the salt mixture over vegetables. Top vegetables with ½ cup eggplant, ¼ cup bell pepper, ¼ cup beans, and 2 tablespoons carrot and sprinkle about ⅓ of remaining salt mixture over carrot; add rice, pork, and remaining sautéed onions, eggplant, bell pepper, beans, and carrot. Sprinkle with half of remaining salt mixture; top with remaining tomato slices and sprinkle tomato with remaining salt mixture. Pour water and remaining teaspoon oil over pork mixture; cover casserole and bake for 1¾ hours. Remove cover and bake for 15 minutes longer.

Each serving provides: 4 Protein Exchanges; 1 Bread Exchange;
  4 Vegetable Exchanges; 1 Fat Exchange
Per serving: 507 calories; 33 g protein; 24 g fat; 39 g carbohydrate;
  929 mg sodium; 111 mg cholesterol

Dolmathes with Lemon Sauce

MAKES 4 SERVINGS, 5 DOLMATHES EACH

Stuffed grape leaves, a classic Greek appetizer or hors d'oeuvre.

2 teaspoons olive oil, divided
½ cup minced onion
2 garlic cloves, minced
2 ounces uncooked regular long-grain rice
2½ cups water, divided
2 medium tomatoes, blanched, peeled, seeded, and finely chopped
½ cup golden raisins
2 tablespoons chopped fresh parsley
1 teaspoon salt
¼ teaspoon ground cinnamon
Dash pepper
20 large bottled grape leaves, drained, soaked, and rinsed several times
2 lemons, cut into thin wedges
Lemon Sauce (see page 171)

In 8-inch nonstick skillet heat 1 teaspoon oil over medium-high heat; add onion and garlic and sauté until onion is golden. Stir in rice and cook for 1 minute. Add 1½ cups water and remaining ingredients except grape leaves, lemons, and Lemon Sauce and stir to combine; bring to a boil. Reduce heat, cover, and let simmer until rice is tender, about 15 minutes.

Spoon an equal amount of rice mixture onto stem end of each grape leaf; fold stem end over, then fold sides of leaves over filling to enclose and, from stem end, roll leaves jelly-roll fashion. Transfer stuffed leaves, seam-side down, to same skillet and add remaining cup water and teaspoon oil; set a heatproof plate onto stuffed leaves. Fill small saucepan with water and set on plate to weight down; cook over high heat until water in skillet comes to a boil and steam forms. Reduce heat; simmer for 15 to 20 minutes. Serve Dolmathes with lemon wedges and Lemon Sauce.

Each serving (including sauce) provides: ½ Protein Exchange; ½ Bread Exchange; 1¾ Vegetable Exchanges; 1 Fat Exchange; 1 Fruit Exchange
Per serving: 224 calories; 7 g protein; 7 g fat; 38 g carbohydrate; 1,036 mg sodium; 137 mg cholesterol

Lemon Sauce

MAKES 4 SERVINGS

Serve this sauce with Dolmathes with Lemon Sauce (see page 170).

2 eggs
1 tablespoon lemon juice
2 teaspoons margarine, divided
½ teaspoon salt
Dash ground red pepper

In small saucepan, using wire whisk, beat together eggs and lemon juice. Set saucepan over low heat and, stirring constantly with whisk, blend in 1 teaspoon margarine, stirring until margarine is melted; stir in remaining teaspoon margarine and cook, stirring constantly, until margarine is melted and sauce thickens *(do not overcook)*. Stir in salt and pepper.

Each serving provides: ½ Protein Exchange; ½ Fat Exchange
Per serving: 57 calories; 3 g protein; 5 g fat; 0.6 g carbohydrate;
 331 mg sodium; 137 mg cholesterol

Greek-Style Vegetables

MAKES 2 SERVINGS

A mélange of fresh vegetables with a cheese topping.

1 cup each thinly sliced tomatoes, divided, diced eggplant (large dice), and chopped spinach
¼ cup each diced celery, sliced onion (¼-inch-thick wedges), and sliced red and green bell peppers (¼-inch-wide strips)
1 tablespoon plus 1½ teaspoons lemon juice
2¼ teaspoons minced fresh dill
2 teaspoons olive oil
1 garlic clove, minced
⅛ teaspoon pepper
2 ounces feta cheese, crumbled

Preheat oven to 400°F. Spray shallow 1-quart casserole with nonstick cooking spray and arrange half of the tomato slices in bottom; set aside.

In medium bowl combine remaining tomato slices with remaining ingredients except cheese and toss to combine; spoon over tomato layer and bake for 15 minutes. Sprinkle cheese over vegetables and continue baking until vegetables are tender-crisp, 5 to 10 minutes longer.

Each serving provides: 1 Protein Exchange; 4 Vegetable Exchanges; 1 Fat Exchange
Per serving: 182 calories; 8 g protein; 11 g fat; 16 g carbohydrate; 369 mg sodium; 25 mg cholesterol

Minted Zucchini Fritters with Feta Cheese

MAKES 2 SERVINGS, 3 FRITTERS EACH

The coolness of mint combines well with the tang of feta, making these fritters extra-special.

¾ cup grated zucchini
⅛ teaspoon salt
1 egg, beaten
1 ounce feta cheese, finely crumbled
1 tablespoon all-purpose flour
¾ teaspoon minced fresh mint or ¼ teaspoon dried
Dash pepper
2 teaspoons vegetable oil

In small mixing bowl combine zucchini and salt and mix well; let stand until zucchini releases moisture, at least 30 minutes. Transfer zucchini to sieve and press to remove as much liquid as possible; discard liquid. Return zucchini to bowl and add remaining ingredients except oil, mixing well to combine.

In 10-inch nonstick skillet heat oil over medium-high heat; drop zucchini mixture by tablespoonfuls into skillet, making 6 equal fritters. Cook until fritters are browned on bottom, about 1 minute; turn fritters over and cook until golden brown on other side, about 1 minute longer.

Each serving provides: 1 Protein Exchange; ¾ Vegetable Exchange; 1 Fat Exchange; 15 calories Optional Exchange
Per serving: 140 calories; 6 g protein; 10 g fat; 6 g carbohydrate; 332 mg sodium; 150 mg cholesterol

Yugoslavian Corn Bread

MAKES 6 SERVINGS

Seltzer is the secret ingredient that makes this bread light.

⅔ cup cottage cheese
½ cup sour cream
1 egg, beaten
1 cup evaporated skimmed milk
½ cup seltzer (no salt added)
2 tablespoons vegetable oil
3¾ ounces (½ cup plus 2 tablespoons) uncooked yellow cornmeal
3 ounces uncooked regular farina
¾ teaspoon double-acting baking powder
½ teaspoon salt

In medium mixing bowl combine cheese, sour cream, and egg, mixing well; add milk, seltzer, and oil and stir until mixture is smooth. Add remaining ingredients and stir until mixture is thoroughly combined; cover with plastic wrap and let stand at room temperature for about 1½ hours (mixture will have batter-like consistency).

Preheat oven to 375°F. Spray 8 x 8 x 2-inch baking pan with nonstick cooking spray; pour batter into pan and bake until golden brown and firm to the touch, 40 to 45 minutes. Serve warm or at room temperature.

Each serving provides: ½ Protein Exchange; 1½ Bread Exchanges; 1 Fat Exchange; ¼ Milk Exchange; 50 calories Optional Exchange
Per serving: 268 calories; 11 g protein; 11 g fat; 31 g carbohydrate; 402 mg sodium; 59 mg cholesterol

Greek Honey Twists

MAKES 6 SERVINGS, 3 COOKIES EACH

A dessert that does honor to the celebrated Greek honey.

3 eggs, beaten
1⅔ cups plus 1 teaspoon all-purpose flour
½ teaspoon double-acting baking powder
¼ teaspoon salt
2 tablespoons each vegetable oil, honey, and granulated sugar
¼ teaspoon ground cinnamon

Measure out and reserve 2 tablespoons egg. In large mixing bowl combine flour, baking powder, and salt; add all but reserved egg, then the oil, and mix well. Turn out onto flat surface and knead until smooth and elastic, 8 to 10 minutes. Let dough rest for 10 to 15 minutes.

Preheat oven to 375°F. Roll dough into an 18 x 8-inch rectangle, about ⅛ inch thick; cut into eighteen 8 x 1-inch strips. Spray baking sheet with nonstick cooking spray; twist each strip of dough and arrange twists on sprayed sheet. Brush each twist with an equal amount of remaining 2 tablespoons egg and bake until golden brown, 8 to 10 minutes. Transfer to wire rack and let cool.

In small saucepan combine honey, sugar, and cinnamon and cook over medium heat, stirring frequently, until sugar melts and mixture is smooth and syrupy, 3 to 4 minutes. Transfer cookie twists to serving plate and drizzle an equal amount of syrup (about ¾ teaspoon) over each.

Each serving provides: ½ Protein Exchange; 1½ Bread Exchanges; 1 Fat Exchange; 40 calories Optional Exchange
Per serving: 245 calories; 7 g protein; 8 g fat; 37 g carbohydrate; 161 mg sodium; 137 mg cholesterol

Koulourakia Cookies

**MAKES 8 SERVINGS,
2 COOKIES EACH**

*Sweet and crunchy,
coil-shaped Greek
sesame cookies.*

1½ cups all-purpose flour
1¼ teaspoons baking soda
1 teaspoon double-acting baking powder
¼ teaspoon ground cinnamon
⅛ teaspoon each ground nutmeg and salt
⅓ cup reduced-calorie margarine
3 tablespoons granulated sugar
1 egg
½ teaspoon vanilla extract
1 teaspoon evaporated skimmed milk
1 tablespoon sesame seed

Onto sheet of wax paper or a paper plate sift together flour, baking soda, baking powder, cinnamon, nutmeg, and salt; set aside.

In medium mixing bowl, using electric mixer at medium speed, beat together margarine and sugar until creamy; add egg and vanilla and continue beating until light and fluffy. Gradually beat in sifted ingredients, beating until mixture forms dough. Form dough into ball, wrap in wax paper or plastic wrap, and refrigerate for 1 hour.

Preheat oven to 350°F. Divide dough into 16 equal pieces. Using palms of hands, roll each piece into a 6-inch-long strip and shape each strip into a coil. Spray cookie sheet with nonstick cooking spray and arrange coils on sheet; brush each with an equal amount of milk, then sprinkle each with an equal amount of sesame seed. Bake until lightly browned, 18 to 20 minutes. Transfer cookies to wire rack and let cool.

Each serving provides: 1 Bread Exchange; 1 Fat Exchange; 40 calories
    Optional Exchange
Per serving: 154 calories; 4 g protein; 5 g fat; 23 g carbohydrate;
    316 mg sodium; 34 mg cholesterol

India

If it hadn't been for India's spices, the history of the world would have been very different, for it was in search of those precious seasonings that Columbus set sail.

They are put to their most renowned use in *kari,* known to us as curry. This isn't the familiar commercially bottled powder but a combination of herbs and spices, with or without sauce. The combinations differ from one family to another, and the secret formulas are handed down like heirlooms. Among the most common ingredients are cardamom, coriander, turmeric, cumin, and ginger. Curry is not necessarily torrid; the "temperature" can be adjusted from hot to mild.

The traditional accompaniment for all curry dishes is chutney, a vegetable or fruit relish. The ingredients also vary, but usually include apples and raisins. Our adaptation uses oranges and dates.

India's eating habits aren't determined as much by region as by religion. Moslems don't eat pork; the vast Hindu population is vegetarian; and most sects revere cattle as sacred. Because of these factors, as well as the economy, vegetables are the core of Indian menus. They appear in curries like our Mixed Vegetable Curry or in raitas, a salad-like combination with a cooling yogurt base. (We offer Radish Raita.) Thrifty bean and lentil combinations are popular too, as in our Sambar.

In Tandoori Chicken, a highly regarded dish, the fowl is marinated in various spices and takes on a reddish coloring. The Indians have also provided us with a soup that's become world-famous, the highly seasoned Mulligatawny, which is aptly named, since it combines pepper *(molegoo)* with water *(tunee).*

For a genuine Indian meal, serve all the courses at the same time and let our dishes put spice into your life.

Some Like It Hot

---

*Radish Raita**

*Tandoori Chicken**

*Naan**

*Mixed Vegetable Curry**

*Orange-Date Chutney**

*Gajar Halva**
(Carrot Halva)

Coffee or Tea

Mulligatawny Soup

MAKES 4 SERVINGS

From exotic India, a delicious version of chicken soup.

1 tablespoon margarine
1 teaspoon vegetable oil
3 pounds chicken parts, skinned
2 cups chopped onions
1 medium green bell pepper, cut into thin strips
1 cup each chopped celery and carrots
3⅓ cups water
2 small tart apples, cored, pared, and chopped
⅔ cup apple juice (no sugar added)
1½ teaspoons salt
1 teaspoon each shredded coconut, curry powder, and lemon juice
⅛ teaspoon each ground cloves, ground mace, and ground coriander
Dash to ⅛ teaspoon ground red pepper

In 5-quart saucepot or Dutch oven combine margarine and oil and heat until margarine is bubbly and hot; in batches, add chicken and brown on all sides. Remove chicken to a plate and set aside.

In same pot combine vegetables and sauté until onions are translucent; return chicken to pot and add remaining ingredients, stirring to combine. Bring to a boil. Reduce heat, cover, and let simmer until thickest piece of chicken is done and carrots are tender, about 30 minutes. Remove chicken parts from pot and let cool; remove meat from bones and chop or shred chicken meat. Return meat to pot and stir to combine; reheat if necessary.

Each serving provides: 4 Protein Exchanges; 2½ Vegetable Exchanges; 1 Fat Exchange; 1 Fruit Exchange; 3 calories Optional Exchange
Per serving: 361 calories; 35 g protein; 13 g fat; 26 g carbohydrate; 1,016 mg sodium; 101 mg cholesterol

Curried Shrimp with Saffron Rice

MAKES 4 SERVINGS

An assortment of spices and a colorful garnish make this special.

RICE

4 ounces uncooked regular long-grain rice
1 cup water
1 tablespoon margarine
1 teaspoon salt
¼ teaspoon ground whole saffron

SHRIMP

1 tablespoon margarine
1 cup thinly sliced onions
1 small apple, cored and cut into small pieces
2 tablespoons each golden raisins and fresh lime
   or lemon juice
1 teaspoon each curry powder and salt
1 bay leaf
1 small garlic clove, minced
½ teaspoon each ground ginger and ground cardamom
¼ teaspoon grated fresh lemon peel
1¼ pounds shelled and deveined large shrimp

GARNISH

½ cup each julienne-cut green bell pepper, diced red bell
   pepper, and diced tomato
¼ cup each cucumber slices and diced onion

To Prepare Rice: In 1½-quart saucepan combine all ingredients for rice and bring to a boil. Reduce heat, cover, and let simmer until rice has absorbed liquid and is tender, 15 to 20 minutes.

To Prepare Shrimp: While rice is cooking, in 10-inch nonstick skillet heat margarine over medium-high heat until bubbly and hot; add sliced onions and sauté until golden. Stir in remaining ingredients except shrimp and garnish. Reduce heat and let simmer until apple is soft, about 5 minutes. Increase heat to high and add shrimp; cook, stirring, just until shrimp turn pink.

(CONTINUED)	*To Serve:* Stir rice and spoon onto 1 side of warmed serving platter; arrange shrimp mixture next to rice and decoratively arrange garnishes on platter.

Each serving provides: 4 Protein Exchanges; 1 Bread Exchange;
 1½ Vegetable Exchanges; 1½ Fat Exchanges; ½ Fruit Exchange
Per serving: 356 calories; 30 g protein; 7 g fat; 42 g carbohydrate;
 1,380 mg sodium; 213 mg cholesterol

Cachumbar

MAKES 2 SERVINGS *This spiced onion salad is a perfect accompaniment to any Indian meal.*	½ cup diced onion 1 medium tomato, diced ½ medium cucumber, diced 1 small hot green chili pepper, seeded and minced 1 tablespoon malt vinegar or white vinegar 1½ teaspoons each chopped fresh cilantro (Chinese parsley) and lemon or lime juice (no sugar added) ½ teaspoon salt Dash each ground cumin and ground turmeric

In 2-cup bowl combine all ingredients; cover with plastic wrap and refrigerate until chilled. Toss again just before serving.

Each serving provides: 2¼ Vegetable Exchanges
Per serving: 47 calories; 2 g protein; 0.3 g fat; 11 g carbohydrate;
 557 mg sodium; 0 mg cholesterol

Tandoori Chicken

MAKES 4 SERVINGS

Serve this with Naan (see page 185) as they do in India. Plan ahead, since the chicken should be marinated for at least 8 hours.

1 cup chopped onions
½ cup plain low-fat yogurt
¼ cup fresh lemon or lime juice
1 tablespoon seeded chopped mild or hot green chili pepper
3 to 6 small garlic cloves
1 teaspoon minced pared ginger root
⅛ teaspoon each ground turmeric, ground cinnamon, ground cardamom, ground cloves, and ground allspice
Dash salt
1 chicken (3 pounds), cut into 8 pieces and skinned
2 teaspoons olive or vegetable oil
Garnish: 1 tablespoon chopped fresh cilantro (Chinese parsley)

In blender container combine onions, yogurt, juice, chili pepper, garlic, and seasonings; process until smooth, scraping down sides of container as necessary.

Using sharp knife, cut slits in chicken but do not pierce to the bone; transfer chicken to 1-quart stainless-steel or glass bowl and add yogurt mixture, rubbing mixture into chicken parts to coat. Cover bowl with plastic wrap and refrigerate for at least 8 hours.

Preheat oven to 475°F. Transfer chicken to rack in roasting pan and brush with any remaining marinade; roast for 15 to 20 minutes. Brush chicken pieces with oil and continue roasting until, when chicken is pierced with a knife, juices run clear, about 10 minutes longer. Transfer chicken to serving platter and pour pan juices over chicken; serve sprinkled with cilantro leaves.

Each serving provides: 4 Protein Exchanges; ½ Vegetable Exchange; ½ Fat Exchange; ¼ Milk Exchange
Per serving: 278 calories; 35 g protein; 11 g fat; 8 g carbohydrate; 155 mg sodium; 103 mg cholesterol

aloo Beef Curry

SERVINGS

Typical of India, redolent with spices of the East.

10 ounces boneless beef round steak
2 teaspoons reduced-calorie margarine
½ cup chopped onion
½ garlic clove, minced
1½ teaspoons white vinegar
1 teaspoon ground coriander
¼ teaspoon ground turmeric
⅛ teaspoon each ground cumin, ground ginger, powdered
  mustard, pepper, crushed red pepper, and salt
¾ cup water
1½ teaspoons to 1 tablespoon lemon juice
1 cup cooked long-grain rice (hot)

On rack in broiling pan broil steak, turning once, until rare; cut into 1-inch cubes.

In 1-quart saucepan heat margarine until bubbly and hot; add onion and garlic and sauté until onion is translucent. Add vinegar and seasonings and stir to combine; add steak and cook, stirring frequently, for 3 minutes. Stir in water, cover pan, and let simmer, stirring occasionally, until meat is tender, about 1 hour. Stir in lemon juice and serve over rice.

Each serving provides: 4 Protein Exchanges; 1 Bread Exchange;
  ½ Vegetable Exchange; ½ Fat Exchange
Per serving: 365 calories; 38 g protein; 9 g fat; 30 g carbohydrate;
  277 mg sodium; 103 mg cholesterol

Indian "Fried" Bread

MAKES 5 SERVINGS, 1 BREAD EACH

This slightly puffed bread is typical of Indian cuisine.

1 cup less 1 tablespoon whole wheat or white flour
½ teaspoon salt
⅓ cup water
1 tablespoon plus 2 teaspoons vegetable oil, divided

In mixing bowl combine flour and salt; using electric mixer at slow speed, add water to flour mixture, beating until mixture resembles coarse meal. Form dough into ball and, on smooth dry surface (*not wood*), knead for 5 minutes; cover with clean damp paper towel or plastic wrap and let rest for 20 minutes.

Cut dough into 5 equal pieces and shape each into a ball; roll each ball to as thin a circle as possible. In 8-inch nonstick skillet heat 1 teaspoon oil; carefully transfer 1 circle to skillet and cook, shaking pan constantly and turning dough frequently, until bread is puffed and golden, about 3 minutes (dough will puff up into a balloon-shaped bread). Transfer bread to warm oven (200°F.) and repeat procedure with remaining dough and oil. Serve hot.

Each serving provides: 1 Bread Exchange; 1 Fat Exchange
Per serving: 115 calories; 3 g protein; 5 g fat; 16 g carbohydrate;
219 mg sodium; 0 mg cholesterol

Variation: After rolling dough into a circle, with index finger make a hole in center; cook as directed.

Naan

MAKES 12 SERVINGS,
1 BUN EACH

In India, these oval buns are usually sprinkled with onion seed; we have substituted poppy or sesame seed. These buns can be frozen and reheated when ready to use. Traditionally, they are served with Tandoori Chicken (see page 182).

1 packet fast-rising active dry yeast
¾ cup warm water (see yeast package directions for temperature), divided
2 teaspoons granulated sugar
¼ cup margarine, melted, divided
¼ cup plain low-fat yogurt
1 egg
2¼ cups plus 1 tablespoon all-purpose flour, divided
1 teaspoon salt
2 teaspoons poppy seed or sesame seed

In cup sprinkle yeast over ¼ cup water; stir in sugar and let stand until foamy, about 5 minutes.

In mixing bowl, using electric mixer at medium speed, combine remaining ½ cup water with 3 tablespoons margarine and the yogurt and egg, beating until blended; add 2¼ cups flour and the salt and yeast mixture and mix to form a soft sticky dough. Spray a bowl with nonstick cooking spray and transfer dough to sprayed bowl; cover with clean damp towel or plastic wrap and let stand in warm draft-free area until dough is doubled in volume, about 30 minutes.

Preheat oven to 450°F. Sprinkle work surface with remaining tablespoon flour; turn dough out onto floured surface, cut into 12 equal pieces, and shape each into a ball. Working on floured surface to prevent sticking, pat each ball into an oval, about 4 inches in diameter and ¼ inch thick. On each of 2 baking sheets arrange 6 ovals; brush each with an equal amount of remaining margarine and sprinkle with poppy (or sesame) seed. Bake until puffed and browned, 10 to 12 minutes. Serve hot.

Each serving provides: 1 Bread Exchange; 1 Fat Exchange; 20 calories Optional Exchange
Per serving: 138 calories; 4 g protein; 5 g fat; 20 g carbohydrate; 238 mg sodium; 23 mg cholesterol

Gajar Halva

MAKES 2 SERVINGS

Carrot halvah, a sweet side dish from Pakistan. May be served hot or chilled.

½ cup skim milk
1 cup shredded carrots
2 tablespoons raisins
1½ teaspoons honey
2 teaspoons unsalted margarine
⅛ teaspoon ground cardamom
Dash ground whole saffron
½ ounce slivered blanched almonds

In heavy-bottom small nonstick saucepan, over medium heat, bring milk to a boil. Reduce heat to low and stir in carrots, raisins, and honey; cook, stirring occasionally, until mixture is thick, 30 to 40 minutes. Stir in remaining ingredients except almonds and cook, stirring constantly, until margarine is melted, about 1 minute. Transfer to work bowl of food processor and process until smooth; transfer to serving dish and, using a spatula, smooth surface. Sprinkle with almonds; serve immediately or let cool, then cover and refrigerate until chilled.

Each serving provides: 1 Vegetable Exchange; 1 Fat Exchange;
 ½ Fruit Exchange; ¼ Milk Exchange; 60 calories Optional Exchange
Per serving: 165 calories; 4 g protein; 8 g fat; 22 g carbohydrate;
 53 mg sodium; 1 mg cholesterol

Mixed Vegetable Curry

MAKES 4 SERVINGS

If your taste turns to hot and spicy, this Pakistani specialty is for you. The rice "cools it down" just a bit.

2 small hot green chili peppers, seeded and minced
2 small garlic cloves, minced
⅛ teaspoon each ground cumin, ground coriander, and ground turmeric
1 tablespoon plus 1 teaspoon olive or vegetable oil
6 ounces diced pared potatoes
1 cup each diced onions, carrots, red bell peppers, and green bell peppers
3 medium tomatoes, blanched, peeled, and chopped
1 teaspoon salt
¾ to 1 cup water
1 cup cooked long-grain rice (hot)
Garnish: chopped fresh cilantro (Chinese parsley) or Italian (flat-leaf) parsley leaves

Using a mortar and pestle, crush together chili peppers, garlic, cumin, coriander, and turmeric to form a paste. In 12- or 14-inch skillet heat oil; add chili pepper mixture and cook, stirring constantly, for 2 to 3 minutes. Add potatoes, onions, carrots, bell peppers, tomatoes, and salt, stirring to combine; add enough water to just cover the vegetables and, stirring constantly, bring to a boil. Reduce heat and let simmer until vegetables are tender, 15 to 20 minutes. To serve, mound vegetable mixture on serving platter, mound rice alongside vegetables, and sprinkle rice and vegetables with cilantro or parsley.

Each serving provides: 1 Bread Exchange; 3¾ Vegetable Exchanges; 1 Fat Exchange
Per serving: 207 calories; 5 g protein; 5 g fat; 37 g carbohydrate; 578 mg sodium; 0 mg cholesterol

Orange-Date Chutney

MAKES 12 SERVINGS, ABOUT 2 TABLESPOONS EACH

No Indian meal is complete without this wonderful accompaniment. Properly refrigerated, this delicious spicy fruit relish will keep for months.

3 small oranges
1 cup diced onions
10 dates, pitted
½ cup raisins
1 small garlic clove
¼ cup white vinegar
2 tablespoons firmly packed brown sugar
1 teaspoon salt
½ teaspoon each ground cinnamon and grated pared ginger root
¼ teaspoon each chili powder and ground nutmeg

Peel oranges over work bowl of food processor to catch juices. Using a sharp knife, remove white pith from peels; add peels to work bowl of processor. Trim any white pith from orange pulp; section oranges, discarding membranes and seeds. Add to work bowl of processor along with onions, dates, raisins, and garlic and, using an on-off motion, process until mixture is finely ground *(do not puree)*.

In 1-quart saucepan combine remaining ingredients and bring to a boil; stir in fruit mixture and bring to a boil again. Cook, stirring constantly, for 3 to 5 minutes. Reduce heat and let simmer, stirring occasionally, until most of liquid has evaporated and mixture is thickened, 30 to 40 minutes. Remove from heat and let cool. Transfer to a container, cover, and store in refrigerator until ready to use.

Each serving provides: ⅛ Vegetable Exchange; 1 Fruit Exchange; 10 calories Optional Exchange
Per serving: 65 calories; 1 g protein; 0.2 g fat; 19 g carbohydrate; 188 mg sodium; 0 mg cholesterol

Spiced "Fried" Potatoes

MAKES 2 SERVINGS

A spicy Pakistani side dish.

9 ounces small potatoes, cut into quarters
1 quart water
¼ teaspoon each salt and ground coriander
⅛ teaspoon each chili powder, ground ginger, and ground cardamom
Dash each ground cumin, ground nutmeg, ground mace, and ground cloves
1½ teaspoons each vegetable oil and margarine

In 2-quart saucepan boil potatoes in water until tender *but not soft;* drain and set aside.

In small cup combine seasonings; set aside. In 8-inch nonstick skillet combine oil and margarine and heat until margarine is bubbly and hot; add potatoes and sauté, stirring occasionally, until lightly browned. Sprinkle with seasonings and continue sautéing until well browned, 10 to 15 minutes.

Each serving provides: 1½ Bread Exchanges; 1½ Fat Exchanges
Per serving: 155 calories; 3 g protein; 6 g fat; 22 g carbohydrate;
309 mg sodium; 0 mg cholesterol

Radish Raita

MAKES 2 SERVINGS

*A raita is a mixture
of yogurt and
vegetables and can be
served as a salad or
an appetizer. Indian
raitas are cooling
accompaniments to
curry dishes.*

1 cup grated radishes
½ teaspoon salt
¼ cup plain low-fat yogurt
Dash each ground cumin and ground red pepper
Garnish: mint sprig

In colander sprinkle radishes with salt; let drain for 30
minutes. Squeeze out any excess water and transfer
radishes to bowl; stir in yogurt and cumin. Serve
sprinkled with red pepper and garnished with mint.

Each serving provides: 1 Vegetable Exchange; ¼ Milk Exchange
Per serving: 28 calories; 2 g protein; 0.5 g fat; 4 g carbohydrate;
    577 mg sodium; 2 mg cholesterol

Sambar

MAKES 4 SERVINGS

A sambar is an Indian puree of legumes that is cooked with vegetables and spices. This lentil puree is excellent as part of a vegetarian meal or as an accompaniment to a meat entrée.

3 ounces sorted uncooked red lentils
2 cups water
1 cup diced onions
2 to 3 garlic cloves, chopped
2 packets instant vegetable or chicken broth and seasoning mix
1 cup diced red or green bell peppers
1 small hot green chili pepper, seeded and minced
4 coriander seeds
Garnish: lime slice and cilantro (Chinese parsley)

Rinse lentils under running cold water. In 3-quart saucepan combine lentils and water and bring to a boil; stir in onions, garlic, and broth mix and return to a boil. Reduce heat to low, cover, and let simmer until lentils are soft, 30 to 40 minutes. Let cool slightly, then transfer mixture to blender container and process until pureed, scraping down sides of container as necessary. Return puree to saucepan and stir in remaining ingredients except garnish; let simmer over low heat until peppers are soft, about 15 minutes. Serve garnished with lime and cilantro.

Each serving provides: 1 Protein Exchange; 1⅛ Vegetable Exchanges; 5 calories Optional Exchange
Per serving: 111 calories; 7 g protein; 0.4 g fat; 21 g carbohydrate; 432 mg sodium; 0 mg cholesterol

Payasam

MAKES 4 SERVINGS

Saffron noodles 'n' raisins, a delicious Indian dessert that can be served hot or lukewarm.

2 tablespoons unsalted margarine
3 ounces uncooked vermicelli (very thin spaghetti), broken into 1-inch pieces
½ cup boiling water
1 cup skim milk
1 tablespoon granulated sugar
Dash ground whole saffron
¼ cup golden raisins
⅛ teaspoon ground cardamom

In 8-inch nonstick skillet heat margarine over medium-high heat until bubbly and hot; add vermicelli and sauté, stirring constantly, until lightly browned. Reduce heat to low, add water, and let simmer until vermicelli is tender, about 5 minutes; stir in milk, sugar, and saffron and cook, stirring occasionally, for 5 minutes longer. Remove from heat and stir in raisins and cardamom.

Each serving provides: 1 Bread Exchange; 1½ Fat Exchanges; ½ Fruit Exchange; ¼ Milk Exchange; 15 calories Optional Exchange
Per serving: 190 calories; 5 g protein; 6 g fat; 29 g carbohydrate; 34 mg sodium; 1 mg cholesterol

Italy

When a strange red fruit reached Europe from the New World in the sixteenth century, botanists classified this so-called love apple as poisonous. Fortunately, it was reevaluated, and Italians have been in love with the tomato ever since.

Along with garlic and olive oil, tomatoes are basic to Italian cookery. But "Italian" means different things, depending on where the dishes are cooked. In the northern regions, garlic is used more sparingly than in the south; butter, rather than oil, dominates their cooking, and rice dishes like our Risotto Pomodoro are preferred to pasta.

Southern Italy's love of pasta has long been recognized. Available in dozens of shapes and sizes, some pastas are eaten with sauces, others encase various stuffings, and some enrich soups like our Minestra di Pasta e Ceci. Pasta dishes frequently take on new coloring—as in our Linguine Verdi, "painted" by spinach.

Served "before the pasta," Italian antipasti, or hors d'oeuvres, customarily include anchovies. We've incorporated this fish into Bagna Cauda, a spicy dip from the Piedmont region.

Italian cooks use seasonings freely, not only garlic but herbs like oregano and the basil that's indispensable in tomato dishes. Cheese is also an essential ingredient, used in a variety of dishes from veal to dumplings, as in our Veal Valdostana and Ricotta Gnocchi.

Desserts are a prime Italian pleasure, and our adaptation of Panettone enables you to savor this holiday cake from Milan, which is eaten throughout the country at Christmas and Easter. Wind up with Cappuccino, which Italy gave to the world. She gave another gift as well: the fork. Our recipes help you use it wisely!

Italian Fare with Flair

Minestra di Pasta e Ceci*
(Pasta and Chick-Pea Soup)

Beef Siciliana*
(Italian Pepper Steak)

Risotto Pomodoro*
(Rice and Tomato)

Vegetable Salad
(Sliced red or Bermuda onion, cucumber, radishes,
and celery with vinegar and herbs)

Fresh Fruit Salad

Red Wine

Mocha Cappuccino*

Bagna Cauda ⏱

**MAKES 2 SERVINGS,
ABOUT ¼ CUP EACH**

*Serve this classic
hot anchovy-garlic
dip with crunchy
breadsticks and
vegetable dippers.*

½ cup skim milk
⅓ cup plus 2 teaspoons buttermilk
1 tablespoon margarine
1½ small garlic cloves, chopped
4 drained canned anchovy fillets, rinsed
½ teaspoon oregano leaves

In small saucepan combine milks; bring to a boil. Reduce heat to lowest possible setting and cook, stirring occasionally, until liquid is reduced by about ⅓; remove from heat.

In small skillet heat margarine until bubbly and hot; add garlic and sauté until golden *(be careful not to burn)*. Transfer sautéed garlic to blender container; add milk, anchovies, and oregano and process until smooth. Pour dip into fondue pot or other heated serving container.

Each serving provides: 1½ Fat Exchanges; ½ Milk Exchange;
    10 calories Optional Exchange
Per serving: 54 calories; 3 g protein; 4 g fat; 3 g carbohydrate;
    107 mg sodium; 4 mg cholesterol

Minestra di Pasta e Ceci

MAKES 2 SERVINGS

This pasta and chick-pea soup is true to the Italian culinary tradition of thick, hearty soups.

2 teaspoons olive oil
½ cup chopped onion
2 garlic cloves, minced
½ cup drained canned Italian tomatoes, chopped
8 ounces drained canned chick-peas (ceci beans), reserve ½ cup liquid
½ cup cooked macaroni (shells, elbows, or ditalini)
1½ teaspoons shredded fresh basil or ½ teaspoon dried
Dash each salt and pepper
Garnish: basil sprigs

In 1-quart saucepan heat oil over medium heat; add onion and garlic and sauté until onion is translucent. Add tomatoes and bring to a boil. Reduce heat and let simmer for 5 minutes. Add chick-peas with reserved liquid and remaining ingredients; cook until heated. Serve garnished with basil sprigs.

Each serving provides: 2 Protein Exchanges; ½ Bread Exchange; 1 Vegetable Exchange; 1 Fat Exchange
Per serving: 222 calories; 8 g protein; 7 g fat; 34 g carbohydrate; 150 mg sodium; 0 mg cholesterol

Linguine Verdi ai Quattro Formaggi

Green linguini with four cheeses.

½ cup part-skim ricotta cheese
2 ounces each mozzarella and Fontina cheeses, shredded
2 ounces grated Parmesan cheese
3 tablespoons skim milk
3 cups cooked spinach linguine (hot)
2 tablespoons plus 2 teaspoons reduced-calorie margarine

In small saucepan heat ricotta cheese until thinned, stirring constantly with a wooden spoon; gradually add remaining cheeses, stirring constantly after each addition until cheeses are melted. Continuing to stir, add milk, 1 tablespoon at a time, stirring until thoroughly combined. Keep warm over lowest possible heat.

In mixing bowl combine hot linguine and margarine, tossing until margarine is completely melted. Transfer linguine to serving dish and top with cheese sauce; toss to combine and serve immediately.

Each serving provides: 2 Protein Exchanges; 1½ Bread Exchanges; 1 Fat Exchange; 5 calories Optional Exchange
Per serving: 362 calories; 21 g protein; 20 g fat; 26 g carbohydrate; 454 mg sodium; 78 mg cholesterol

Veal Valdostana

MAKES 4 SERVINGS

Breaded veal with cheese, made from tender cutlets and enhanced with Fontina cheese.

¾ cup plain dried bread crumbs
3 tablespoons all-purpose flour
½ teaspoon salt
Dash pepper
4 veal cutlets (4 ounces each), preferably cut from leg
1 egg, beaten with 2 tablespoons water
¼ cup reduced-calorie margarine
4 ounces Fontina cheese, shredded
Garnish: 8 lemon wedges

On sheet of wax paper or a paper plate spread bread crumbs; set aside. In bowl combine flour, salt, and pepper; dredge cutlets in flour mixture, coating all sides. Dip each cutlet into beaten egg, then into bread crumbs, thoroughly coating all sides.

In 12-inch nonstick skillet heat margarine over medium heat until bubbly and hot; add cutlets and brown on both sides. Transfer cutlets to jelly-roll pan or baking sheet; top each with 1 ounce cheese and broil just until cheese melts. Serve each portion garnished with 2 lemon wedges.

Each serving provides: 4 Protein Exchanges; 1 Bread Exchange;
    1½ Fat Exchanges; 40 calories Optional Exchange
Per serving: 451 calories; 34 g protein; 26 g fat; 19 g carbohydrate;
    643 mg sodium; 183 mg cholesterol

Beef Siciliana ⏱

MAKES 2 SERVINGS

Italian pepper steak, a Sicilian favorite.

1 tablespoon lemon juice
2 teaspoons olive oil
1½ teaspoons chopped fresh mint
¼ teaspoon minced fresh garlic or shallot
Dash salt
¼ teaspoon peppercorns, crushed
1 T-bone or porterhouse steak (12 ounces)

In small bowl combine all ingredients except peppercorns and steak; set aside. Press crushed peppercorns into steak; on rack in broiling pan broil steak 2 inches from heat source, turning once, for about 3 minutes on each side or until done to taste. Remove to warmed platter and brush with mint mixture; serve immediately.

Each serving provides: 4 Protein Exchanges; 1 Fat Exchange
Per serving: 277 calories; 37 g protein; 13 g fat; 0.8 g carbohydrate;
   157 mg sodium; 103 mg cholesterol

Pasta e Piselli

MAKES 2 SERVINGS

Although called "pasta and peas," this easy-to-prepare side dish is embellished with mushrooms, onion, and cheese.

2 teaspoons olive oil or margarine
¼ cup chopped onion
1 garlic clove, minced
½ cup sliced mushrooms
1 cup tomato juice
½ cup frozen tiny peas
2 ounces Fontina or mozzarella cheese, shredded
½ cup cooked ditalini or other tube macaroni
1 tablespoon plus 2 teaspoons chopped fresh parsley
Dash each salt and pepper

In 1-quart saucepan heat oil; add onion and garlic and sauté until onion is translucent. Add mushrooms and sauté over high heat until mushrooms exude liquid, about 2 minutes; add juice and bring to a boil. Cook until sauce is slightly thickened, about 15 minutes; add peas and cook, stirring occasionally, for about 3 minutes longer. Add remaining ingredients and cook, stirring, until cheese is melted.

Each serving provides: 1 Protein Exchange; 1 Bread Exchange; ¾ Vegetable Exchange; 1 Fat Exchange; 25 calories Optional Exchange
Per serving: 260 calories; 13 g protein; 14 g fat; 22 g carbohydrate; 379 mg sodium; 33 mg cholesterol

Pasta Primavera

MAKES 2 SERVINGS

Garden vegetables brighten this "springtime" pasta.

½ cup part-skim ricotta cheese
¼ cup skim milk
2 teaspoons reduced-calorie margarine
2 garlic cloves, minced
1½ cups cooked fettuccine, linguine, or tagliatelli
½ medium red bell pepper, seeded and cut into matchstick pieces
⅓ cup each cooked diagonally sliced asparagus and carrot
⅓ cup cooked sliced zucchini
1 ounce grated Parmesan cheese
¼ teaspoon salt
Dash pepper

In blender container combine ricotta cheese and milk and process until smooth; set aside.

In 12-inch skillet heat margarine over medium heat until bubbly and hot; add garlic and sauté briefly *(do not brown)*. Pour in ricotta mixture and bring to a boil. Reduce heat and add remaining ingredients; using 2 forks, toss well until pasta and vegetables are thoroughly coated with sauce. Serve immediately.

Each serving provides: 1½ Protein Exchanges; 1½ Bread Exchanges; 1½ Vegetable Exchanges; ½ Fat Exchange; 10 calories Optional Exchange
Per serving: 328 calories; 19 g protein; 12 g fat; 37 g carbohydrate; 696 mg sodium; 31 mg cholesterol

Ricotta Gnocchi

MAKES 4 SERVINGS

These delicious little cheese dumplings are a wonderful side dish; for a complete entrée, serve with Bolognese Meat Sauce (see page 204).

¾ cup part-skim ricotta cheese
2 ounces grated Parmesan cheese
1 egg, lightly beaten
2 teaspoons olive or vegetable oil
⅛ teaspoon ground nutmeg
Dash salt
¾ cup all-purpose flour
2 quarts water

In mixing bowl thoroughly combine first 6 ingredients; add flour gradually, mixing well to form dough. Divide dough into 4 equal balls and roll each into a rope, about ¾ inch in diameter; cut each rope into 1-inch lengths and, using your thumb and forefinger, press the middle of each piece to form an indent.

In 3-quart saucepan bring water to a boil; drop in gnocchi, a few at a time; when gnocchi rise to the surface, cook for 5 to 7 minutes (until al dente). Using slotted spoon, remove from water. Serve hot.

Each serving provides: 1½ Protein Exchanges; 1 Bread Exchange;
  ½ Fat Exchange
Per serving: 254 calories; 15 g protein; 12 g fat; 21 g carbohydrate;
  372 mg sodium; 94 mg cholesterol

Risotto Pomodoro

MAKES 4 SERVINGS

Risotto is a culinary gift from Milan. The method of preparation as well as the flavor of this rice and tomato side dish is classically Italian.

1 tablespoon plus 1 teaspoon margarine
½ cup chopped onion
2 garlic cloves, minced
4 ounces uncooked aborio rice (or any medium- or short-grain rice)
1 packet instant chicken broth and seasoning mix, dissolved in 1 cup hot water
1 medium tomato, blanched, peeled, seeded, and chopped
Dash each salt and pepper

In 10-inch skillet heat margarine until bubbly and hot; add onion and garlic and sauté until onion is soft *(do not brown)*. Add rice and cook, stirring frequently, until golden, about 3 minutes; stir in ¼ cup dissolved broth mix and cover skillet. Cook over medium heat until rice begins to absorb liquid, about 3 minutes (watch carefully so that rice does not burn). Stir in tomato, salt, pepper, and about ¼ cup more broth; cover skillet and cook, checking rice frequently, until liquid has been almost absorbed. Continue cooking and adding broth as described until rice is tender but still moist, about 15 minutes (be careful that rice does not dry out completely).

Each serving provides: 1 Bread Exchange; ¾ Vegetable Exchange; 1 Fat Exchange; 3 calories Optional Exchange
Per serving: 157 calories; 3 g protein; 4 g fat; 27 g carbohydrate; 291 mg sodium; 0 mg cholesterol

Bolognese Meat Sauce

MAKES 4 SERVINGS, ABOUT ¾ CUP EACH

Wonderful with any cooked pasta. This sauce can be kept in the refrigerator for up to 3 days or it can be frozen for future use.

1 tablespoon plus 1 teaspoon olive oil
½ cup chopped onion
2 garlic cloves, minced
¼ cup each minced carrot and celery
8 ounces ground veal
½ cup skim milk
2 cups drained canned Italian tomatoes, finely chopped
1 teaspoon salt
Dash each pepper and ground nutmeg

In heavy 1½-quart saucepan heat oil; add onion and garlic and sauté until onion is translucent. Add carrot and celery and sauté for about 2 minutes; add veal and cook, stirring constantly with a fork, until meat is crumbly and loses its pink color. Add milk and cook over low heat, stirring frequently, until some of liquid has evaporated, about 3 minutes; add remaining ingredients and bring to a boil. Reduce heat and let simmer, stirring occasionally, until sauce is thick and creamy, about 30 minutes.

Each serving provides: 1½ Protein Exchanges; 1½ Vegetable Exchanges; 1 Fat Exchange; 10 calories Optional Exchange
Per serving: 188 calories; 14 g protein; 10 g fat; 10 g carbohydrate; 776 mg sodium; 41 mg cholesterol

Pesche Ripiene

MAKES 4 SERVINGS

Serve these baked stuffed peaches warm or chilled.

4 medium peaches, cut into halves and pitted
2 tablespoons margarine, divided
1 tablespoon each granulated sugar and shredded coconut
2 teaspoons unsweetened cocoa
1 egg
½ teaspoon almond extract
10 amaretti biscuits (Italian cookies), finely crushed
2 tablespoons Marsala wine

Scoop out some pulp from center of each peach half and reserve. In small mixing bowl combine 1 tablespoon plus 1 teaspoon margarine with the sugar, mixing until well blended; add coconut and cocoa and combine thoroughly. Add egg, extract, and reserved peach pulp and beat well; sprinkle with amaretti crumbs and stir until crumbs are thoroughly moistened.

Preheat oven to 375°F. In 8 x 8 x 2-inch baking pan arrange peach halves, cut-side up; fill each half with ⅛ of the crumb mixture. Pour wine into pan; cut remaining 2 teaspoons margarine into small pieces and add to wine. Bake until peaches are browned, about 30 minutes. For each portion, serve 2 peach halves topped with ¼ of the pan juices.

Each serving provides: 1½ Fat Exchanges; 1 Fruit Exchange; 140 calories Optional Exchange
Per serving: 350 calories; 9 g protein; 25 g fat; 25 g carbohydrate; 94 mg sodium; 69 mg cholesterol

Rice Cakes

MAKES 6 SERVINGS, 1 CAKE EACH

Rice and dried fruit combine to make these delightful Italian cakes. Arborio rice is short-grain Italian rice and gives these little cakes their authentic texture.

1½ cups evaporated skimmed milk
3 ounces uncooked arborio rice (or any short-grain rice)
Dash salt
1 tablespoon plus 2 teaspoons margarine
1 teaspoon granulated sugar
4 dried apricot halves, chopped
¾ ounce dried pineapple (no sugar added), chopped
2 tablespoons each golden raisins and light rum
½ teaspoon grated lemon peel
1 egg, separated
½ teaspoon vanilla extract
1 teaspoon each olive oil and confectioners' sugar

In 2-quart saucepan, over medium heat, bring milk to a boil; add rice and salt and simmer, stirring constantly with wooden spoon, for 10 minutes. Add margarine and granulated sugar and cook until rice is almost tender, about 10 minutes longer. Transfer mixture to medium mixing bowl and stir in dried fruit, rum, and lemon peel; let cool to lukewarm, 10 to 15 minutes.

Preheat oven to 375°F. Add egg yolk and vanilla to cooled rice mixture and stir well. In separate bowl beat egg white until soft peaks form; fold into rice mixture. Using pastry brush, grease six 2½-inch-diameter muffin pan cups with ⅙ of the oil each; spoon ⅙ of rice batter into each greased cup and partially fill remaining cups with water (this will prevent pan from burning and/or warping). Bake until lightly browned, 20 to 25 minutes. Let cakes cool in pan for 5 minutes; carefully drain water from pan and transfer cakes to wire rack. Let cool for 5 minutes longer, then sift an equal amount of confectioners' sugar over each; serve warm.

Each serving provides: ½ Bread Exchange; 1 Fat Exchange;
    ½ Fruit Exchange; ½ Milk Exchange; 30 calories Optional Exchange
Per serving: 176 calories; 7 g protein; 5 g fat; 25 g carbohydrate;
    145 mg sodium; 48 mg cholesterol

Panettone

MAKES 4 SERVINGS

The classic Italian version of fruitcake.

1 cup plus 2 tablespoons all-purpose flour
⅛ teaspoon salt
1 packet fast-rising active dry yeast
2 tablespoons warm water (see yeast package
   directions for temperature)
3 tablespoons granulated sugar, divided
2 eggs
2 tablespoons plus 2 teaspoons reduced-calorie margarine
½ teaspoon each grated orange peel and brandy extract
3 ounces mixed dried fruit, coarsely chopped

Onto sheet of wax paper or a paper plate sift together flour and salt; set aside.

In small bowl sprinkle yeast over water; add 1 teaspoon sugar and stir to dissolve. Let stand until foamy, about 5 minutes.

In mixing bowl, using electric mixer at medium speed, beat eggs with remaining sugar until frothy; add margarine and beat until well combined. Continuing to beat, add orange peel and brandy extract. Add yeast mixture, then gradually beat in sifted flour; beat at high speed for 5 minutes. Add dried fruit, beating until thoroughly combined. Cover bowl with clean damp towel or plastic wrap and let stand in warm draft-free area until dough is doubled in volume, about 30 minutes.

Preheat oven to 400°F. Spray 3-cup fluted mold with nonstick cooking spray. Punch dough down, then turn into sprayed mold; bake in middle of center oven rack for 10 minutes. Reduce oven tmperature to 325°F. and bake until top is browned and cake begins to pull away from mold, about 30 minutes longer (cover with foil if Panettone is browning too quickly). Unmold onto wire rack and let cool.

Each serving provides: ½ Protein Exchange; 1½ Bread Exchanges;
  1 Fat Exchange; 1 Fruit Exchange; 45 calories Optional Exchange
Per serving: 295 calories; 8 g protein; 7 g fat; 51 g carbohydrate;
  200 mg sodium; 137 mg cholesterol

Cassata

MAKES 8 SERVINGS

This chocolate-frosted, cheese-filled cake is a chocolate lover's delight.

¾ cup all-purpose flour
1½ teaspoons double-acting baking powder
⅓ cup unsalted margarine, divided
¼ cup granulated sugar
3 eggs
1½ teaspoons vanilla extract
6 ounces semisweet mini chocolate pieces, divided
¼ cup strong black coffee (hot)
1¼ cups part-skim ricotta cheese
2 tablespoons each confectioners' sugar, sifted, and cherry liqueur
½ teaspoon grated fresh orange peel
¼ ounce shelled pistachio nuts, crushed

Preheat oven to 375°F. Spray 8½ x 4½ x 2½-inch loaf pan with nonstick baking spray; set aside. Onto sheet of wax paper or a paper plate sift together flour and baking powder; set aside. Measure out 1 tablespoon margarine; cut into pieces and set aside. In mixing bowl cream remaining margarine, gradually adding granulated sugar, until mixture is light and fluffy; add eggs and extract and beat to combine. Add sifted flour and mix until thoroughly blended; scrape into sprayed pan and bake for 25 to 30 minutes (until golden and cake tester, inserted in center, comes out dry). Invert loaf onto wire rack and let cool.

In double boiler combine 5 ounces chocolate with coffee; cook over hot (*not boiling*) water until chocolate is melted and mixture is smooth. Remove from heat and stir in margarine, adding 1 piece at a time and stirring until margarine is melted. Cover and refrigerate until spreadable.

In small bowl combine cheese, remaining 1 ounce chocolate pieces, confectioners' sugar, liqueur, and orange peel, mixing well. Cut cooled loaf horizontally into 3 equal slices; spread half of cheese mixture over bottom slice, then top with middle slice and spread with remaining cheese mixture. Replace top slice and spread chocolate mixture

| (CONTINUED) | over entire loaf; garnish with pistachio nuts and refrigerate until chilled.

Each serving provides: 1 Protein Exchange; ½ Bread Exchange; 2 Fat Exchanges; 175 calories Optional Exchange
Per serving: 350 calories; 9 g protein; 21 g fat; 33 g carbohydrate; 155 mg sodium; 115 mg cholesterol

Variation: Substitute licorice-flavored or coffee liqueur for the cherry liqueur. |

Mocha Cappuccino

| MAKES 2 SERVINGS

A very special coffee for a grand occasion. | **1 cup strong coffee (hot)**
2 teaspoons unsweetened cocoa
½ cup skim milk (hot)
2 tablespoons thawed frozen dairy whipped topping
¼ ounce semisweet or milk chocolate, shaved or grated

Combine hot coffee and cocoa, stirring until cocoa is dissolved; pour into 2 cappuccino or coffee cups. Add ¼ cup hot skim milk to each portion and stir; top each with 1 tablespoon whipped topping, then sprinkle each with half of the chocolate.

Each serving provides: ¼ Milk Exchange; 35 calories Optional Exchange
Per serving: 59 calories; 3 g protein; 3 g fat; 7 g carbohydrate; 34 mg sodium; 1 mg cholesterol |

Japan

The Japanese use plates the way artists use easels, for their aim is to make food as pleasing to the eye as it is to the palate. Great care is taken to harmonize shapes and colors, and tiny vegetable stars or petals decorate each course or float beguilingly on the top of clear soups.

Since Japan is a series of islands, foods from the sea—including seaweed—are menu mainstays. One of the most typical Japanese ways of eating fish is as sushi—thin slices of raw fish laid over vinegar-flavored boiled rice. Nigiri Zushi (which we've duplicated) adds pungent wasabi (horseradish) powder. When these fillets of raw fish are served without rice, the dish is called sashimi. Try our version of Tuna Sashimi.

Chicken is very popular and often appears in the form of Yakitori, a skewered barbecued dish. Beef is less popular, although two beef specialties have also scored hits in the western world: Teriyaki, marinated meat cut into strips, and Sukiyaki, sautéed beef with vegetables.

As in other Asian cooking, rice is basic; Japanese rice is meant to be sticky, which is why it adheres as a hub for sushi. We've included a recipe for Sushi Rice and used it in a quartet of dishes, including Vegetarian Sushi Rolls. Vegetables play a major role in Japanese cuisine, especially the soybean, which appears in various forms: as miso, a fermented bean paste that is a base for soups; as tofu, the bean curd that is used in many dishes; and as soy sauce, used for seasoning.

Desserts are rarely served, but tea—especially green tea, served plain—is a ritual, enhanced by a beautiful teapot and special cups.

A Taste of Japan

———

*Suimono**
(Clear Japanese Soup)

*Gingered Shrimp Appetizer**

*Fukusa Zushi**

*Tuna Sashimi**

*Cucumber and Bean Sprouts with Sesame Dressing**

Melon Wedge with Lemon Slice

Tea

Gingered Shrimp Appetizer

MAKES 4 SERVINGS

Chilled shrimp with a teriyaki marinade.

2 tablespoons teriyaki sauce
1½ teaspoons chopped pared ginger root
2 tablespoons rice vinegar
1 teaspoon dry sherry
½ teaspoon granulated sugar
Dash salt
8 ounces shelled and deveined cooked large shrimp
½ medium cucumber, pared and cut into sticks

In metal measuring cup or other small flameproof container bring teriyaki sauce to a boil. Reduce heat to low, add ginger, and let simmer until liquid is slightly reduced, about 3 minutes. Add vinegar, sherry, sugar, and salt and stir to combine; let simmer 3 minutes.

In glass or stainless-steel container that is large enough to hold shrimp in a single layer arrange shrimp; pour in teriyaki mixture and toss to coat. Cover with plastic wrap and refrigerate for at least 3 hours.

Using slotted spoon, remove shrimp from marinade to serving plate; pour marinade into bowl and serve as dipping sauce with shrimp and cucumber.

Each serving provides: 2 Protein Exchanges; ¼ Vegetable Exchange;
  5 calories Optional Exchange
Per serving: 82 calories; 14 g protein; 1 g fat; 4 g carbohydrate;
  413 mg sodium; 85 mg cholesterol

Misoshiru with Shrimp, Tofu, and Radish Sprouts

MAKES 2 SERVINGS

Miso soup, with an assortment of delicious ingredients.

2 tablespoons bottled clam juice
1 packet instant chicken broth and seasoning mix
¾ teaspoon soy sauce
2 cups water
1 tablespoon plus 1 teaspoon miso
   (fermented soybean paste)
6 shelled and deveined small shrimp
1½ ounces drained firm-style tofu (soybean curd),
   cut into ¼-inch cubes
2 tablespoons radish sprouts*

In 1-quart saucepan combine clam juice, broth mix, and soy sauce; add water and, over high heat, bring to a boil. Add miso and stir to dissolve. Reduce heat to medium, add shrimp and tofu, and cook until shrimp turn pink, 2 to 3 minutes. Ladle soup into 2 soup bowls and top each portion with 1 tablespoon radish sprouts.

Each serving provides: 1 Protein Exchange; ⅛ Vegetable Exchange;
   45 calories Optional Exchange
Per serving: 72 calories; 9 g protein; 2 g fat; 5 g carbohydrate;
   684 mg sodium; 44 mg cholesterol

*Radish sprouts, like bean sprouts, can be found in the produce section of the supermarket.

Suimono ⏱

2 packets instant chicken broth and seasoning mix
1 teaspoon teriyaki sauce or soy sauce
1½ cups water
2 tablespoons each thinly sliced carrot and mushrooms
1 tablespoon thinly sliced scallion (green onion)
8 each celery leaves and thin lemon or lime slices
  (or 4 lemon slices and 4 lime slices)

In small saucepan combine broth mix and teriyaki (or soy) sauce; add water and bring to a boil. Pour into 2 soup bowls. To each bowl add 1 tablespoon each carrot and mushrooms, 1½ teaspoons scallion, 4 celery leaves, and 4 lemon or lime slices (or 2 each lemon and lime slices); serve immediately.

Each serving provides: ¼ Vegetable Exchange; 10 calories Optional Exchange
Per serving with teriyaki sauce: 26 calories; 2 g protein; 0.1 g fat; 7 g carbohydrate; 939 mg sodium; 0 mg cholesterol
With soy sauce: 25 calories; 2 g protein; 0.2 g fat; 6 g carbohydrate; 1,061 mg sodium; 0 mg cholesterol

Cucumber and Bean Sprouts with Sesame Dressing

MAKES 2 SERVINGS

Subtle flavors in a specially seasoned sauce.

½ cup bean sprouts
2 cups boiling water
1 medium cucumber, pared, cut in half lengthwise, and thinly sliced
2 tablespoons water
1 tablespoon each rice vinegar and soy sauce
2 teaspoons Chinese sesame oil
⅛ teaspoon seven-pepper spice* or dash each ground red pepper and Japanese powdered mustard (karashi)
2 teaspoons sesame seed, toasted

In 1-quart saucepan add bean sprouts to boiling water; blanch for 1 minute, then drain and immediately rinse with cold water. Transfer sprouts to medium bowl; add cucumber slices.

In 1-cup measure or small bowl combine 2 tablespoons water with the vinegar, soy sauce, sesame oil, and spice powder (or red pepper and mustard); stir well. Pour over sprouts and cucumber, tossing to coat with dressing. Spoon cucumber-sprout mixture onto 2 salad plates and top each portion with 1 teaspoon sesame seed.

Each serving provides: 1½ Vegetable Exchanges; 1 Fat Exchange; 20 calories Optional Exchange
Per serving: 84 calories; 3 g protein; 6 g fat; 6 g carbohydrate; 671 mg sodium; 0 mg cholesterol

*Seven-pepper spice is available at Oriental and specialty food shops.

Fukusa Zushi

MAKES 4 SERVINGS,
2 FILLED PANCAKES
EACH

*Crab- and rice-
filled pancakes.*

4 large dried Chinese mushrooms*
2 tablespoons soy sauce
1 teaspoon dry sherry
2 cups Sushi Rice (see page 223), at room temperature
2 ounces well-drained thawed frozen crab meat, flaked
Tomago Pancakes (see page 227)
1 teaspoon wasabi powder (green horseradish powder),*
    mixed with 1 teaspoon water
Ginger Dipping Sauce (see page 228)

In small bowl combine mushrooms with enough water to
cover; let soak for 1 hour. Drain mushrooms well; trim off
and discard stems and finely chop caps.

Spray 8-inch nonstick skillet with nonstick cooking
spray and heat over medium heat; add chopped mushroom
caps, soy sauce, and sherry and sauté for 3 to 4 minutes.
Transfer to medium mixing bowl; add rice and crab meat
and mix well to combine.

Spoon ⅛ of rice mixture onto quarter of 1 pancake. Fold
pancake in half to enclose filling; top with ⅛ of the wasabi
mixture. Fold pancake in half again, forming a triangle
shape; repeat procedure with remaining rice mixture,
pancakes, and wasabi mixture. Serve with Ginger Dipping
Sauce.

Each serving (including rice, pancakes, and dipping sauce) provides:
    1½ Protein Exchanges; 1 Bread Exchange; ½ Vegetable Exchange;
    35 calories Optional Exchange
Per serving: 248 calories; 13 g protein; 7 g fat; 34 g carbohydrate;
    2,528 mg sodium; 288 mg cholesterol

*If Chinese mushrooms are not available, substitute fresh white
mushroom caps; omit soaking and proceed as directed. Both Chinese
mushrooms and wasabi powder are available in Oriental and specialty
food shops.

Nigiri Zushi

MAKES 4 SERVINGS, 2 SHRIMP EACH *Rectangles of rice, topped with shrimp.*	**8 large shrimp (about ¾ ounce each)** **2¼ cups water, divided** **1 tablespoon rice vinegar** **2 cups Sushi Rice (see page 223), at room temperature** **1 teaspoon wasabi powder (green horseradish powder),*** **mixed with 1 teaspoon water** **Ginger Dipping Sauce (see page 228)**

Insert toothpick or wooden skewer lengthwise along inner curve of each shrimp (to prevent shrimp from curling during cooking). In 1-quart saucepan over high heat bring 2 cups water to a boil; add shrimp and cook until shrimp turn pink, 2 to 3 minutes. Drain shrimp and rinse with cold water; remove toothpicks (or skewers) and shell and devein shrimp. Using sharp knife, cut each shrimp along inner curve butterfly-fashion (being careful not to cut shrimp all the way through). Carefully spread shrimp open and, using side of knife, gently pound to flatten slightly.

In small bowl combine remaining ¼ cup water with the vinegar; moisten hands with vinegar mixture and form Sushi Rice into 8 equal rectangles. Spread ⅛ of wasabi mixture along inside center of each shrimp and top each rice rectangle with 1 shrimp, wasabi-side down. Serve with Ginger Dipping Sauce.

Each serving (including rice and dipping sauce) provides: 1 Protein Exchange; 1 Bread Exchange; 15 calories Optional Exchange
Per serving: 156 calories; 10 g protein; 1 g fat; 27 g carbohydrate; 1,701 mg sodium; 53 mg cholesterol

*Wasabi powder is available in Oriental and specialty food shops.

Hidden Sushi

**MAKES 4 SERVINGS,
3 RICE BALLS EACH**

*The hidden ingredient
is sherry-marinated
cubes of chicken.*

3 tablepoons soy sauce
1 teaspoon each dry sherry and rice vinegar
2 ounces skinned and boned cooked chicken breast, cut
    into 12 equal cubes (about ½ inch each)
2 cups Sushi Rice (see page 223), at room temperature
1 tablespoon each white sesame seed and black sesame
    seed, lightly toasted and combined
Ginger Dipping Sauce (see page 228)

In small mixing bowl combine soy sauce, sherry, and
vinegar; add chicken and toss to coat. Cover with plastic
wrap and refrigerate for at least 30 minutes.

Using slotted spoon, remove chicken from marinade and
set aside. Add rice to marinade and mix until thoroughly
combined.

Moisten a 5 x 10-inch piece of cheesecloth; squeeze out
excess moisture. Divide rice into 12 equal portions. Using
wet hands, place one portion rice in center of cheesecloth
and flatten slightly; place a chicken cube in center of rice.
Gather corners of cheesecloth together and twist to
enclose rice, shaping rice into a ball around chicken cube.
Remove rice ball from cheesecloth and place on serving
plate. Repeat procedure with remaining rice and chicken,
making 11 more balls; sprinkle each rice ball with
½ teaspoon sesame seed. Serve with Ginger Dipping Sauce.

Each serving (including rice and dipping sauce) provides: ½ Protein
    Exchange; 1 Bread Exchange; 45 calories Optional Exchange
Per serving: 179 calories; 9 g protein; 3 g fat; 28 g carbohydrate;
    2,659 mg.sodium; 12 mg cholesterol

Variation: Substitute 6 small shelled and deveined cooked
shrimp, cut crosswise into halves, for the chicken.

Per serving: 184 calories; 8 g protein; 3 g fat; 28 g carbohydrate;
    2,669 mg sodium; 21 mg cholesterol

Vegetarian Sushi Rolls

MAKES 4 SERVINGS, 6 SUSHI ROLL SLICES EACH

Nori are sheets of dried seaweed and are available in plastic packages of 10 to 20 sheets.

Four 8 x 7-inch nori sheets (dried seaweed)
2 cups Sushi Rice (see page 223), at room temperature
1 cup well-drained cooked spinach
Tomago Pancakes (see page 227), cut into thin strips, divided
¾ cup drained pickled ginger slices,* divided
1 tablespoon plus 1 teaspoon wasabi powder (green horseradish powder),* mixed with 2 teaspoons water
Ginger Dipping Sauce (see page 228)
Garnish: decoratively cut cucumber, carrot, and red bell pepper

Preheat broiler. Place 1 nori sheet on baking sheet and broil just until toasted, 3 to 5 seconds *(do not overcook)*. Transfer to sudaré (bamboo rolling mat), flexible place mat, or linen towel. Using wet hands, spread ½ cup Sushi Rice in an even layer over nori sheet to within 1 inch of long ends of sheet; spread ¼ cup spinach along center of rice, then arrange ¼ of pancake strips over rice and top with 2 tablespoons pickled ginger.

Holding inner filling with fingertips, flip long side of mat over filling; roll mat, lifting edge as you roll, to form sushi into a cylinder. Press firmly, then remove mat (the ends of nori will be sealed, making a long roll). Using sharp knife, cut roll into 6 equal slices, wiping knife with damp cloth after every few slices. Repeat procedure with remaining ingredients, making 3 more rolls and 18 more slices.† Arrange sushi on serving plate and serve with wasabi mixture, remaining ¼ cup ginger slices, and Ginger Dipping Sauce; garnish platter with decoratively cut vegetables.

Each serving (including rice, pancakes, and dipping sauce) provides:
1 Protein Exchange; 1 Bread Exchange; ½ Vegetable Exchange;
30 calories Optional Exchange
Per serving: 255 calories; 12 g protein; 6 g fat; 37 g carbohydrate;
2,736 mg sodium; 274 mg cholesterol

*Pickled ginger and wasabi powder are available in Oriental and specialty food shops.
†To add interest, cut roll into thirds; then, cutting on the diagonal, slice each third in half.

Red Snapper Sashimi

MAKES 4 SERVINGS

Since, following Japanese tradition, this fish is served raw, purchase it just before using and be sure it is extremely fresh when purchased.

8 ounces red snapper fillet, chilled
1 cup seeded and shredded pared cucumbers
¾ cup grated carrots
¼ cup finely chopped scallions (green onions)
2 teaspoons wasabi powder (green horseradish powder),*
** mixed with 2 teaspoons water**
Ginger Dipping Sauce (see page 228)

Chill a serving tray. On clean cutting board place fillet skin-side down. Using sharp knife held at an angle, thinly slice fillet into ⅛- to ¼-inch-thick slices, wiping knife on clean damp cloth after every few slices. Arrange fish slices on chilled tray and surround with cucumbers, carrots, and scallions; serve with wasabi mixture and Ginger Dipping Sauce.

Each serving (including dipping sauce) provides: 2 Protein Exchanges; 1 Vegetable Exchange; 10 calories Optional Exchange
Per serving: 83 calories; 13 g protein; 1 g fat; 7 g carbohydrate; 1,424 mg sodium; 31 mg cholesterol

*Wasabi powder is available in Oriental and specialty food stores.

Tuna Sashimi ⏱

MAKES 4 SERVINGS

Since sashimi is served raw, purchase fish just before using and be sure it is extremely fresh when purchased.

8 ounces tuna fillet (preferably 1 piece), chilled
1 cup grated carrots
½ cup grated pared daikon (Japanese radish)
2 teaspoons wasabi powder (green horseradish powder),*
   mixed with 2 teaspoons water
Lemon-Soy Dipping Sauce (see page 228)

Chill a serving tray. On clean cutting board place fillet and, using sharp knife, cut lengthwise into ½-inch-thick slices, wiping knife on clean damp cloth after every few slices; cut slices into ½-inch cubes. Decoratively arrange on chilled tray and surround with carrots and daikon. Serve with wasabi mixture and Lemon-Soy Dipping Sauce.

Each serving provides: 2 Protein Exchanges; ¾ Vegetable Exchange
Per serving (including dipping sauce): 115 calories; 16 g protein; 3 g fat; 7 g carbohydrate; 1,362 mg sodium; 32 mg cholesterol

Serving Suggestion: For a complete meal, serve with Red Snapper Sashimi (see page 221). Each serving of this combination provides: 4 Protein Exchanges; 1¾ Vegetable Exchanges; 10 calories Optional Exchange.

*Wasabi powder is available in Oriental and specialty food shops.

Sushi Rice

YIELDS 2 CUPS COOKED RICE

Use with Vegetarian Sushi Rolls, Hidden Sushi, Fukusa Zushi, and Nigiri Zushi (see pages 220, 219, 217, and 218).

2 tablespoons rice vinegar
1 tablespoon dry sherry
½ teaspoon each granulated sugar and salt
2 cups cooked short-grain rice*

In small saucepan combine vinegar, sherry, sugar, and salt and, over high heat, bring mixture to a boil; cook for 1 minute longer. Set aside and let cool to room temperature.

In wooden bowl, using wooden spoon, gradually fold vinegar mixture into rice, combining thoroughly.

Each ½-cup serving provides: 1 Bread Exchange; 5 calories Optional Exchange

Per serving: 111 calories; 2 g protein; 0.1 g fat; 24 g carbohydrate; 275 mg sodium; 0 mg cholesterol

*It's important that short-grain rice be used. This can be purchased in most Oriental and specialty food shops. Do not substitute long-grain rice.

Yakitori

MAKES 2 SERVINGS

*Pieces of chicken,
chicken livers,
mushrooms,
and scallions
on a skewer.*

2 tablespoons each dry sherry and canned chicken broth
1 tablespoon teriyaki sauce
½ garlic clove, thinly sliced
¼ teaspoon thinly sliced pared ginger root
5 ounces skinned and boned chicken breast,
  cut into 1-inch pieces
5 ounces chicken livers
8 small mushroom caps
4 medium scallions (green onions), about 2 ounces,
  cut into 1-inch pieces

In small stainless-steel or glass mixing bowl combine sherry, chicken broth, teriyaki sauce, garlic, and ginger; mix well. Add chicken and livers and toss to coat with marinade. Cover with plastic wrap and refrigerate for at least 1 hour.

Onto each of four 12-inch wooden or metal skewers, starting and ending with a mushroom cap and alternating remaining ingredients, thread 2 mushroom caps and ¼ each of the chicken pieces, livers, and scallions. Remove and discard garlic and ginger from marinade, reserving marinade. Set skewers on nonstick baking sheet and broil 4 to 5 inches from heat source, turning once and brushing frequently with marinade, until livers are browned and firm and chicken is tender, 2 to 3 minutes on each side. Arrange skewers on serving plate and brush or pour any pan drippings over skewers.

Each serving provides: 4 Protein Exchanges; ¾ Vegetable Exchange; 20 calories Optional Exchange
Per serving: 234 calories; 32 g protein; 5 g fat; 10 g carbohydrate; 452 mg sodium; 359 mg cholesterol

Steak Teriyaki

MAKES 2 SERVINGS

Gingered sherry marinade lends special flavor to thick strips of tender sirloin steak.

¼ cup canned beef broth
2 tablespoons each dry sherry and reduced-sodium soy sauce
½ teaspoon granulated sugar
¼ teaspoon minced pared ginger root
⅛ teaspoon minced fresh garlic
10 ounces boneless beef sirloin steak
½ teaspoon cornstarch, dissolved in 1 teaspoon water

In glass or stainless-steel bowl combine broth, sherry, soy sauce, sugar, ginger root, and garlic, stirring to dissolve sugar; add steak and turn several times to coat with marinade. Cover with plastic wrap and refrigerate for at least 30 minutes.

Transfer steak to rack in broiling pan; set aside. Pour marinade into small saucepan and cook over high heat until mixture comes to a boil; stir in dissolved cornstarch. Reduce heat to medium and cook, stirring frequently, until mixture is clear and thickened, 5 to 10 minutes. Reduce heat to low and keep warm.

Broil steak 5 to 6 inches from heat source for 4 to 5 minutes; turn steak over, brush with 2 tablespoons marinade, and broil 4 to 5 minutes longer or until done to taste.

Remove steak to cutting board and cut into 1-inch-thick strips. Arrange on serving plate and top with remaining marinade.

Each serving provides: 4 Protein Exchanges; 30 calories Optional Exchange
Per serving: 274 calories; 38 g protein; 9 g fat; 4 g carbohydrate; 795 mg sodium; 103 mg cholesterol

Variation: To prepare Chicken Teriyaki, substitute ¼ cup chicken broth for the beef broth and use 10 ounces skinned and boned chicken breasts instead of sirloin steak; proceed according to directions.

Per serving: 198 calories; 34 g protein; 2 g fat; 4 g carbohydrate; 797 mg sodium; 82 mg cholesterol

Sukiyaki

MAKES 2 SERVINGS

A flavorful mix of fresh vegetables and steak slices.

½ cup each canned beef broth and dried Chinese mushrooms
¼ cup reduced-sodium soy sauce
2 tablespoons plus 2 teaspoons dry sherry
10 ounces boneless beef sirloin steak
1 teaspoon Chinese sesame oil
½ cup trimmed Chinese snow peas (stem ends and strings removed)
4 medium scallions (green onions), about 2 ounces, cut into 1½-inch pieces
¼ cup sliced onion
½ garlic clove, minced
¼ teaspoon minced pared ginger root
1 cup shredded Chinese cabbage
¼ cup drained canned sliced bamboo shoots

In small bowl combine beef broth and mushrooms; let stand for 15 minutes. Using slotted spoon, remove mushrooms from broth, reserving broth; trim off and discard stems from mushrooms and cut caps into quarters. Add soy sauce and sherry to broth and mix well; set aside broth mixture and mushrooms.

On rack in broiling pan broil steak 5 to 6 inches from heat source, turning once, until rare, about 3 minutes on each side. Remove steak to cutting board and cut into ¼-inch-thick slices.

In 12-inch nonstick skillet heat oil over medium-high heat; add snow peas, scallions, onion, garlic, and ginger and sauté for 1 minute. Add ¼ cup reserved broth mixture and continue cooking for 1 to 2 minutes longer. Move vegetables to one side of skillet; add mushrooms, cabbage, and bamboo shoots to center of skillet and pour in an additional ¼ cup broth mixture. Cook until vegetables are tender-crisp, 2 to 3 minutes; move vegetables to opposite side of pan from snow pea mixture. Add steak slices and remaining broth mixture to center of skillet and cook, turning once, until steak is heated through, about

(CONTINUED) 30 seconds on each side. Decoratively arrange steak and vegetables on serving plate and top with any juices remaining in pan.

Each serving provides: 4 Protein Exchanges; 2¾ Vegetable Exchanges; ½ Fat Exchange; 30 calories Optional Exchange
Per serving: 364 calories; 43 g protein; 11 g fat; 21 g carbohydrate; 1,519 mg sodium; 103 mg cholesterol

Tomago Pancakes

MAKES 4 SERVINGS, 2 PANCAKES EACH

Use with Fukusa Zushi and Vegetarian Sushi Rolls (see pages 217 and 220).

4 eggs
2 teaspoons granulated sugar
2 teaspoons cornstarch, dissolved in 2 tablespoons water

In small mixing bowl combine eggs, sugar, and dissolved cornstarch and beat; force mixture through fine sieve into another bowl.

Spray 8-inch nonstick skillet with nonstick cooking spray and heat over medium-high heat (to test, sprinkle skillet with drop of water; if water sizzles, skillet is hot enough). Pour ⅛ of batter into skillet and quickly swirl batter so that it covers entire bottom of pan; cook until edges and center are dry and bright yellow, about 1 minute. Using pancake turner, carefully turn pancake over; cook other side briefly (just to dry), about 15 seconds. Line plate with wax paper and slide pancake onto plate. Repeat procedure 7 more times, making 7 more pancakes and placing a sheet of wax paper between each to separate.

Each serving provides: 1 Protein Exchange; 15 calories Optional Exchange
Per serving: 92 calories; 6 g protein; 6 g fat; 4 g carbohydrate; 70 mg sodium; 274 mg cholesterol

Lemon-Soy Dipping Sauce

MAKES 4 SERVINGS, ABOUT 2 TABLE-SPOONS EACH

Serve with Tuna Sashimi (see page 222).

¼ cup soy sauce
2 tablespoons each rice vinegar and lemon juice
¼ teaspoon grated lemon peel

In small bowl combine all ingredients, mixing well. Serve immediately or transfer to resealable plastic container, cover, and store in refrigerator for up to 6 months; serve at room temperature.

Per serving: 15 calories; 1 g protein; 0.3 g fat; 3 g carbohydrate; 1,329 mg sodium; 0 mg cholesterol

Ginger Dipping Sauce

MAKES 4 SERVINGS, ABOUT 2 TABLE-SPOONS EACH

Serve with Red Snapper Sashimi, Vegetarian Sushi Rolls, Hidden Sushi, Nigiri Zushi, and Fukusa Zushi (see pages 221, 220, 219, 218, and 217).

¼ cup each canned chicken broth and dark soy sauce
1 tablespoon plus 1 teaspoon dry sherry
1 tablespoon slivered pared ginger root

In small saucepan combine broth, soy sauce, and sherry and cook over high heat until mixture comes to a boil; add ginger and cook for 1 minute longer. Remove from heat and let cool to room temperature.

Each serving provides: 10 calories Optional Exchange
Per serving: 22 calories; 1 g protein; 0.3 g fat; 2 g carbohydrate; 1,376 mg sodium; 0 mg cholesterol

Latin America

Latin America combines the culinary legacy of the Spanish conquistadors with native Indian dishes; throughout South America foods are generally spicy and paired with rice.

Brazil is an exception—first, because its settlers were primarily Portuguese, and second, because that heritage was expanded by the African slaves, who incorporated much of Brazil's familiar tropical produce into the cuisine. The Portuguese influence can be seen in the abundant use of olives and olive oil, as well as the tomatoes that typically flavor our Brazilian Rice.

When it comes to the cooking of Mexico, the magic word is "chilies." Nearly one hundred varieties of capsicum (the plant from which both chilies and bell peppers come) thrive on Mexican soil. One of the most familiar peppers is the jalapeño, which helps convert squash into our Chayotes Rellenos. However, not all Mexican fare is necessarily hot, and you can always adjust the seasonings to your taste.

Mexico's cuisine also owes a debt to its Aztec and Mayan past. These Indians contributed their reliance on corn as a staple. Another legacy is beans, now a basic dish at every Mexican meal, including breakfast. The Aztecs also ate *ahyacatl*, or avocado, which is used in a multitude of Mexican recipes today, including our Avocado Soup.

The Spanish-Indian combination is best illustrated by the tortilla. The original Spanish omelet became transformed on Mexican shores into Aztec-style bread. When fried, tortillas become tostada shells; fried and spicily filled (with our Picadillo, for example), they become tacos. Tortillas are also delightfully edible substitutes for forks.

The best news about our south-of-the-border imports is that they can help keep you heading down on the scale.

A Latin American Fiesta

Tostadas[*]

Empanaditas[*]
(Mini Turnovers)

Chayotes Rellenos[*]
(Stuffed Squash Mexican Style)

Green Beans with Creamy Tomato Sauce[*]

Pudim de Abóbora[*]
(Mexican Pumpkin Custard)

Sangria with Lemon and Lime Slices

Avocado Soup

MAKES 4 SERVINGS, ABOUT ½ CUP EACH

Enjoy this Mexican soup either warm or chilled.

2 teaspoons olive oil
½ cup diced onion
1 garlic clove, minced
1 teaspoon all-purpose flour
1 packet instant chicken broth and seasoning mix, dissolved in ½ cup hot water
1 teaspoon dry white wine
1 cup skim milk
¼ avocado (about 2 ounces), pared
Dash white pepper
¼ cup sour cream

In 1-quart saucepan heat oil; add onion and garlic and sauté until onion is translucent. Sprinkle with flour and stir quickly to combine; cook, stirring constantly, for 1 minute. Gradually stir in dissolved broth mix; add wine and, stirring constantly, bring to a boil. Reduce heat and let simmer for 2 minutes.

In blender container combine milk and avocado and process until smooth. Add pureed avocado and white pepper to saucepan and stir to combine; let simmer until heated. Divide soup into 4 bowls and top each portion with 1 tablespoon sour cream.

Each serving provides: ¼ Vegetable Exchange; ½ Fat Exchange; ¼ Milk Exchange; 65 calories Optional Exchange
Per serving: 110 calories; 3 g protein; 8 g fat; 8 g carbohydrate; 251 mg sodium; 8 mg cholesterol

Serving Suggestion: Break 2 taco shells into pieces and top each portion of soup with ¼ of the taco pieces. Add ½ Bread Exchange to Exchange Information.

Per serving: 135 calories; 3 g protein; 9 g fat; 11 g carbohydrate; 251 mg sodium; 8 mg cholesterol

Sopa de Lima

MAKES 4 SERVINGS, ABOUT 1½ CUPS EACH

This Yucatan tortilla soup is a Mexican version of chicken soup that has a subtle lime flavor.

2 teaspoons olive oil
4 annatto (achiote) seeds*
¾ cup diced onions
½ cup diced green bell pepper
1 garlic clove, minced
1½ quarts water
6 ounces skinned and boned cooked chicken, diced
¾ cup drained canned Italian tomatoes, seeded and diced
4 packets instant chicken broth and seasoning mix
1 teaspoon oregano leaves
½ teaspoon pepper
1 lime, cut in half
1 strip grapefruit peel (about 2 x ¼-inch strip)
2 corn tortillas (6-inch diameter each)

In 2½- or 3-quart saucepan heat oil over medium-high heat; add annatto seeds and cook until seeds release their color, 1 to 2 minutes. Remove and discard seeds. To saucepan add onions, bell pepper, and garlic and sauté until onions are translucent, 3 to 4 minutes; add water, chicken, tomatoes, broth mix, oregano, and pepper. Squeeze lime halves into soup, then add squeezed halves and grapefruit peel to soup and stir to combine. Reduce heat to low and let simmer for 15 minutes. Using slotted spoon, remove and discard lime halves and grapefruit peel; let soup simmer for 15 minutes longer.

While soup is simmering, spray 9-inch skillet with nonstick cooking spray and heat over medium heat; 1 at a time add tortillas and cook, turning once, until lightly browned on both sides. Cut tortillas into thin strips.

To serve, ladle soup into 4 bowls and top each portion with ¼ of the tortilla strips.

Each serving provides: 1½ Protein Exchanges; ½ Bread Exchange; 1 Vegetable Exchange; ½ Fat Exchange; 10 calories Optional Exchange
Per serving: 165 calories; 15 g protein; 6 g fat; 14 g carbohydrate; 946 mg sodium; 38 mg cholesterol

*This rust-red seed gives food a delicate flavor and a deep golden-orange color. It is usually readily available in the section of the supermarket that stocks Spanish products.

Avocado-Chicken Salad

MAKES 2 SERVINGS

A spicy sour cream dressing adds zest to the mild flavors of chicken and avocado.

3 tablespoons sour cream
2 tablespoons reduced-calorie mayonnaise
1½ teaspoons each drained capers, rinsed, and lemon juice
Dash each crushed red pepper, garlic powder, and
  chili powder
6 ounces skinned and boned cooked chicken (preferably
  white meat), diced
⅛ avocado (about 1 ounce), pared and diced
2 cups shredded lettuce
1 medium tomato, cut into 4 wedges
4 large pimiento-stuffed green olives

In small bowl combine sour cream, mayonnaise, capers, lemon juice, and seasonings; cover with plastic wrap and refrigerate for about 30 minutes to blend flavors.

In another bowl combine chicken and avocado; add dressing and toss to coat. Line 2 salad plates with 1 cup lettuce each and top each portion of lettuce with half of the chicken mixture, 2 tomato wedges, and 2 olives.

Each serving provides: 3 Protein Exchanges; 3 Vegetable Exchanges;
  1½ Fat Exchanges; 85 calories Optional Exchange
Per serving: 287 calories; 29 g protein; 16 g fat; 64 g carbohydrate;
  421 mg sodium; 87 mg cholesterol

Empanaditas

MAKES 8 SERVINGS, 3 TURNOVERS EACH

These mini turnovers make wonderful hors d'oeuvres that will spice up any party.

2 tablespoons plus 2 teaspoons chilled margarine
¾ cup all-purpose flour
3 tablespoons ice water
2 ounces cooked ground pork, crumbled, or finely chopped cooked ham
2 ounces Monterey Jack or Cheddar cheese, shredded
1 teaspoon prepared spicy brown mustard
Dash crushed red pepper
1 egg, separated
1 tablespoon skim milk
Paprika
Garnish: red bell pepper strips and cilantro leaves (Chinese parsley)

In small bowl, with pastry blender or 2 knives used scissors-fashion, cut margarine into flour until mixture resembles coarse meal; sprinkle with water and, using fork, mix to form soft dough. Between 2 sheets of wax paper roll dough, forming a rectangle about ¼ inch thick; remove paper and, using 2-inch-diameter plain or fluted round cookie cutter, cut dough into rounds. Roll scraps of dough and continue cutting until all dough has been used (should yield 24 rounds).

In small bowl, combine pork (or ham), cheese, mustard, and red pepper; set aside.

Preheat oven to 375°F. Beat egg white lightly and brush an equal amount onto each pastry round. Spoon an equal amount of meat mixture (about ½ rounded teaspoon) onto center of each round; fold pastry over, turnover-fashion, to enclose filling. Press edges of dough together to seal. Transfer turnovers to nonstick cookie sheet.

Add milk to egg yolk and beat lightly; brush an equal amount of mixture over each turnover and sprinkle each with dash paprika. Bake until turnovers are golden brown, 15 to 20 minutes. Transfer to warmed serving tray; garnish with red pepper strips and cilantro.

Each serving provides: ½ Protein Exchange; ½ Bread Exchange; 1 Fat Exchange; 10 calories Optional Exchange

(CONTINUED)	Per serving with pork and Monterey Jack cheese: 133 calories; 6 g protein; 8 g fat; 9 g carbohydrate; 104 mg sodium; 47 mg cholesterol With ham and Monterey Jack cheese: 125 calories; 5 g protein; 7 g fat; 9 g carbohydrate; 184 mg sodium; 44 mg cholesterol With pork and Cheddar cheese: 135 calories; 6 g protein; 8 g fat; 9 g carbohydrate; 110 mg sodium; 49 mg cholesterol With ham and Cheddar cheese: 127 calories; 5 g protein; 7 g fat; 9 g carbohydrate; 190 mg sodium; 45 mg cholesterol *Serving Suggestion:* Serve ¼ cup chili sauce alongside turnovers for dipping. Increase Optional Exchange to 20 calories.

Seviche

MAKES 2 SERVINGS *The lime juice in this Peruvian recipe is what "cooks" the scallops; it's a real energy saver.*	**8 ounces bay scallops (or sea scallops, cut into ½-inch pieces)** **½ cup each thinly sliced red onion and freshly squeezed lime juice** **1 small garlic clove, sliced** **1 bay leaf** **½ teaspoon salt** **Dash each freshly ground pepper and crushed red pepper*** **4 lettuce leaves** **Garnish: parsley sprigs** In glass dish that is large enough to hold scallops in a single layer combine all ingredients except lettuce and garnish. Cover with plastic wrap and refrigerate at least 3 hours. 　　To serve, line serving plate with lettuce and, using slotted spoon, transfer scallops and onions onto lettuce; discard liquid, garlic slices, and bay leaf. Garnish with parsley. Each serving provides: 4 Protein Exchanges; 1 Vegetable Exchange Per serving: 115 calories; 18 g protein; 0.3 g fat; 9 g carbohydrate; 842 mg sodium; 40 mg cholesterol *Finely chopped dried red chili pepper can be substituted for the crushed red pepper. If your taste runs to spicy hot, increase peppers to ⅛ teaspoon each.

Tostadas

MAKES 2 SERVINGS

Highly seasoned meat and beans on a tostada shell, served with cooling sour cream.

1 teaspoon olive oil
¼ cup chopped onion
1 garlic clove, minced
½ teaspoon seeded and minced jalapeño or poblano pepper
4 ounces cooked ground beef, crumbled
2 ounces drained canned red kidney beans, mashed
½ cup canned Italian tomatoes (with liquid), drain, seed, and chop tomatoes, reserving liquid
¼ cup canned beef broth
¾ teaspoon chili powder
¼ teaspoon each ground cumin and oregano leaves
⅛ teaspoon salt
2 tostada shells (6-inch diameter each)
1 ounce Cheddar cheese, shredded
½ cup shredded lettuce
¼ cup chopped tomato
¼ cup sour cream
Garnish: cilantro sprig (Chinese parsley)

Preheat oven to 350°F. In 10-inch skillet heat oil over medium-high heat; add onion, garlic, and jalapeño (or poblano) pepper and sauté until onion is translucent, 3 to 4 minutes. Add beef, kidney beans, canned tomatoes with reserved liquid, broth, and seasonings. Reduce heat to medium and let simmer until liquid is reduced and mixture thickens, 5 to 10 minutes.

Place tostada shells on nonstick baking sheet and bake until heated through, 3 to 5 minutes; transfer to serving plate. Spread half of meat mixture over each shell; sprinkle each with ½ ounce cheese, then top each with ¼ cup lettuce and 2 tablespoons chopped tomato. Serve with sour cream garnished with cilantro.

Each serving provides: 3 Protein Exchanges; 1 Bread Exchange; 1½ Vegetable Exchanges; ½ Fat Exchange; 70 calories Optional Exchange
Per serving: 440 calories; 24 g protein; 29 g fat; 21 g carbohydrate; 643 mg sodium (estimated); 81 mg cholesterol

Filetes de Pescado Rellenos

MAKES 4 SERVINGS, 1 STUFFED FILLET EACH

Although these stuffed fish fillets are often prepared with red snapper, our version, which uses flounder, is just as delicious.

2 tablespoons margarine
¼ cup each finely chopped scallions (green onions) and green bell pepper
2 slices white bread, made into crumbs
1 egg, beaten
⅓ cup chopped fresh parsley, divided
½ teaspoon salt
Dash each crushed red pepper and ground nutmeg
4 flounder fillets (5 ounces each)
1 tablespoon lemon juice

Preheat oven to 350°F. In 10-inch skillet melt margarine; remove 1 tablespoon and set aside. Heat remaining margarine until bubbly and hot; add scallions and bell pepper to skillet and sauté over medium heat until vegetables are softened, about 3 minutes. Remove from heat and let cool slightly. Add bread crumbs, egg, ¼ cup parsley, and the seasonings to vegetables and mix until all ingredients are moistened.

Preheat oven to 350°F. Spoon ¼ of vegetable mixture onto center of each fillet and roll fish to enclose. Transfer stuffed fillets, seam-side down, to 8 x 8 x 2-inch baking pan; spoon any remaining stuffing mixture around fillets. Drizzle reserved tablespoon margarine over fillets and sprinkle each with ¾ teaspoon lemon juice. Bake until fish flakes easily when tested with a fork, 15 to 20 minutes. Serve sprinkled with remaining parsley.

Each serving provides: 4 Protein Exchanges; ½ Bread Exchange; ¼ Vegetable Exchange; 1½ Fat Exchanges; 20 calories Optional Exchange
Per serving: 223 calories; 27 g protein; 9 g fat; 8 g carbohydrate; 533 mg sodium; 140 mg cholesterol

Picadillo ⏱

MAKES 2 SERVINGS

*Serve this beef hash
with rice or as a
filling for tacos
or tortillas.*

2 teaspoons olive oil
8 ounces cooked ground beef (sirloin or top round)
¼ cup diced onion
½ garlic clove, minced
1 medium tomato, blanched, peeled, seeded, and chopped
1 small apple, pared, cored, and chopped
1 canned jalapeño pepper, drained, seeded, and
    thinly sliced
2 tablespoons raisins
2 each large pimiento-stuffed green olives and pitted black
    olives, sliced crosswise
¼ teaspoon each salt and pepper
Dash each ground cinnamon and ground cloves

In 10-inch skillet heat oil over medium heat; add beef and
cook, breaking up large pieces with a wooden spoon, until
crumbly. Add onion and garlic and sauté until onion is
softened, about 5 minutes; stir in remaining ingredients.
Reduce heat to low and cook, stirring occasionally, until
flavors are well blended, about 20 minutes.

Each serving provides: 4 Protein Exchanges; 1½ Vegetable Exchanges;
    1 Fat Exchange; 1 Fruit Exchange; 10 calories Optional Exchange
Per serving with sirloin steak: 374 calories; 38 g protein; 15 g fat;
    21 g carbohydrate; 771 mg sodium; 103 mg cholesterol
With round steak: 353 calories; 37 g protein; 14 g fat; 21 g carbohydrate;
    769 mg sodium; 103 mg cholesterol

Steak Rancheros

MAKES 2 SERVINGS

Mexican country steaks, a hearty meat-and-potatoes casserole.

10 ounces boneless chuck steak (about ½ inch thick)
2 teaspoons olive oil
½ cup sliced onion
2 garlic cloves, minced
1 cup canned Italian tomatoes (with liquid), drain, seed, and chop tomatoes, reserving liquid
2 teaspoons minced fresh cilantro (Chinese parsley)
6 ounces new potatoes, scrubbed and sliced (¼-inch-thick slices)
¼ cup seeded and sliced mild green chili peppers (1-inch strips)

On rack in broiling pan broil steak, turning once, until well browned but rare, 3 to 4 minutes on each side. Transfer to 1-quart flameproof casserole; set aside.

In 9-inch skillet heat oil over medium-high heat; add onion and garlic and sauté until onion is softened. Add tomatoes with reserved liquid and cilantro and sauté for 5 minutes.

Arrange potato slices over steak in casserole, pour in tomato mixture, and top with chili pepper strips; cover and bake at 350°F. for 20 to 25 minutes. Remove cover and bake until steak is tender and potatoes are browned, about 30 minutes longer. (If potatoes are not browned, place casserole under broiler during last 5 minutes of cooking.)

Each serving provides: 4 Protein Exchanges; 1 Bread Exchange; 1¾ Vegetable Exchanges; 1 Fat Exchange
Per serving: 440 calories; 37 g protein; 21 g fat; 26 g carbohydrate; 222 mg sodium; 103 mg cholesterol

Brazilian Rice

MAKES 2 SERVINGS

Capers accent this rice and tomato mixture.

2 teaspoons olive oil
¼ cup chopped onion
2 ounces uncooked regular long-grain rice
½ cup canned chicken broth
¼ cup drained canned Italian tomatoes, chopped
1½ teaspoons drained capers, rinsed
Dash each salt and pepper

In 1-quart saucepan heat oil over medium heat; add onion and cook until translucent *(do not brown)*. Add rice and cook, stirring constantly, for 2 minutes; add remaining ingredients, stir to combine, and bring to a boil. Reduce heat to low, cover, and cook until all liquid has been absorbed and rice is tender, 15 to 20 minutes.

Each serving provides: 1 Bread Exchange; ½ Vegetable Exchange; 1 Fat Exchange; 10 calories Optional Exchange
Per serving: 167 calories; 4 g protein; 5 g fat; 26 g carbohydrate; 358 mg sodium; 0 mg cholesterol

Chayotes Rellenos

MAKES 2 SERVINGS,
2 STUFFED SQUASH
HALVES EACH

*Jalapeño enlivens the
tomato 'n' cheese
stuffing in this
stuffed squash
Mexican style.*

2 medium chayotes, 9 to 10 ounces each (also known as
   mirliton, vegetable pear, or mango squash)*
¼ cup minced onion
3 tablespoons minced green bell pepper
1 tablespoon seeded and minced drained canned jalapeño
   pepper
½ cup drained canned whole tomatoes, seeded and chopped
2 garlic cloves, minced
1 teaspoon minced fresh cilantro (Chinese parsley)
2 ounces mild Cheddar cheese, shredded, divided

In 4-quart saucepan place chayotes and fill pan with water
to a depth of about 1 inch. Bring water to a boil, cover
saucepan, and cook until chayotes are fork-tender, about
30 minutes. Drain off water and run cold water over
chayotes; set aside and let cool.

Spray 9-inch skillet with nonstick cooking spray and heat
over medium heat; add onion and peppers and cook, stirring
frequently, until onion is translucent. Add tomatoes, garlic,
and cilantro and sauté for 3 minutes longer; transfer to
medium bowl and set aside.

Preheat oven to 375°F. Slice each chayote in half
lengthwise; remove and discard pit and fibrous core. Using
spoon, carefully scoop out pulp, leaving skin intact; reserve
chayote shells. Finely chop pulp and add to vegetable
mixture; stir in 1 ounce cheese. Spoon ¼ of mixture into
each chayote shell and sprinkle each with ¼ ounce cheese.
Set stuffed shells on baking sheet and bake until heated
through and cheese is melted, 15 to 20 minutes.

Each serving provides: 1 Protein Exchange; 3 Vegetable Exchanges
Per serving: 218 calories; 10 g protein; 10 g fat; 26 g carbohydrate;
   334 mg sodium; 30 mg cholesterol

*A 9- to 10-ounce chayote will yield about 1 cup squash.

Green Beans with Creamy Tomato Sauce

MAKES 2 SERVINGS

Fresh beans in a tomato-cheese sauce, a side dish that adds color to any meal.

2 teaspoons margarine
¼ cup chopped scallions (green onions)
1½ teaspoons all-purpose flour
½ cup drained canned Italian tomatoes, chopped
½ teaspoon chopped fresh cilantro (Chinese parsley)
   or curly parsley
⅛ teaspoon salt
Dash each oregano leaves and pepper
2 tablespoons each skim milk and part-skim ricotta cheese
1½ ounces Monterey Jack or part-skim mozzarella cheese,
   shredded
8 ounces whole green beans, trimmed and cooked
   (about 2 cups), hot

In 1-quart saucepan heat margarine until bubbly and hot; add scallions and sauté until softened, about 2 minutes. Sprinkle with flour and stir quickly to combine; add tomatoes, cilantro (or curly parsley), and seasonings and cook over medium heat, stirring constantly, until mixture comes to a boil. Reduce heat to low.

In small bowl combine milk and ricotta cheese and stir until well blended; add ricotta mixture and Monterey Jack (or mozzarella) cheese to saucepan and cook, stirring constantly, until cheeses melt and sauce becomes creamy, about 2 minutes *(do not boil)*.

To serve, arrange green beans on serving plate and top with sauce.

Each serving provides: 1 Protein Exchange; 2¾ Vegetable Exchanges;
   1 Fat Exchange; 15 calories Optional Exchange
Per serving with Monterey Jack cheese: 197 calories; 10 g protein;
   12 g fat; 14 g carbohydrate; 409 mg sodium; 24 mg cholesterol
With mozzarella cheese: 172 calories; 10 g protein; 9 g fat;
   15 g carbohydrate; 395 mg sodium; 17 mg cholesterol

Mexican Potato Salad

MAKES 4 SERVINGS

A fiesta of colorful ingredients makes this potato salad outstanding.

12 ounces peeled cooked potatoes, cut into cubes
½ medium tomato, cut into 4 wedges
¼ cup each diced red bell pepper and drained canned
  whole-kernel corn
2 tablespoons each diced red onion and celery
4 pitted black olives, sliced
1½ teaspoons seeded and minced green chili pepper
2 tablespoons vegetable oil
1 tablespoon plus 1½ teaspoons red wine vinegar
1 teaspoon chili powder
½ teaspoon salt
Dash pepper

In salad bowl combine potatoes, tomato, bell pepper, corn, onion, celery, olives, and chili pepper.

In small bowl combine remaining ingredients; pour over salad and toss to coat. Cover with plastic wrap and refrigerate for at least 2 hours. Toss again just before serving.

Each serving provides: 1 Bread Exchange; ½ Vegetable Exchange;
  1½ Fat Exchanges; 15 calories Optional Exchange
Per serving: 144 calories; 2 g protein; 8 g fat; 17 g carbohydrate;
  344 mg sodium; 0 mg cholesterol

Polvorones

**MAKES 10 SERVINGS,
2 CAKES EACH**

*Sugar and spice
combined with the
tang of sour cream
make these Mexican
tea cakes special.*

2 cups less 1 tablespoon cake flour, divided
½ teaspoon each baking soda and cream of tartar
¼ teaspoon salt
½ cup less 1 tablespoon margarine
¼ cup sifted confectioners' sugar, divided
1 egg
¼ cup sour cream
1 teaspoon each almond and vanilla extracts
¼ teaspoon ground cinnamon

Into small mixing bowl sift all but 1 tablespoon flour with the baking soda, cream of tartar, and salt; set aside.

In large deep mixing bowl cream margarine with 3 tablespoons sugar; add egg, sour cream, and extracts and, using electric mixer, beat until thoroughly combined. Beat in sifted ingredients, ⅓ at a time, and continue beating until thoroughly combined, scraping dough from beaters as necessary. Transfer dough to sheet of plastic wrap; enclose dough in wrap and form into a ball. Refrigerate for 15 to 20 minutes.

Preheat oven to 400°F. Spray baking sheet with nonstick cooking spray. Cut dough into 20 equal pieces (about ¾ ounce each); working directly over dough, dust hands with remaining 1 tablespoon flour, allowing excess to sprinkle over dough. Using hands, form each piece into a ball; arrange balls on sprayed sheet, leaving a space of about 1 inch between each. Bake until lightly browned, 8 to 10 minutes. Sift remaining tablespoon sugar with the cinnamon onto plate. Roll warm tea cakes in sugar mixture to coat, transfer to wire rack, and let cool for 10 minutes before serving.

Each serving provides: 1 Bread Exchange; 2 Fat Exchanges; 50 calories Optional Exchange
Per serving: 187 calories; 3 g protein; 10 g fat; 21 g carbohydrate; 195 mg sodium; 30 mg cholesterol

Paella

Hawaiian Cheese-Filled Papaya

Orange Chicken

Tourtière

Curried Shrimp
with Saffron Rice

Facing:
Polvorones
Koulourakia Cookies
Greek Honey Twists

Almond Apples

Chocolate-Raspberry
Fondue

Pudim de Abóbora

MAKES 4 SERVINGS

A creamy, spiced Mexican pumpkin custard.

1 cup skim milk
½ cup evaporated skimmed milk
2 eggs
1 cup canned or pureed cooked fresh pumpkin
½ teaspoon ground cinnamon
¼ teaspoon each ground ginger, salt, and grated
   orange peel
2 teaspoons firmly packed brown sugar

Preheat oven to 350°F. In medium mixing bowl beat together skim milk, evaporated milk, and eggs; add pumpkin, cinnamon, ginger, salt, and orange peel and, using wooden spoon, stir until mixture is thoroughly combined and smooth.

Lightly spray four 6-ounce custard cups with nonstick cooking spray; fill each cup with ¼ of pumpkin mixture. Place cups in 13 x 9 x 2-inch baking pan and fill pan with boiling water to a depth of about 1 inch; bake until surface of custard is firm, about 30 minutes. Sprinkle ½ teaspoon sugar over each custard and bake 10 to 15 minutes longer (until knife, inserted in center of custard, comes out clean). Remove baking pan from oven and carefully remove cups from water bath (water will be boiling hot); let custard cool, then cover and refrigerate for at least 30 minutes.

Each serving provides: ½ Protein Exchange; ½ Vegetable Exchange; ½ Milk Exchange; 10 calories Optional Exchange
Per serving with canned pumpkin: 116 calories; 8 g protein; 3 g fat; 14 g carbohydrate; 242 mg sodium; 139 mg cholesterol
With cooked fresh pumpkin: 108 calories; 8 g protein; 3 g fat; 12 g carbohydrate; 240 mg sodium; 139 mg cholesterol

The Middle East

The nations of this area are in general accord on the subject of food. Because of religious restrictions, pork is rarely eaten in Israel and the Arab world, and many Arab dishes, like the chick-pea mixture called Hummus, have been adopted by the Israelis, who serve it on pita bread, another shared specialty.

Throughout most of the Middle East, lamb is the basic meat. It is often combined with bulgur (cracked wheat), as in our Lebanese Meatball Soup. Sis Kebab—cubed lamb cooked on skewers—is another favorite, often served with Pilav, a rice dish that is also typical of the region. Both of these originated in Turkey, whose well-seasoned cuisine reflects the Balkans as well as the Arab nations.

In Israel, which blends the heritages of its European immigrants with those of neighboring countries, chicken is the exclusive Sabbath eve (Friday) entrée. Try our version of Israeli Sweet and Spiced Chicken, flavored with fresh fruits and honey. In the proverbial "land of milk and honey," honey enhances everything from poultry dishes to Israel's famous Honey Cake.

In most of the Mideast, Mediterranean vegetables such as squash, eggplant, and tomato are served either stuffed or encased in grape leaves. Sesame seeds are used freely, and mint is valued for its cooling qualities. We use it to flavor our Arabian Mint Tea, a ritual drink.

The most popular beverage across all the borders is coffee. For an authentic touch, serve it in small glasses, the way it's drunk in Israel, or Egyptian-style, in miniature cups that hold only a few sips, or make our Arabian Coffee, black, strong, and spiced with cardamom seeds—the fabled "grains of Paradise."

A Mideast Feast

Lebanese Meatball Soup[*]

Turkish Sis Kebab[*]
(Skewered Lamb)

Domates Dolmasi[*]
(Stuffed Tomatoes)

Salade Aubergine[*]
(Eggplant Salad)

Mahallebi[*]
(Rose Water Pudding)

Arabian Coffee[*]

Lebanese Meatball Soup

MAKES 2 SERVINGS

This is excellent for lunch or as a first course for dinner.

1 ounce cracked wheat (bulgur)
2½ cups water, divided
4 ounces ground lamb
¼ cup minced onion
¼ teaspoon each salt and pepper
⅛ teaspoon ground cumin
Dash ground allspice
2 tablespoons each diced celery and carrot
½ garlic clove, minced
2 ounces drained canned chick-peas
2 packets instant chicken broth and seasoning mix
1 teaspoon lemon juice
½ bay leaf

In small bowl combine cracked wheat with ½ cup water; let stand for 30 minutes. Using a fine sieve, drain cracked wheat, extracting as much water as possible; transfer wheat to medium mixing bowl and add lamb, onion, salt, pepper, cumin, and allspice, mixing well. Form mixture into 1-inch-diameter meatballs and transfer meatballs to rack in broiling pan; broil until browned, 4 to 6 minutes. Remove from heat and set aside.

Spray 1½- or 2-quart saucepan with nonstick cooking spray; add celery, carrot, and garlic and cook over medium-high heat, stirring constantly, until vegetables are softened, 1 to 2 minutes. Add chick-peas, broth mix, lemon juice, bay leaf, and remaining 2 cups water, stirring to combine; let simmer for 10 minutes. Add meatballs and cook until vegetables are tender and meatballs are heated through, 10 to 15 minutes. Remove bay leaf before serving.

Each serving provides: 2 Protein Exchanges; ½ Bread Exchange; ½ Vegetable Exchange; 10 calories Optional Exchange
Per serving: 198 calories; 16 g protein; 5 g fat; 22 g carbohydrate; 1,245 mg sodium (estimated); 43 mg cholesterol

Munkaczina

MAKES 2 SERVINGS

An easy-to-prepare orange, onion, and olive salad.

2 small navel oranges, peeled and thinly sliced crosswise
¼ cup thinly sliced red or Bermuda onion
   (separated into rings)
4 pitted black olives, whole or sliced
1 tablespoon lemon juice
2 teaspoons olive or vegetable oil
¼ teaspoon salt
Garnish: mint leaves

In salad bowl combine oranges, onion rings, and olives. In small bowl, using a whisk, combine lemon juice, oil, and salt; pour over salad and toss to coat. Serve at room temperature or cover and refrigerate until chilled. Just before serving, garnish with mint leaves.

Each serving provides: ¼ Vegetable Exchange; 1 Fat Exchange;
   1 Fruit Exchange; 10 calories Optional Exchange
Per serving: 120 calories; 2 g protein; 6 g fat; 17 g carbohydrate;
   329 mg sodium; 0 mg cholesterol

Salade Aubergine

MAKES 4 SERVINGS

This eggplant salad is a variation of the popular Syrian dish, baba ganosh.

1 large eggplant (about 1½ pounds)
½ cup diced green bell pepper
1 tablespoon plus 1 teaspoon olive oil
2 teaspoons sesame seed, toasted and ground
2 garlic cloves, mashed
1 teaspoon minced fresh mint
½ teaspoon salt
⅛ teaspoon each pepper and paprika

Preheat oven to 500°F. Pierce eggplant in several places and bake until skin is charred, 20 to 30 minutes. Remove eggplant from oven, place in paper bag, and let cool. Remove and discard skin; in bowl mash pulp. Add remaining ingredients, mixing well to combine; cover with plastic wrap and refrigerate for at least 2 hours.

Each serving provides: 2¼ Vegetable Exchanges; 1 Fat Exchange;
   10 calories Optional Exchange
Per serving: 97 calories; 3 g protein; 6 g fat; 11 g carbohydrate;
   280 mg sodium; 0 mg cholesterol

Çerkes Tavuğu

MAKES 4 SERVINGS

Chicken Circassian, regarded by Iranians as a national dish, is usually served as a first course or as an hors d'oeuvre. Our version converts this into a main course.

3 packets instant chicken broth and seasoning mix, dissolved in 2 cups boiling water
4 slices 2-day-old whole wheat or white bread, torn into pieces
1 tablespoon plus 1 teaspoon walnut or olive oil
½ teaspoon paprika
Dash pepper
1 ounce shelled walnuts, ground
1 pound skinned and boned boiled chicken, cut into strips (warm)

In blender container combine all ingredients except walnuts and chicken; process into a smooth, thick sauce, scraping down sides of container as necessary. Add walnuts and stir to combine. Arrange chicken strips on serving platter and pour sauce over chicken; serve warm.

Each serving provides: 4 Protein Exchanges; 1 Bread Exchange; 1 Fat Exchange; 55 calories Optional Exchange
Per serving: 367 calories; 37 g protein; 18 g fat; 13 g carbohydrate; 844 mg sodium; 102 mg cholesterol

Israeli Sweet and Spiced Chicken

MAKES 4 SERVINGS

Olives, onions, and oranges add interest to this casserole.

1 tablespoon plus 1 teaspoon vegetable oil
1 whole chicken (3 pounds), cut into 8 or 12 pieces and skinned
2 cups thinly sliced onions
1 cup orange juice (no sugar added)
2 tablespoons honey
1 teaspoon each salt and paprika
½ teaspoon each ground ginger and ground nutmeg
8 large pitted black olives, sliced or whole
1 tablespoon water
2 teaspoons cornstarch
2 small oranges, peeled and sectioned, or 1 cup canned mandarin orange sections (no sugar added)

Preheat oven to 350°F. In 10-inch nonstick skillet heat oil; in batches, brown chicken pieces on all sides. Over bottom of shallow 3-quart casserole spread onion slices; top onions with chicken pieces. In 2-cup measure or bowl combine juice, honey, and seasonings; pour mixture evenly over chicken and top chicken with olives. Cover casserole and bake until chicken is tender, about 45 minutes.

Transfer chicken and olives to serving platter and keep warm. Scrape onions and pan juices into 1-quart saucepan and bring to a boil. In small cup combine water and cornstarch, stirring to dissolve cornstarch; stir into onion mixture. Reduce heat and simmer, stirring constantly, until mixture thickens; pour over chicken. Serve garnished with orange sections.

Each serving provides: 4 Protein Exchanges; 1 Vegetable Exchange; 1 Fat Exchange; 1 Fruit Exchange; 45 calories Optional Exchange
Per serving with fresh oranges: 353 calories; 33 g protein; 11 g fat; 32 g carbohydrate; 731 mg sodium; 99 mg cholesterol
With canned orange sections: 348 calories; 33 g protein; 11 g fat; 31 g carbohydrate; 734 mg sodium; 99 mg cholesterol

Turkish Sis Kebab

MAKES 2 SERVINGS

For an elegant meal, serve this skewered lamb with a tossed green salad and red wine.

1 tablespoon lemon juice
½ teaspoon salt
½ teaspoon coarsely ground pepper
10 ounces lamb cubes (1-inch cubes)
½ cup onion wedges
6 cherry tomatoes
2 medium mild or hot green chili peppers, seeded and each cut into thirds
4 bay leaves
1 cup cooked long-grain rice (hot)

In stainless-steel or glass bowl combine first 3 ingredients; add lamb and toss to coat with marinade. Cover and refrigerate for 1 hour.

Remove meat from marinade, reserving marinade. Onto each of two 12-inch skewers, alternating ingredients, thread 5 ounces lamb, ¼ cup onion wedges, 3 cherry tomatoes, 3 pepper pieces, and 2 bay leaves. Set skewers on rack in broiling pan and broil for 3 to 5 minutes; brush with reserved marinade, turn skewers over, and broil until lamb is done to taste. Serve over hot rice.

Each serving provides: 4 Protein Exchanges; 1 Bread Exchange; 2½ Vegetable Exchanges
Per serving: 399 calories; 37 g protein; 9 g fat; 43 g carbohydrate; 653 mg sodium; 113 mg cholesterol

Domates Dolmasi

MAKES 4 SERVINGS

Stuffed tomatoes, a popular Turkish side dish.

4 medium tomatoes
1 tablespoon plus 1 teaspoon olive or vegetable oil, divided
½ cup diced onion
1 garlic clove, minced
¼ cup dried currants
1 teaspoon salt
⅛ teaspoon pepper
1 cup cooked long-grain rice (hot)
1 ounce pignolias (pine nuts), lightly toasted
1 tablespoon each chopped fresh Italian (flat-leaf)
parsley and mint
2 teaspoons sunflower seed
1 tablespoon plain dried bread crumbs

Cut thin slice from stem end of each tomato; reserve slices. Set a sieve over a bowl. Scoop out pulp from tomatoes and place pulp in sieve to drain; set shells upside down on paper towels and let drain. Discard seeds from tomato pulp; reserve liquid. Chop pulp and set aside.

In small nonstick skillet heat 2 teaspoons oil; add onion and garlic and sauté until onion is golden. Stir in currants, salt, pepper, and 2 tablespoons of reserved tomato liquid; remove from heat and stir in rice, nuts, parsley, mint, and sunflower seed.

Preheat oven to 375°F. In 8 x 8 x 2-inch baking dish set tomato shells upright; spoon ¼ of rice mixture into each tomato and top each with a reserved tomato slice. Brush ½ teaspoon oil over each tomato and pour remaining tomato liquid into baking dish (to prevent sticking). Sprinkle each tomato with ¾ teaspoon bread crumbs and bake until filling is hot and skin begins to split, about 30 minutes.

Each serving provides: ½ Bread Exchange; 2¼ Vegetable Exchanges; 1 Fat Exchange; ½ Fruit Exchange; 60 calories Optional Exchange
Per serving: 215 calories; 6 g protein; 9 g fat; 30 g carbohydrate; 570 mg sodium; 0.1 mg cholesterol

Hummus

MAKES 4 SERVINGS

Serve this chick-pea spread with pita or crudités.

4 ounces drained canned chick-peas (reserve 1 tablespoon liquid)
1 tablespoon lemon juice
2 teaspoons sesame seed, toasted
½ teaspoon Chinese sesame oil
1 small garlic clove

In work bowl of food processor combine chick-peas and reserved liquid with remaining ingredients; process into a smooth paste.

Each serving provides: ½ Protein Exchange; 15 calories Optional Exchange
Per serving: 42 calories; 2 g protein; 2 g fat; 5 g carbohydrate; 1 mg sodium; 0 mg cholesterol

Pilav ⏱

MAKES 4 SERVINGS

A rice pilaf indigenous to Turkey.

2 teaspoons olive oil
4 ounces uncooked regular long-grain rice
1 cup water
2 packets instant beef broth and seasoning mix
⅛ teaspoon pepper
1 medium tomato, thinly sliced
2 teaspoons margarine
1 tablespoon chopped fresh mint

In 1-quart saucepan heat oil; add rice and sauté, stirring constantly, until browned. Stir in water, broth mix, and pepper and bring to a boil. Reduce heat to low, cover pan, and let simmer until rice is tender but not soft, about 15 minutes.

Spoon rice onto flameproof serving platter; arrange tomato slices around rice and dot rice with margarine. Place platter under broiler and broil until tomatoes are cooked and margarine is melted, 2 to 3 minutes. Serve sprinkled with chopped mint.

Each serving provides: 1 Bread Exchange; ½ Vegetable Exchange; 1 Fat Exchange; 5 calories Optional Exchange
Per serving: 153 calories; 3 g protein; 4 g fat; 25 g carbohydrate; 398 mg sodium; 0 mg cholesterol

Honey Cake

MAKES 8 SERVINGS

A delicious dessert from "the land of milk and honey."

½ cup raisins
1½ cups all-purpose flour, divided
2 tablespoons plus 2 teaspoons vegetable oil, divided
1 teaspoon double-acting baking powder
¼ teaspoon each baking soda and ground cinnamon
⅛ teaspoon ground allspice
Dash ground cloves
4 eggs, separated
3 tablespoons granulated sugar
2 tablespoons honey
1 teaspoon each instant coffee, dissolved in 1 tablespoon hot water, and grated lemon peel
⅛ teaspoon salt

In small bowl combine raisins with 2 teaspoons flour, tossing to coat; set aside. Brush a 7⅜ x 3⅝ x 2¼-inch loaf pan with 1 teaspoon oil, then dust with 1 teaspoon flour; set aside. Onto sheet of wax paper or a paper plate sift together remaining flour, baking powder, baking soda, and spices; set aside.

Preheat oven to 325°F. In mixing bowl, using electric mixer at medium speed, beat egg yolks with sugar until frothy; add remaining oil and the honey and beat until mixture is fluffy. Beat in dissolved coffee and lemon peel; gradually beat in sifted ingredients. Add raisins and stir to combine. In separate bowl, using clean beaters, beat egg whites with salt until stiff peaks form; using rubber scraper, stir about ⅓ of whites into batter. Gently fold in remaining whites; pour into greased pan and bake for 40 to 45 minutes (until cake tester, inserted in center, comes out clean). Let cake cool in pan for 5 minutes, then invert cake onto wire rack and let cool completely.

Each serving provides: ½ Protein Exchange; 1 Bread Exchange; 1 Fat Exchange; ½ Fruit Exchange; 40 calories Optional Exchange
Per serving: 227 calories; 6 g protein; 8 g fat; 35 g carbohydrate; 150 mg sodium; 137 mg cholesterol

Israeli Apple Pancakes

MAKES 2 SERVINGS, 3 PANCAKES EACH

These matzo meal pancakes are best served warm.

½ cup applesauce (no sugar added)
1 egg, lightly beaten
3 tablespoons matzo meal
1 teaspoon double-acting baking powder
Dash ground cinnamon
2 teaspoons vegetable oil, divided
1 teaspoon confectioners' sugar, mixed with dash ground nutmeg, then sifted

In small bowl, using a fork, combine applesauce and egg; add matzo meal, baking powder, and cinnamon and combine thoroughly.

In 10-inch nonstick skillet heat 1 teaspoon oil; using half of batter, drop batter by rounded tablespoonfuls into skillet, forming 3 equal pancakes. Using back of spoon, flatten pancakes to form 4-inch circles; cook until bottom and edges are lightly browned and bubbles appear on surface. Using pancake turner, turn pancakes over; cook until browned on other side. Transfer pancakes to warmed serving platter and keep warm. Using remaining oil and batter, repeat procedure, making 3 more pancakes.

Using half of the sugar mixture, sprinkle each pancake with an equal amount of mixture; roll pancakes jelly-roll fashion and sprinkle each with an equal amount of remaining sugar mixture.

Each serving provides: ½ Protein Exchange; ½ Bread Exchange; 1 Fat Exchange; ½ Fruit Exchange; 10 calories Optional Exchange
Per serving: 161 calories; 4 g protein; 7 g fat; 19 g carbohydrate; 249 mg sodium; 137 mg cholesterol

Mahallebi

MAKES 4 SERVINGS

This rose water pudding is a true Turkish delight.

2 cups skim milk, divided
¼ cup rose water, divided*
3 tablespoons all-purpose flour
2 tablespoons granulated sugar
½ ounce shelled pistachio nuts, ground

In small bowl combine ¼ cup milk with 3 tablespoons plus 1½ teaspoons rose water and the flour and sugar, mixing to a smooth thin paste. In small saucepan, over low heat, bring remaining 1¾ cups milk to a boil; add rose water mixture and cook over low heat, stirring constantly, until pudding thickens, about 5 minutes. Remove from heat. Moisten inside of 4 dessert dishes with remaining 1½ teaspoons rose water and divide pudding into dishes; let cool. Sprinkle each portion with ¼ of the ground nuts, then cover with plastic wrap and refrigerate until chilled.

Each serving provides: ½ Milk Exchange; 75 calories Optional Exchange
Per serving: 109 calories; 5 g protein; 2 g fat; 17 g carbohydrate; 64 mg
    sodium; 2 mg cholesterol

*Rose water can be purchased in specialty food stores, health food stores, and some supermarkets.

Arabian Coffee

MAKES 2 SERVINGS

Cardamom is the secret of this brew.

1 tablespoon coarsely ground espresso coffee beans
2 to 3 whole cardamom, split and crushed
Dash ground ginger
1 cup cold water
1 teaspoon granulated sugar (optional)

In small saucepan combine coffee, cardamom, and ginger; add water and bring to a boil. Reduce heat and let simmer for 15 to 20 minutes. Pour coffee through a filter into a serving pot. Serve in demitasse cups and, if desired, add ½ teaspoon sugar to each portion.

Each serving with sugar provides: 10 calories Optional Exchange
Per serving: 10 calories; trace protein; trace fat; 2 g carbohydrate;
   1 mg sodium; 0 mg cholesterol
Without sugar: 2 calories; trace protein; trace fat; 0.1 g carbohydrate;
   1 mg sodium; 0 mg cholesterol

Arabian Mint Tea

**MAKES 2 SERVINGS,
1 CUP EACH**

*Mint tea is a favorite
round the world.*

**1 tablespoon each green China tea leaves (or 3 tea bags)
and chopped fresh mint**
2 teaspoons granulated sugar
2 cups boiling water

In heated teapot combine tea leaves (or tea bags), mint,
and sugar; add water, cover pot, and let stand for 5 to 10
minutes (the longer the tea steeps, the stronger the flavor
will be).

Each serving provides: 20 calories Optional Exchange
Per serving: 20 calories; 0.2 g protein; trace fat; 5 g carbohydrate;
    trace sodium; 0 mg cholesterol

North America

The menus of North America with their diverse ethnic recipes reflect the history of the many immigrants who came to the shores of Canada and the United States. In our national melting pot, there is no real United States cuisine but rather myriad regional specialties.

From New England comes one of our most famous dishes, Boston Baked Beans, traditionally made with white beans and dark molasses. From New Orleans comes Creole cookery—a lively and unique combination of provincial French and Spanish styles with an African accent. One of the best-known Creole dishes is Jambalaya, a risotto-like dish customarily made with shrimp and pork or ham, although other shellfish and chicken can be used. A coast-to-coast tradition is the pairing of fried potatoes with steak, a duo that dates back to Colonial times, for it was Thomas Jefferson who concocted the idea. Our baked version of these "fries" helps you declare your independence from the tyranny of excess pounds.

Much of Canada's cuisine mirrors her British ancestry, but French-speaking Quebec retains Gallic specialties like Tourtière, a pie made with pork, veal, or chicken. Because it's especially popular at Christmas, Tourtière is also known as *pâté de Noël*.

During the snowy Canadian winters, hot, nourishing soups are welcome, among them the chowder brought by the French settlers. The name comes from the *chaudière,* or cauldron, in which it was cooked. Corn Chowder, relished throughout Canada, is also very popular in the southern United States, proving that culinary customs can migrate freely across the border of these two neighbors.

An All-American Affair

Canadian Yellow Split-Pea Soup*

Jambalaya*

Spinach and Mushroom Salad

White Wine Spritzer

Blueberry Crumb*

Coffee or Tea

Oysters Rockefeller

**MAKES 2 SERVINGS,
3 OYSTERS EACH**

*An elegant
beginning to a
dinner party.*

6 small oysters, scrubbed and shucked
  (reserve liquid and 6 deep shell halves)
1 cup spinach leaves, washed well and drained
¼ ounce Canadian-style bacon
1 tablespoon chopped Italian (flat-leaf) parsley
½ medium scallion (green onion)
1 drained canned anchovy fillet
½ teaspoon imitation bacon bits, crushed
½ small garlic clove
Dash each crushed red pepper and hot sauce
2 teaspoons margarine
1 teaspoon each all-purpose flour and dry white wine
Coarse salt (optional)

In 1-cup liquid measure combine reserved oyster liquid
with enough water so that liquid measures 1 cup; set aside
liquid and oysters.

In work bowl of food processor combine remaining
ingredients except margarine, flour, wine, and salt and
process until pureed; set aside.

In 8-inch skillet heat margarine until bubbly and hot; add
flour and cook, stirring constantly, for 1 minute. Gradually
stir in reserved oyster liquid; stir in spinach mixture and
wine. Reduce heat to low and cook, stirring constantly, for
5 minutes. Remove from heat and set aside.

Preheat oven to 425°F. In bottom of 8 x 8 x 2-inch
baking pan spread coarse salt (if salt is not used, line pan
with crumpled foil); set reserved oyster shells on salt (or
foil) and bake until heated, about 10 minutes. Remove
from oven and set 1 oyster into each shell; spoon an equal
amount of spinach mixture over each oyster. Bake until
oysters and topping are heated through, about 10 minutes.

Each serving provides: 1 Protein Exchange; 1 Vegetable Exchange;
  1 Fat Exchange; 20 calories Optional Exchange
Per serving: 81 calories; 5 g protein; 5 g fat; 4 g carbohydrate;
  177 mg sodium; 17 mg cholesterol

Canadian Corn Chowder

MAKES 2 SERVINGS

A thick, warming soup for those chilly winter days.

2 teaspoons margarine
2 ounces diced Canadian-style bacon
½ cup diced onion
2 tablespoons each diced celery and shredded carrot
1½ teaspoons all-purpose flour
½ cup skim milk
3 ounces pared potato, diced
½ teaspoon salt
Dash each marjoram leaves and pepper
½ cup frozen or drained canned whole-kernel corn
Water, if necessary

In 2-quart saucepan heat margarine until bubbly and hot; add bacon, onion, celery, and carrot and sauté until onion is translucent. Sprinkle with flour and stir quickly to combine; cook, stirring, for 1 minute. Stirring constantly, gradually add milk and bring to a boil. Reduce heat and add potato and seasonings; cover and let simmer until potato is tender, about 15 minutes. Stir in corn and let simmer until heated through. If mixture gets too thick, add water, 1 tablespoon at a time, until desired consistency.

Each serving provides: 1 Protein Exchange; 1 Bread Exchange;
    ¾ Vegetable Exchange; 1 Fat Exchange; ¼ Milk Exchange;
    10 calories Optional Exchange
Per serving with frozen corn: 194 calories; 11 g protein; 6 g fat;
    25 g carbohydrate; 1,041 mg sodium; 15 mg cholesterol
With canned corn: 195 calories; 11 g protein; 6 g fat; 25 g carbohydrate;
    1,138 mg sodium; 15 mg cholesterol

Canadian Yellow Split-Pea Soup

MAKES 4 SERVINGS

Sage and allspice lend an accent to this bacon-flavored soup.

4½ ounces sorted uncooked yellow split peas
1 quart water
½ teaspoon salt
2 teaspoons vegetable oil
2 ounces diced Canadian-style bacon
1 cup each chopped onions and sliced carrots
¼ teaspoon each crumbled sage leaves and ground allspice
Dash white pepper, or to taste
2 tablespoons chopped fresh parsley

Rinse peas. In 4-quart saucepan combine peas, water, and salt and bring to a boil; remove from heat and let soak for 1 hour.

In 10-inch nonstick skillet heat oil over medium-high heat; add bacon and cook, stirring frequently, until browned. Stir in onions and carrots and cook, stirring occasionally, until onions are translucent; add to peas in saucepan and stir to combine. Add remaining ingredients except parsley and bring to a boil. Reduce heat to low, cover, and let simmer, stirring occasionally to prevent mixture from sticking to bottom of pan, until peas are softened and mixture thickens, about 45 minutes (if soup becomes too thick, add up to an additional 1 cup water). Serve each portion sprinkled with 1½ teaspoons parsley.

Each serving provides: 2 Protein Exchanges; 1 Vegetable Exchange; ½ Fat Exchange
Per serving: 183 calories; 12 g protein; 4 g fat; 27 g carbohydrate; 501 mg sodium; 7 mg cholesterol

Oysters Bienville

MAKES 4 SERVINGS,
3 OYSTERS EACH

From Canada, an
Acadian delight.

8 ounces cooked shelled and deveined large shrimp
½ cup mushrooms
3 tablespoons chopped fresh parsley
1 shallot
12 small oysters, scrubbed and shucked (reserve liquid and
    12 deep shell halves)
½ cup skim milk
2 teaspoons dry vermouth
1 tablespoon plus 1 teaspoon margarine
1 tablespoon all-purpose flour
1 egg, lightly beaten
Coarse salt (optional)
1 tablespoon grated Parmesan cheese

In work bowl of food processor combine shrimp, mushrooms, parsley, and shallot; using an on-off motion, process until finely chopped *(do not puree)*. Set aside.

In 1-cup liquid measure combine reserved oyster liquid, milk, and vermouth (if necessary add enough water so that liquid measures 1 cup); set aside liquid and oysters. In 8-inch skillet heat margarine until bubbly and hot; sprinkle with flour and, stirring constantly, cook for 1 minute. Stirring constantly, gradually add milk mixture and bring to a boil. Stir in shrimp mixture and cook until heated, 1 to 2 minutes. Reduce heat to low. Add ¼ cup shrimp mixture to egg and stir to combine; gradually add egg mixture to skillet, stirring rapidly to prevent lumping. Cook, stirring constantly, for 1 to 2 minutes. Remove from heat and set aside.

Preheat oven to 425°F. In bottom of 15 x 10½ x 1-inch jelly-roll pan spread coarse salt (if salt is not used, line pan with crumpled foil); set reserved oyster shells on salt (or foil) and bake until heated, about 10 minutes. Remove pan from oven and place 1 oyster into each shell; spoon an equal amount of shrimp mixture over each oyster and sprinkle each with ¼ teaspoon cheese. Bake until oysters

(CONTINUED) and topping are heated through and cheese is browned, about 10 minutes.

Each serving provides: 3 Protein Exchanges; ¼ Vegetable Exchange;
   1 Fat Exchange; 45 calories Optional Exchange
Per serving: 169 calories; 20 g protein; 7 g fat; 5 g carbohydrate;
   204 mg sodium; 169 mg cholesterol

Crab Cakes

**MAKES 2 SERVINGS,
2 CAKES EACH**

*A favorite from the
U.S. South.*

7 ounces drained thawed frozen crab meat, minced
12 unsalted saltines, made into fine crumbs
1 egg
**2 tablespoons each minced onion, minced red bell pepper,
   and finely chopped fresh parsley**
1 tablespoon each mayonnaise and lemon juice
¼ teaspoon powdered mustard
Dash each ground red pepper and white pepper
1½ teaspoons vegetable oil

In large bowl thoroughly combine all ingredients except oil and garnish; divide mixture into 4 equal portions, forming each into a patty. Arrange patties on a plate in 1 layer, or stack patties, using sheet of wax paper between each to separate; cover and refrigerate for at least 30 minutes.

In 8-inch skillet heat oil over high heat. Reduce heat to medium and add patties; cook, turning once, until browned, about 3 minutes on each side. Serve on warmed platter.

Each serving provides: 4 Protein Exchanges; 1 Bread Exchange;
   ¼ Vegetable Exchange; 2 Fat Exchanges; 10 calories Optional
   Exchange
Per serving: 299 calories; 22 g protein; 16 g fat; 16 g carbohydrate;
   427 mg sodium; 242 mg cholesterol

Tourtière

MAKES 8 SERVINGS

This Canadian pork pie is particularly popular at holiday time.

PASTRY

1½ cups all-purpose flour
½ teaspoon salt
⅓ cup less 2 teaspoons margarine
½ cup plain low-fat yogurt

FILLING

2 teaspoons vegetable oil
½ cup diced onion
2 garlic cloves, minced
1 pound cooked ground pork, crumbled
12 ounces peeled cooked potatoes, mashed
1 teaspoon salt
½ teaspoon each sage leaves, crumbled, and
   ground nutmeg
¼ teaspoon pepper

GLAZE

1 egg, beaten

To Prepare Pastry: In mixing bowl combine flour and salt; with pastry blender, or 2 knives used scissors-fashion, cut in margarine until mixture resembles coarse meal. Add yogurt and mix thoroughly. Form dough into 2 equal balls; wrap in plastic wrap and refrigerate for at least 1 hour.

To Prepare Filling: In small nonstick skillet heat oil over medium-high heat; add onion and garlic and cook, stirring frequently, until onion is golden. Transfer to large bowl and add remaining ingredients for filling; stir to combine.

To Prepare Pie: Preheat oven to 425°F. Roll each dough ball between 2 sheets of wax paper, forming two 9-inch circles; fit 1 circle into 8-inch pie pan and add filling. Place second circle over filling and fold edges under; if desired, flute edges. Gently pierce dough to allow steam to escape; brush

(CONTINUED) pastry with beaten egg and bake until top crust is golden brown, 25 to 30 minutes.

Each serving provides: 2 Protein Exchanges; 1½ Bread Exchanges; ⅛ Vegetable Exchange; 2 Fat Exchanges; 20 calories Optional Exchange
Per serving: 352 calories; 19 g protein; 19 g fat; 26 g carbohydrate; 552 mg sodium; 91 mg cholesterol

Boston Baked Beans

MAKES 2 SERVINGS

Serve with Boston Brown Bread (see page 276).

6 ounces drained canned great northern or small white beans
¼ cup water
2 tablespoons finely chopped onion
2¼ teaspoons dark molasses
½ teaspoon powdered mustard
⅛ teaspoon ground ginger
Dash ground cloves
1½ teaspoons firmly packed dark brown sugar

Preheat oven to 350°F. In 2-cup flameproof casserole combine all ingredients except brown sugar and mix thoroughly; bake until bean mixture is hot and bubbly, 40 to 45 minutes. Sprinkle with brown sugar; turn oven control to broil and broil beans until sugar is melted.

Each serving provides: 1½ Protein Exchanges; ⅛ Vegetable Exchange; 40 calories Optional Exchange
Per serving: 132 calories; 7 g protein; 1 g fat; 26 g carbohydrate; 300 mg sodium (estimated); 0 mg cholesterol

Jambalaya

MAKES 2 SERVINGS

The popularity of this dish spans time and distance, from seventeenth-century Acadia to current Creole cuisine.

1 tablespoon olive or vegetable oil, divided
½ cup each diced onion and green bell pepper
2 small garlic cloves, minced
8 ounces shelled and deveined large shrimp
2 ounces diced boiled ham
2 ounces uncooked regular long-grain rice
2 cups canned Italian tomatoes (with liquid), drain and coarsely chop tomatoes, reserving liquid
½ cup water
1½ teaspoons lemon juice
1 packet instant chicken broth and seasoning mix
1 bay leaf
Dash each crushed red pepper, thyme leaves, pepper, and hot sauce
1½ teaspoons chopped fresh parsley

In small skillet heat 1½ teaspoons oil; add onion, bell pepper, and garlic and cook until onion is translucent. Add shrimp and cook, stirring constantly, until shrimp just turn pink, 2 to 3 minutes. Stir in ham; remove from heat and set aside.

In 2-quart saucepan heat remaining 1½ teaspoons oil; add rice and cook, stirring constantly, until rice is browned, about 2 minutes. Add tomatoes, reserved liquid, water, lemon juice, broth mix, bay leaf, red pepper, thyme, pepper, and hot sauce and stir to combine; bring to a boil. Reduce heat to low, cover, and let simmer until rice is tender, about 20 minutes. Stir in shrimp mixture and cook, stirring frequently, until heated through, 3 to 5 minutes. Remove bay leaf before serving; serve sprinkled with chopped parsley.

Each serving provides: 4 Protein Exchanges; 1 Bread Exchange; 3 Vegetable Exchanges; 1½ Fat Exchanges; 5 calories Optional Exchange
Per serving: 393 calories; 33 g protein; 10 g fat; 43 g carbohydrate; 1,243 mg sodium; 185 mg cholesterol

Oven-Baked Steak "Fries"

MAKES 2 SERVINGS

Our delicious version of the "french fry."

1 pared baking potato (6 ounces), cut into ½-inch wedges
1 teaspoon each vegetable oil and paprika
Dash pepper, or to taste

Preheat oven to 425°F. Spray an aluminum baking sheet with nonstick cooking spray. Using pastry brush, brush all sides of potato wedges with oil; arrange wedges on sprayed sheet and sprinkle with paprika and pepper. Bake until wedges are browned and tender, 15 to 20 minutes.

Each serving provides: 1 Bread Exchange; ½ Fat Exchange
Per serving: 88 calories; 2 g protein; 2 g fat; 15 g carbohydrate;
   3 mg sodium; 0 mg cholesterol

Pennsylvania Dutch
Corn Fritters

**MAKES 6 SERVINGS,
1 FRITTER EACH**

*Two styles of corn
make these fritters
extra-good.*

1 egg, separated
1 teaspoon granulated sugar
¾ cup frozen whole-kernel corn, thawed
¼ cup canned cream-style corn
3 tablespoons all-purpose flour
1 tablespoon chopped chives
⅛ teaspoon each salt and pepper
2 tablespoons vegetable oil

In medium mixing bowl beat together egg yolk and sugar.
Using wooden spoon, stir in kernel and cream-style corn,
flour, chives, salt, and pepper; mix well.

In small mixing bowl, using electric mixer, beat egg
white until stiff but not dry; gently fold into corn mixture.

In 10-inch skillet heat oil over medium-high heat; drop
batter by ¼-cup measures into skillet, forming 6 equal
fritters. Cook until fritters are golden on bottom, about
1 minute; using pancake turner, turn fritters over. Cook
until golden on other side, about 1 minute longer.

Each serving provides: ½ Bread Exchange; 1 Fat Exchange; 15 calories
Optional Exchange
Per serving: 96 calories; 2 g protein; 6 g fat; 10 g carbohydrate;
83 mg sodium; 46 mg cholesterol

Vegetable Medley Canadian Style

MAKES 2 SERVINGS

A touch of lemon, sugar, and dillweed lend the dash to this dish.

1 tablespoon margarine
1 cup sliced carrots
½ cup each diced onion and celery
¼ teaspoon each granulated sugar and dillweed
Dash grated lemon peel

In 1-quart saucepan melt margarine; add remaining ingredients and stir to coat vegetables with margarine. Reduce heat to lowest possible setting, cover pan, and let cook until vegetables are tender, 10 to 15 minutes. Serve vegetables with accumulated pan juices.

Each serving provides: 2 Vegetable Exchanges; 1½ Fat Exchanges;
   3 calories Optional Exchange
Per serving: 98 calories; 2 g protein; 6 g fat; 11 g carbohydrate;
   128 mg sodium; 0 mg cholesterol

Boston Brown Bread

**MAKES 8 SERVINGS,
1 SLICE EACH**

*In keeping with
tradition, serve this
bread with Boston
Baked Beans
(see page 271), or for
a delicious breakfast,
spread with
margarine
and serve with
skim milk.*

1 cup plus 2 tablespoons whole wheat flour, divided
**2¼ ounces (⅓ cup plus 2 teaspoons) uncooked
    yellow cornmeal**
1 teaspoon salt
¼ cup dark molasses
2 teaspoons water
½ teaspoon baking soda
1 cup skim milk, mixed with 1 tablespoon lemon juice
½ cup raisins

In large mixing bowl combine 1 cup flour with the
cornmeal and salt. In small bowl combine molasses, water,
and baking soda, mixing until foamy and caramel-colored;
gradually add molasses and milk mixtures to flour mixture,
stirring until no lumps remain. In small bowl toss raisins
with remaining 2 tablespoons flour; stir into batter.

Spray clean 1-pound coffee can with nonstick cooking
spray; pour batter into can. Tightly cover can with foil; set
cooking rack into deep kettle or 8-quart Dutch oven and
set coffee can on rack. Pour boiling water into kettle (or
Dutch oven) until it reaches middle of can; tightly cover
kettle (or Dutch oven) and let simmer, adding additional
water if necessary, for 2½ to 3 hours (until cake tester,
inserted in center of bread, comes out clean). Invert coffee
can on plate (bread will slip out); let cool slightly before
serving. To serve, cut into 8 equal slices.

Each serving provides: 1 Bread Exchange; ½ Fruit Exchange; 50 calories
    Optional Exchange
Per serving: 145 calories; 4 g protein; 1 g fat; 33 g carbohydrate;
    354 mg sodium; 1 mg cholesterol

Tea Scones

Plum Tart
Salmon en Papillote

Linguine Verdi
ai Quattro Formaggi

Szechuan Squid

Indian "Fried" Bread
Couscous
Flat Onion Bread

Scandinavian
Kringler

Orange-Date Bread

**MAKES 8 SERVINGS,
1 SLICE EACH**

*Toasted slices of this
bread, spread with
reduced-calorie
orange marmalade,
cottage cheese, or
margarine, will
brighten your
breakfast table.
Also delicious
as a dessert
or snack.*

1½ cups all-purpose flour
3 tablespoons granulated sugar
2 teaspoons double-acting baking powder
½ teaspoon salt
1 tablespoon grated orange peel
1 cup orange juice (no sugar added)
¼ cup margarine, melted
1 egg
2 ounces pecan pieces, chopped
4 pitted dates, chopped

Preheat oven to 350°F. Into medium mixing bowl sift
together flour, sugar, baking powder, and salt; stir in
orange peel. In small mixing bowl beat together orange
juice, margarine, and egg; add to dry ingredients and stir
until thoroughly combined. Fold in nuts and dates.

Spray 7⅜ x 3⅝ x 2¼-inch loaf pan with nonstick cooking
spray; pour in batter and bake for 50 to 60 minutes (until
cake tester, inserted in center, comes out clean). Remove
loaf from pan and transfer to wire rack; let cool for at least
10 minutes before slicing. To serve, cut into 8 equal slices.

Each serving provides: 1 Bread Exchange; 1½ Fat Exchanges; ½ Fruit
 Exchange; 80 calories Optional Exchange
Per serving: 240 calories; 4 g protein; 12 g fat; 30 g carbohydrate;
 320 mg sodium; 34 mg cholesterol

Blueberry Crumb ⏱

MAKES 4 SERVINGS

This delicious dessert from Canada is wonderful served warm.

2 cups blueberries (fresh or frozen, no sugar added)
1 tablespoon lemon juice
2 tablespoons firmly packed brown sugar, divided
1½ teaspoons cornstarch
2¼ ounces uncooked quick oats
3 tablespoons all-purpose flour
Dash ground cinnamon
2 tablespoons margarine, softened

Preheat oven to 350°F. In 1-quart shallow casserole toss blueberries with lemon juice. In small bowl combine 1 tablespoon sugar with the cornstarch; add to blueberries, stir to combine, and set aside.

In medium bowl combine oats, flour, remaining 1 tablespoon sugar, and the cinnamon; with pastry blender, or 2 knives used scissors-fashion, cut in margarine until mixture resembles coarse crumbs. Sprinkle mixture over blueberries and bake until berries are bubbly and crumbs are lightly browned, 25 to 30 minutes.

Each serving provides: 1 Bread Exchange; 1½ Fat Exchanges; 1 Fruit Exchange; 35 calories Optional Exchange
Per serving: 204 calories; 4 g protein; 7 g fat; 33 g carbohydrate; 75 mg sodium; 0 mg cholesterol

Serving Suggestion: Top each portion of Blueberry Crumb with ¼ cup vanilla ice milk. Increase Optional Exchange to 95 calories.

Per serving: 264 calories; 6 g protein; 9 g fat; 43 g carbohydrate; 101 mg sodium (estimated); 5 mg cholesterol (estimated)

Canadian "Butter" Cups

MAKES 12 SERVINGS,
1 CUP EACH

These fruit-filled pastries are a perfect party dessert.

PASTRY CUPS

1 cup plus 2 tablespoons all-purpose flour
2 tablespoons confectioners' sugar, sifted
⅓ cup plus 2 teaspoons margarine, softened

FILLING

1 egg, beaten
2 tablespoons each margarine, melted, and light
  corn syrup
1½ cups raisins, plumped in hot water, then drained
¼ cup thawed frozen dairy whipped topping

To Prepare Pastry Cups: Preheat oven to 350°F. In mixing bowl combine flour and sugar; with pastry blender, or 2 knives used scissors-fashion, cut in margarine until mixture resembles coarse meal. Divide mixture into 12 equal portions and, using hands, shape each into a smooth ball. Into each of twelve 2½-inch-diameter nonstick muffin pan cups press 1 dough ball, pressing dough into bottom and about 1 inch up sides of cup; set aside.

To Prepare "Butter" Cups: In small mixing bowl combine egg, margarine, and corn syrup; stir in raisins. Spoon an equal amount of raisin mixture into each pastry cup and bake until pastry is lightly browned and filling is set, 15 to 20 minutes. Remove from oven and let cool slightly, 2 to 5 minutes. Using tip of knife, carefully lift cups from pan; transfer to wire rack and let cool completely. To serve, top each cup with 1 teaspoon whipped topping.

Each serving provides: ½ Bread Exchange; 2 Fat Exchanges; 1 Fruit
  Exchange; 30 calories Optional Exchange
Per serving: 190 calories; 2 g protein; 8 g fat; 28 g carbohydrate;
  99 mg sodium; 23 mg cholesterol

Variation: Before topping with whipped topping, top each portion with ¼ cup ice milk; increase Optional Exchange to 90 calories.

Per serving: 250 calories; 4 g protein; 10 g fat; 38 g carbohydrate;
  125 mg sodium (estimated); 27 mg cholesterol (estimated)

Deep-Dish Apple Pie

MAKES 8 SERVINGS, ⅛ OF 9-INCH PIE EACH

The most famous American dessert, especially delicious topped with vanilla ice milk.

⅓ cup margarine, divided
2¼ cups all-purpose flour, divided
¼ cup plain low-fat yogurt
1 teaspoon each salt and white vinegar
¼ to ⅓ cup cold water
⅓ cup granulated sugar, divided
8 small Golden Delicious apples, cored, pared, and thinly sliced*
1 tablespoon lemon juice
1 teaspoon ground cinnamon
¼ teaspoon each ground allspice and ground nutmeg
1 tablespoon skim milk

Measure out and reserve 2 tablespoons margarine. Into medium mixing bowl measure 2 cups flour; with pastry blender, or 2 knives used scissors-fashion, cut in all but reserved margarine until mixture resembles coarse meal. Add yogurt, salt, and vinegar and mix until combined. Stir in water, 1 tablespoon at a time, adding just enough water so that mixture clings together and forms soft dough; form dough into a ball, wrap in plastic wrap, and refrigerate for at least 1 hour (may be refrigerated overnight).

Measure out and reserve 2 teaspoons sugar. In medium bowl combine apples, all but reserved sugar, 2 tablespoons flour, and the lemon juice and spices; set aside. Cut chilled pastry dough into 2 pieces, making 1 piece slightly larger than the other. Sprinkle work surface with 1 tablespoon flour; on floured surface roll larger piece of dough into a circle, about ⅛ inch thick. Fit dough into 9-inch pie plate; spoon apple mixture into pie plate and dot with reserved 2 tablespoons margarine.

Preheat oven to 375°F. Sprinkle work surface with remaining tablespoon flour; on floured surface roll remaining dough into ⅛-inch-thick circle. Carefully lift pastry and fit over filling; fold edges of dough under and

(CONTINUED)

flute. Cut slashes in top of pastry to allow steam to escape; brush top of pie with milk, then sprinkle with reserved 2 teaspoons sugar. Cover fluted edges with foil to prevent burning and transfer pie to baking sheet. Bake for 20 minutes; remove foil and continue baking until crust is golden, 20 to 30 minutes longer.

Each serving provides: 1½ Bread Exchanges; 2 Fat Exchanges; 1 Fruit Exchange; 45 calories Optional Exchange
Per serving: 290 calories; 4 g protein; 8 g fat; 51 g carbohydrate; 371 mg sodium; 0.5 mg cholesterol

*Small baking apples may be substituted.

Scandinavia

The smörgåsbord is undoubtedly the single best-known Scandinavian repast. Swedish etiquette requires at least three trips to the table: first for fish, then for cold meats and salads, third (but not necessarily last!) for hot dishes. However, the weight-conscious Swedes are modifying their approach, and in restaurants today there is a simplified "one-trip" version, in which half a dozen items are placed on a single plate.

Although the Scandinavian countries have their individual specialties, together they share a talent for design—not just in tableware but also in the way the foods are placed on the dishes. The Scandinavians also share a love of fish; their smoked salmon, in particular, is superb. Try it on Smørrebrød, the famous Danish open sandwich. Herring, which is abundant in the North Sea, is even eaten for breakfast by Norwegians, and Finnish families literally buy herring by the barrel.

Beef is also enjoyed, particularly in dishes like our Swedish Meatballs or Beef à la Lindstrom. Nourishing hot creamed soups are popular on the long winter nights, and cucumber soups or chilled fruit soups like our Orange Soup are served on the balmier days of the "midnight sun."

Desserts are usually fresh fruits, predominantly cloudberries. (Our Almond Apples recipe substitutes a more available fruit.) Swedes like to end a meal with miniature pancakes served with lingonberries. The sweet-toothed Danes like cake even for breakfast, but the rich pastry that Americans call "Danish" is known locally as "Vienna Bread" (shifting the caloric blame?). There'll be nothing but praise when you offer our Scandinavian Kringler and bring your guests to the table with a *"Velkommen til bords"* (welcome to the table).

A Smörgåsbord Designed to Delight

Orange Soup[*]

Smørrebrød[*]

Swedish Meatballs[*]

Fruit Slaw[*]

Omenapuuro[*]
(Apple Porridge Dessert)

Coffee or Tea

Cauliflower Soup

MAKES 4 SERVINGS

*Norwegians
warm up with
this on chilly
winter evenings.*

5½ cups cauliflower florets
2 cups water
1 teaspoon salt
2 tablespoons margarine
½ cup diced onion
2 teaspoons all-purpose flour
1 packet instant chicken broth and seasoning mix
·1 cup skim milk
Dash white pepper
Ground nutmeg (optional)

In 4-quart saucepan combine cauliflower, water, and salt; bring to a boil. Reduce heat and let simmer until cauliflower is tender; let cool slightly.

Transfer 2 cups cauliflower (including cooking liquid) to blender container and process until smooth; transfer to large bowl and repeat procedure, 2 cups at a time, until all cauliflower and liquid have been processed. Set aside.

In same saucepan heat margarine over medium-high heat until bubbly and hot; add onion and sauté until translucent. Sprinkle with flour and broth mix and stir quickly to combine; cook, stirring, for 1 minute. Gradually add milk and cook, stirring constantly, until flour mixture is completely dissolved and liquid thickens; stir in pureed cauliflower. Reduce heat and let simmer, stirring occasionally, until cauliflower is heated; stir in pepper. Ladle into 4 soup bowls and, if desired, sprinkle each portion with dash nutmeg.

Each serving provides: 3 Vegetable Exchanges; 1½ Fat Exchanges;
   ¼ Milk Exchange; 10 calories Optional Exchange
Per serving: 134 calories; 7 g protein; 6 g fat; 16 g carbohydrate;
   893 mg sodium; 1 mg cholesterol

Orange Soup

MAKES 2 SERVINGS

Finland gives fruit a new twist in this delicious soup, which may be served warm or chilled. For the true Finnish flavor, use freshly squeezed orange juice.

1½ teaspoons cornstarch
½ teaspoon granulated sugar
½ cup water
1 cup orange juice (no sugar added)
2 tablespoons thawed frozen dairy whipped topping
Garnish: julienne-cut orange peel

In small saucepan combine cornstarch and sugar; add water and stir to dissolve. Over medium-low heat and stirring constantly, bring to a slow boil; continue cooking and stirring until mixture is slightly thickened. Remove from heat and stir in juice; serve immediately or transfer to container, cover, and refrigerate until chilled.

To serve, ladle soup into 2 bowls and top each portion with 1 tablespoon whipped topping; garnish with orange peel.

Each serving provides: 1 Fruit Exchange; 25 calories Optional Exchange
Per serving: 81 calories; 1 g protein; 1 g fat; 17 g carbohydrate;
    2 mg sodium; trace cholesterol

Fruit Slaw

MAKES 4 SERVINGS

Oranges, apples, and grapes make a super slaw.

¼ cup buttermilk
2 tablespoons reduced-calorie mayonnaise
2 teaspoons lemon juice
1 teaspoon cider vinegar
¼ teaspoon caraway seed
⅛ teaspoon each salt and pepper
2¼ cups shredded green cabbage
1 small apple, cored and diced
10 small seedless grapes, cut into halves
¼ cup each orange sections, diced, and sliced scallions
   (green onions)

In large mixing bowl combine milk, mayonnaise, lemon juice, vinegar, caraway seed, salt, and pepper, mixing well; add remaining ingredients and toss to thoroughly combine. Cover with plastic wrap and refrigerate for at least 30 minutes. Toss again just before serving.

Each serving provides: 1¼ Vegetable Exchanges; ½ Fat Exchange;
   ½ Fruit Exchange; 20 calories Optional Exchange
Per serving: 72 calories; 2 g protein; 2 g fat; 12 g carbohydrate;
   153 mg sodium; 3 mg cholesterol

Västkustsallad

MAKES 4 SERVINGS

Shrimp and mussels combine with dill to make this wonderful west coast salad, a piquant treat from the waters of Scandinavia.

6 ounces shelled and deveined cooked medium shrimp (about 12 shrimp), cut lengthwise into halves
18 small mussels, steamed and shelled
1 cup thinly sliced mushrooms
¼ cup water
1 tablespoon plus 1 teaspoon olive oil
1 tablespoon each lemon juice and red wine vinegar
2 teaspoons minced fresh dill
1 teaspoon Dijon-style mustard
2 garlic cloves, minced
¼ teaspoon each salt and pepper
2 cups shredded lettuce

In medium mixing bowl (not aluminum) combine shrimp, mussels, and mushrooms. In 1-cup measure combine remaining ingredients except lettuce, mixing well; pour over seafood mixture and toss well to coat. Cover with plastic wrap and refrigerate for at least 2 hours. Serve on bed of shredded lettuce.

Each serving provides: 3 Protein Exchanges; 1½ Vegetable Exchanges; 1 Fat Exchange
Per serving: 157 calories; 19 g protein; 6 g fat; 5 g carbohydrate; 403 mg sodium; 92 mg cholesterol

Danish Liver Pâté

MAKES 4 SERVINGS

This homemade pâté is great for entertaining.

1 tablespoon plus 1 teaspoon margarine
½ cup minced onion
1 tablespoon plus 1½ teaspoons all-purpose flour
1 cup skim milk
8 ounces finely minced or ground calf liver
2 eggs, beaten
½ teaspoon salt
½ medium tomato, thinly sliced
4 lettuce leaves
12 saltines

In 8-inch nonstick skillet heat margarine until bubbly and hot; add onion and sauté until translucent. Sprinkle flour over onion and stir quickly to combine; cook, stirring, for 1 minute. Stirring constantly, gradually add milk and bring to a boil. Reduce heat and simmer, stirring, until mixture thickens; remove skillet from heat, set aside, and let cool slightly. Add liver, eggs, and salt and combine thoroughly.

Preheat oven to 375°F. Transfer liver mixture to 7⅜ x 3⅝ x 2¼-inch nonstick loaf pan; bake in middle of center oven rack until mixture is set and top is browned, 45 to 55 minutes. Transfer pan to wire rack and let cool for 5 minutes. Invert pâté onto serving platter, cover with plastic wrap, and refrigerate until thoroughly chilled, about 4 hours.

To serve, arrange tomato slices down center of pâté and surround pâté with lettuce leaves and saltines.

Each serving provides: 2 Protein Exchanges; ½ Bread Exchange; ¾ Vegetable Exchange; 1 Fat Exchange; ¼ Milk Exchange; 10 calories Optional Exchange
Per serving: 235 calories; 18 g protein; 10 g fat; 17 g carbohydrate; 523 mg sodium; 308 mg cholesterol

Smørrebrød

MAKES 12 SERVINGS

In Denmark, an open-faced sandwich is a smørrebrød. For a great party, let guests have the fun of making their own sandwiches.

8 large lettuce leaves
6 eggs, hard-cooked and cut into quarters
12 shelled and deveined cooked small shrimp
3 ounces each smoked salmon and smoked herring or whitefish, thinly sliced
2 ounces each sliced boiled ham and rare roast beef
2 ounces each Danish blue cheese and Danish hard cheese, cut into cubes
3 medium tomatoes, cut into wedges or sliced
3 small apples, cored, cut into wedges, and dipped in lemon juice
3 small oranges, peeled and sectioned
½ cup sliced onion
24 pimiento-stuffed green olives
6 dill pickles, cut lengthwise into quarters
⅓ cup plus 2 teaspoons each mayonnaise, prepared mustard, prepared horseradish, and seafood cocktail sauce
12 thin slices rye bread (½ ounce each)
4½ ounces crispbread

Line 2 large wooden serving boards or 2 trays with 4 lettuce leaves each. On each board (or tray) decoratively arrange 12 egg quarters, 6 shrimp, 1½ ounces each salmon and herring (or whitefish), 1 ounce each ham, roast beef, and cheeses, half each of the tomatoes and fruits, ¼ cup onion slices, 12 olives, and 12 pickle spears. Spoon mayonnaise, mustard, horseradish, and cocktail sauce into individual serving dishes and set out near serving boards. Serve bread slices and crispbread in napkin-lined basket.

Each serving provides: 2 Protein Exchanges; 1 Bread Exchange; 1¾ Vegetable Exchanges; 1½ Fat Exchanges; ½ Fruit Exchange; 20 calories Optional Exchange
Per serving: 318 calories; 17 g protein; 14 g fat; 31 g carbohydrate; 2,087 mg sodium; 179 mg cholesterol

Finnish Rye "Fried" Fish

MAKES 2 SERVINGS

Rye flour and a dash of caraway seed give this fish its distinctive flavor.

10 ounces fish fillets (halibut, cod, flounder, or sole)
3 tablespoons rye flour
2 teaspoons vegetable oil
1 cup sliced mushrooms
¼ cup each canned chicken broth and bottled clam juice
2 tablespoons lemon juice
2 teaspoons minced fresh parsley
¼ teaspoon caraway seed
⅛ teaspoon pepper

On sheet of wax paper or a paper plate dredge fish in flour, coating both sides. In 10- or 12-inch skillet heat oil over medium-high heat; add fish and cook, turning once, until golden brown on both sides, 2 to 3 minutes on each side. Using pancake turner, carefully transfer fish to warmed platter; keep warm.

In same skillet sauté mushrooms for 2 minutes; add remaining ingredients and stir well. Stirring occasionally, bring to a boil, then cook for 1 minute longer. Pour sauce over fish.

Each serving provides: 4 Protein Exchanges; ½ Bread Exchange;
   1 Vegetable Exchange; 1 Fat Exchange; 15 calories Optional Exchange
Per serving with halibut: 236 calories; 33 g protein; 7 g fat;
   10 g carbohydrate; 303 mg sodium; 74 mg cholesterol
Per serving with cod: 205 calories; 28 g protein; 5 g fat;
   10 g carbohydrate; 325 mg sodium; 74 mg cholesterol
Per serving with flounder or sole: 207 calories; 27 g protein;
   6 g fat; 10 g carbohydrate; 337 mg sodium; 74 mg cholesterol

Beef à la Lindstrom

MAKES 4 SERVINGS

Tasty beef patties topped with eggs.

5 eggs
½ cup finely chopped onion
14 ounces ground beef (chuck, sirloin, or round)
6 ounces peeled cooked potatoes, mashed
½ cup chopped drained canned beets
3 tablespoons chopped drained capers
2 tablespoons minced fresh parsley
1 tablespoon each red wine vinegar and
  Worcestershire sauce
1 teaspoon salt
½ teaspoon white pepper

In medium mixing bowl beat 1 egg; reserve remaining eggs. Spray 8-inch nonstick skillet with nonstick cooking spray; add onion and cook until softened, 2 to 3 minutes. Thoroughly combine cooked onion and remaining ingredients, except reserved eggs, with beaten egg in bowl; shape mixture into 4 equal patties. Transfer patties to rack in broiling pan; broil 6 inches from heat source, turning once, for 5 to 7 minutes or until done to taste.

While meat is broiling, spray 12-inch nonstick skillet with nonstick cooking spray and heat; add remaining 4 eggs and cook sunny-side up. Top each beef patty with 1 cooked egg.

Each serving provides: 4 Protein Exchanges; ½ Bread Exchange;
  ½ Vegetable Exchange
Per serving with chuck: 403 calories; 29 g protein; 26 g fat;
  12 g carbohydrate; 932 mg sodium; 416 mg cholesterol
With sirloin: 450 calories; 27 g protein; 32 g fat; 12 g carbohydrate;
  941 mg sodium; 416 mg cholesterol
With round: 352 calories; 31 g protein; 19 g fat; 12 g carbohydrate;
  952 mg sodium; 416 mg cholesterol

Sailor's Beef

MAKES 2 SERVINGS

Beer is the basis of the sauce for this Swedish favorite.

10 ounces boneless chuck steak
2 teaspoons mayonnaise
¾ cup sliced onions
½ teaspoon salt, mixed with ⅛ teaspoon pepper
1 teaspoon Dijon-style mustard
½ cup beer
¼ cup water
6 ounces pared potatoes, thinly sliced
2 teaspoons chopped fresh parsley

On rack in broiling pan broil meat 3 to 4 inches from heat source, turning once, until thoroughly browned on both sides. Cut meat into ¼-inch-thick slices and set aside.

In 8-inch skillet heat mayonnaise until bubbly and hot; add onions and sauté until softened. Add meat and sprinkle with half of salt mixture; stir in mustard and remove from heat. Using slotted spoon, remove meat mixture from skillet, reserving pan drippings; add beer and water to drippings and bring to a boil. Remove from heat.

Preheat oven to 350°F. In shallow 1-quart casserole arrange half of the potato slices; sprinkle with half of remaining salt mixture and top with meat mixture, then remaining potato slices. Sprinkle with remaining salt mixture and pour in beer mixture; cover casserole and bake for 1¼ hours. Remove cover and continue baking until beef and potatoes are tender, about 15 minutes longer. Serve sprinkled with parsley.

Each serving provides: 4 Protein Exchanges; 1 Bread Exchange;
 ¾ Vegetable Exchange; 1 Fat Exchange; 25 calories Optional Exchange
Per serving: 394 calories; 37 g protein; 15 g fat; 23 g carbohydrate;
 721 mg sodium; 106 mg cholesterol

Swedish Meatballs

MAKES 4 SERVINGS

These meatballs are popular fare around the world.

1 tablespoon plus 1 teaspoon margarine, divided
½ cup minced onion
1 cup evaporated skimmed milk, divided
1 egg
1 slice white bread, made into crumbs
15 ounces ground beef
4 ounces ground pork
2 teaspoons salt, divided
1½ teaspoons granulated sugar, divided
½ teaspoon ground allspice
¼ teaspoon ground nutmeg
3 tablespoons all-purpose flour
1 cup water
⅛ teaspoon white pepper

Preheat oven to 350°F. In small skillet heat 1 teaspoon margarine; add onion and sauté until golden. Transfer to mixing bowl and add ¼ cup milk, the egg, and bread crumbs, stirring well to combine; let stand for 5 minutes. Add meat, 1 teaspoon each salt and sugar, and the allspice and nutmeg; using a fork, blend well. Using a teaspoon, form meat mixture into small balls, each about ½ inch in diameter; set on rack in roasting pan and bake, turning once, for 10 minutes. Remove from oven and set aside.

In 2-quart saucepan heat remaining tablespoon margarine until bubbly and hot; add flour and cook over low heat, stirring constantly, for 3 minutes. Gradually stir in remaining ¾ cup milk; add water, remaining teaspoon salt and ½ teaspoon sugar, and the pepper and cook, stirring constantly, until thickened. Add meatballs and cook until heated.

Each serving provides: 4 Protein Exchanges; ½ Bread Exchange; ¼ Vegetable Exchange; 1 Fat Exchange; ½ Milk Exchange; 10 calories Optional Exchange
Per serving: 497 calories; 35 g protein; 30 g fat; 19 g carbohydrate; 1,339 mg sodium; 172 mg cholesterol

Swedish Hasselback Potatoes

**MAKES 4 SERVINGS,
½ POTATO EACH**

Special baked potatoes, sprinkled with cheese and bread crumbs.

**2 tablespoons each grated Parmesan cheese and plain
   dried bread crumbs**
½ teaspoon paprika
Dash white pepper
2 baking potatoes (6 ounces each), scrubbed
**2 tablespoons plus 2 teaspoons reduced-calorie margarine,
   melted, divided**

Preheat oven to 375°F. In small bowl combine cheese, bread crumbs, paprika, and pepper, mixing well; set aside.

Spray 8 x 8 x 2-inch baking pan with nonstick cooking spray. Cutting potatoes ¾ of the way through, cut each crosswise into ⅛-inch-thick slices; set in sprayed pan, cut-side up. Brush each with ¼ of the margarine and bake for 45 minutes. Sprinkle each potato with half of the cheese mixture and drizzle each with half of the remaining margarine; return to oven and bake until potatoes are tender and topping is browned, 10 to 15 minutes. To serve, cut each potato in half.

Each serving provides: 1 Bread Exchange; 1 Fat Exchange; 30 calories
   Optional Exchange
Per serving: 123 calories; 3 g protein; 5 g fat; 17 g carbohydrate;
   163 mg sodium; 2 mg cholesterol

Scandinavian Kringler

MAKES 2 LOAVES,
10 SERVINGS EACH

A wonderful frosted pastry for party time. May be prepared ahead and frozen until needed.

PASTRY CRUST
⅓ cup plus 2 teaspoons chilled margarine
1 cup less 1 tablespoon all-purpose flour
2 to 3 tablespoons ice water

PUFF TOPPING
1 cup water
⅓ cup plus 2 teaspoons margarine
1 cup less 1 tablespoon all-purpose flour
3 eggs
½ teaspoon almond extract

FROSTING
¾ cup confectioners' sugar, sifted
3 tablespoons skim milk
1 tablespoon plus 1 teaspoon margarine, softened
½ teaspoon almond extract

GARNISH
2 ounces sliced almonds
2 small oranges, each cut in half, then each half cut into 10 slices

To Prepare Pastry Crust: In medium bowl, with pastry blender or 2 knives used scissors-fashion, cut margarine into flour until mixture resembles coarse meal; sprinkle with water and, using a fork, stir to form soft dough. Divide dough in half and transfer both halves to nonstick cookie sheet; shape each into a 12 x 3-inch rectangular strip and set aside.

To Prepare Topping: In 1-quart saucepan combine water and margarine and bring to a boil, stirring until margarine is melted; add flour and stir vigorously until mixture leaves sides of pan. Remove from heat; beat in eggs 1 at a time, beating after each addition until thoroughly blended. Stir in extract.

To Prepare Loaves: Preheat oven to 350°F. Fill pastry bag with puff topping; without using a tip, pipe topping onto crust, making 5 or 6 lengthwise strips, all touching each other, leaving a border of about ½ inch of crust all around. Bake

(CONTINUED) until loaves are golden brown and strips are puffed, 55 to 60 minutes. Transfer pastries to wire rack and let cool completely.

To Prepare Frosting and Serve: In bowl combine all ingredients for frosting, mixing with electric mixer on low speed until smooth. Spread half of frosting over each loaf and sprinkle each with 1 ounce almonds; serve each loaf garnished with 20 orange slices.

Each serving provides: ½ Bread Exchange; 2 Fat Exchanges; 70 calories Optional Exchange
Per serving: 163 calories; 3 g protein; 10 g fat; 16 g carbohydrate; 101 mg sodium; 41 mg cholesterol

Omenapuuro

MAKES 2 SERVINGS

This apple porridge dessert is a Finnish cousin to our rice pudding. Serve warm.

1 ounce uncooked regular long-grain rice
¼ cup water
1 small apple, cored, pared, and diced
¼ cup evaporated skimmed milk
1½ teaspoons granulated sugar
1½-inch cinnamon stick
1 lemon strip, blanched
2 tablespoons thawed frozen dairy whipped topping

In small saucepan combine rice and water and bring to a boil. Reduce heat to low, cover pan, and let simmer for 10 minutes; stir in remaining ingredients except topping. Cover and let simmer, stirring occasionally, until rice is tender, about 15 minutes; remove cinnamon and lemon and spoon dessert into 2 dishes. Top each portion with 1 tablespoon whipped topping.

Each serving provides: ½ Bread Exchange; ½ Fruit Exchange; ¼ Milk Exchange; 30 calories Optional Exchange
Per serving: 129 calories; 3 g protein; 1 g fat; 27 g carbohydrate; 38 mg sodium; 1 mg cholesterol

Almond Apples

MAKES 4 SERVINGS,
1 APPLE EACH

A delicious dessert
from Finland.
Serve warm.

4 small Golden Delicious apples, pared
2 tablespoons plus 2 teaspoons reduced-calorie margarine, melted
4 zwieback, made into fine crumbs, divided
¼ cup raisins
1 ounce blanched almonds, lightly toasted and finely chopped
2 teaspoons granulated sugar
¼ teaspoon ground cinnamon
⅛ teaspoon almond extract

Core each apple to about ½ inch from bottom, leaving bottom intact. Spray 2-quart shallow casserole with nonstick cooking spray. Dip apples into margarine, then into crumbs, reserving remaining margarine; stand apples upright in sprayed casserole.

Preheat oven to 350°F. In small bowl combine remaining margarine with the raisins, almonds, sugar, cinnamon, and extract, mixing well; fill cavity of each apple with ¼ of raisin mixture. Bake for 40 minutes; cover casserole to prevent overbrowning and bake until apples are tender, about 10 minutes longer.

Each serving provides: ½ Bread Exchange; 1 Fat Exchange; 1½ Fruit Exchanges; 55 calories Optional Exchange
Per serving: 196 calories; 3 g protein; 8 g fat; 30 g carbohydrate; 102 mg sodium; 1 mg cholesterol

Variation: Reserve 1 teaspoon chopped toasted almonds. Top each baked apple with 1 tablespoon thawed frozen dairy whipped topping and sprinkle each with ¼ teaspoon chopped almonds. Increase Optional Exchange to 65 calories.

Per serving: 208 calories; 3 g protein; 9 g fat; 31 g carbohydrate; 102 mg sodium; 1 mg cholesterol

The South Pacific and Southeast Asia

Voyage to the South Seas without ever leaving home. The islands are a nautical crossroads of culinary styles brought by traders from other lands (including American tourists!) and blended with native dishes. Hawaii's traditional feast—the luau—invariably features barbecued pig, but the authentic cooking method might be difficult to duplicate in your backyard. The pig is placed in an underground "oven," sandwiched between alternating layers of rocks, sticks, and leaves. You might prefer to cook our Pork Adobo, a version brought by the Spanish. There's one Hawaiian custom you may want to emulate, though: all the outdoor cooking is done by the men!

As might be expected, seafood, especially Hawaii's superb shellfish, has a featured place on the island menus. Poi, a starchy, tapioca-like paste made from taro root, is an age-old substitute for rice or bread. You can simulate it with our Banana-Tapioca Pudding. The incomparable South Pacific fruits—pineapples, papayas, bananas, and coconuts—enhance a variety of dishes, including our Hawaiian Cheese-Filled Papaya.

Southeast Asian dishes reflect the spice of Indian life, with sauces enlivened by ginger, garlic, curry, and hot chili peppers. Rice is the standard accompaniment to these spicy dishes, and it is the center of the famous Indonesian *rijsttafel*, which features rice surrounded by as many as twenty other dishes. Dahl Soup, Thai Hot 'n' Sour Shrimp Soup, and Indonesian Shrimp Balls offer a provocative mix of flavors, as does Chicken Saté with Peanut Sauce. Saté—meat or poultry cooked on skewers—is now a universal Asian dish although it actually originated in Dutch Indonesia. It's a small world when it comes to cookery.

Island Luau

Thai Hot 'n' Sour Shrimp Soup[*]

Indonesian Shrimp Balls with Dipping Sauce[*]

Chicken Saté with Peanut Sauce[*]

Hawaiian Sweet Potatoes[*]

Banana-Tapioca Pudding[*]

Thai Hot 'n' Sour Shrimp Soup

MAKES 4 SERVINGS

Lemon grass, also known as citronella grass, adds a sweetish lemon flavor to this dish. It looks like a large scallion and it can be purchased in most produce stores that carry Oriental vegetables. If not available, substitute 1 scallion and ½ teaspoon grated lemon peel.

8 ounces shelled and deveined small shrimp,
  reserve shells
1 quart water
1 stalk lemon grass, cut into 1-inch lengths (about ¼ cup)
2 tablespoons lime juice (no sugar added)
3 packets instant chicken broth and seasoning mix
1½ teaspoons sliced seeded serrano chili pepper, divided
½ cup sliced mushrooms
¼ cup sliced scallions (green onions)
1 tablespoon each minced cilantro (Chinese parsley)
  and Oriental fish sauce (nuoc nam nhi)*
1 teaspoon grated lime peel
¼ teaspoon minced dried red chili pepper

Cut each shrimp in half lengthwise; set aside. In 2-quart saucepan bring water to a boil; add reserved shrimp shells, lemon grass, lime juice, broth mix, and 1 teaspoon serrano chili pepper. Reduce heat to low, cover pan, and let simmer for 20 minutes. Line a sieve with cheesecloth and place over large bowl; strain lime juice mixture through sieve, discarding solids. Return liquid to pan and bring to a boil; add vegetables, cilantro, fish sauce, lime peel, dried chili pepper, shrimp, and remaining ½ teaspoon serrano chili pepper. Let simmer until shrimp turn pink, 5 to 7 minutes. Ladle into 4 soup bowls.

Note: For a spicier soup, add an additional ¼ teaspoon dried pepper; for a more sour soup, add 1 tablespoon lime juice when vegetables and other ingredients are added.

Each serving provides: 1½ Protein Exchanges; ¼ Vegetable Exchange;
  10 calories Optional Exchange
Per serving: 71 calories; 12 g protein; 1 g fat; 4 g carbohydrate;
  1,039 mg sodium; 85 mg cholesterol

*The sauce can usually be found in the section of the supermarket that stocks Oriental products; if fish sauce is not available, substitute soy sauce.

Chicken Saté with Peanut Sauce

MAKES 4 SERVINGS

An easy-to-prepare delicious hors d'oeuvre from Indonesia.

1 tablespoon plus 1½ teaspoons soy sauce, divided
1 tablespoon lemon juice, divided
1 teaspoon peanut or vegetable oil, divided
¼ teaspoon each firmly packed brown sugar and salt
½ garlic clove, minced
Dash each white pepper and ground ginger
4 ounces chicken cutlets, cut into cubes
2 tablespoons minced onion
1 tablespoon chunky-style peanut butter
½ packet (about ½ teaspoon) instant chicken broth and seasoning mix
⅛ teaspoon ground coriander

In shallow glass or stainless-steel bowl combine 1 tablespoon soy sauce, half each lemon juice and oil, and next 3 ingredients; add chicken and toss to coat. Let stand at room temperature for 1 hour (if preferred, chicken may be covered and marinated in refrigerator overnight).

Onto each of four 8-inch wooden skewers thread ¼ of the chicken cubes, reserving marinade; transfer skewers to nonstick baking sheet and brush chicken with half of the marinade. Broil for 3 to 4 minutes; turn skewers over and brush chicken with remaining marinade. Broil until chicken is tender, about 3 minutes. Remove skewers to warmed serving platter, reserving any remaining pan juices. Keep chicken warm.

In small saucepan heat remaining oil; add onion and sauté until golden. Reduce heat to low and add remaining ingredients and any reserved pan juices; cook, stirring constantly, until sauce is heated. Serve sauce alongside chicken.

Each serving provides: 1 Protein Exchange; ½ Fat Exchange; 3 calories Optional Exchange
Per serving: 75 calories; 8 g protein; 4 g fat; 3 g carbohydrate; 781 mg sodium; 16 mg cholesterol

Dahl Soup

MAKES 4 SERVINGS

A hot and spicy yellow lentil soup from the Fiji Islands.

½ cup each chopped onion and seeded and diced pared eggplant
¼ cup seeded and diced drained canned whole tomatoes
2 tablespoons each minced seeded red bell pepper and hot green chili pepper
3 garlic cloves, minced
2 teaspoons minced cilantro (Chinese parsley)
1 teaspoon curry powder
1 quart water
4½ ounces uncooked yellow lentils (dahl)
4 packets instant chicken broth and seasoning mix

Spray 2-quart saucepan with nonstick cooking spray; add onion, eggplant, tomatoes, red and green peppers, and garlic. Cook over medium-high heat, stirring frequently, until onion is translucent; stir in cilantro and curry powder and continue cooking for about 1 minute longer. Add water, lentils, and broth mix and stir to combine. Reduce heat to low and let simmer, stirring occasionally, until lentils are tender, 30 to 35 minutes.

Each serving provides: 1½ Protein Exchanges; ¾ Vegetable Exchange; 10 calories Optional Exchange
Per serving: 141 calories; 10 g protein; 1 g fat; 26 g carbohydrate; 866 mg sodium; 0 mg cholesterol

Indonesian Shrimp Balls with Dipping Sauce

SHRIMP BALLS

10 ounces shelled and deveined small shrimp
⅓ cup plus 2 teaspoons plain dried bread crumbs
¼ cup minced scallions (green onions)
2 tablespoons minced cilantro (Chinese parsley)
1 tablespoon Oriental fish sauce (nuoc nam nhi) or
   soy sauce
2 garlic cloves, minced
1 teaspoon lemon juice
½ teaspoon grated lemon peel
⅛ teaspoon pepper
1 tablespoon plus 1 teaspoon vegetable oil

DIPPING SAUCE

¼ cup canned chicken broth
1 tablespoon each soy sauce and Oriental fish sauce
   (nuoc nam nhi) or 2 tablespoons soy sauce
1 teaspoon each lemon juice and molasses
¼ teaspoon minced pared ginger root

To Prepare Shrimp Balls: Preheat oven to 400°F. In blender container process 5 ounces shrimp to smooth paste; transfer to mixing bowl. Add remaining shrimp to blender container and, using an on-off motion, process until coarsely chopped *(do not allow to become a paste)*. Add to shrimp in mixing bowl along with 3 tablespoons bread crumbs and the scallions, cilantro, fish (or soy) sauce, garlic, lemon juice, lemon peel, and pepper; mix until thoroughly combined. Using a wet tablespoon, form shrimp mixture into small balls, making 20 shrimp balls; roll in remaining 3 tablespoons bread crumbs, coating all sides. Spray baking sheet with nonstick cooking spray and arrange shrimp balls on sheet, leaving about 1 inch between each. Drizzle oil evenly over shrimp balls and bake until golden brown, 10 to 15 minutes.

To Prepare Sauce: While shrimp balls are baking, in small saucepan combine all ingredients for sauce; over medium-high heat, bring to a boil. Serve with shrimp balls.

| (CONTINUED) | Each serving provides: 2 Protein Exchanges; ½ Bread Exchange; ⅛ Vegetable Exchange; 1 Fat Exchange; 10 calories Optional Exchange
Per serving: 165 calories; 16 g protein; 6 g fat; 11 g carbohydrate; 1,195 mg sodium; 86 mg cholesterol

Note: If dipping sauce is not used, omit Optional Exchange from Exchange Information.

Per serving: 155 calories; 15 g protein; 6 g fat; 9 g carbohydrate; 482 mg sodium; 86 mg cholesterol |

Beef-Spinach Soup

| MAKES 4 SERVINGS

On cold nights, serve up this delicious Korean soup. | **8 ounces boneless round steak**
2 teaspoons vegetable oil
¼ cup chopped scallions (green onions)
1 tablespoon sesame seed
1 garlic clove, minced
1 quart water
2 tablespoons soy sauce
2 cups spinach leaves
1 tablespoon cornstarch, dissolved in 2 tablespoons water
¼ teaspoon pepper

On rack in broiling pan broil steak, turning once, for 3 minutes on each side; cut into thin strips and set aside.
    In 2-quart saucepan heat oil over medium heat; add scallions, sesame seed, and garlic and sauté until seeds are lightly browned. Add beef and sauté for 2 minutes; add water and soy sauce and bring to a boil. Reduce heat, cover pan, and let simmer for 25 minutes. Stir in spinach, dissolved cornstarch, and pepper and cook, stirring, for 5 minutes longer.

Each serving provides: 1½ Protein Exchanges; 1⅛ Vegetable Exchanges; ½ Fat Exchange; 25 calories Optional Exchange
Per serving: 137 calories; 15 g protein; 6 g fat; 5 g carbohydrate; 717 mg sodium; 39 mg cholesterol |

Vietnamese Fish with Sweet and Sour Sauce

MAKES 2 SERVINGS

Soy sauce, rice vinegar, and fish sauce combine flavors to set off this colorful dish.

1 tablespoon each soy sauce, rice vinegar, Oriental fish sauce (nuoc nam nhi),* and cornstarch
2 teaspoons granulated sugar
Dash pepper
½ cup water
10 ounces fish fillets (sole or flounder)
3 tablespoons all-purpose flour
1 tablespoon vegetable oil
¼ cup sliced scallions (green onions)
2 garlic cloves, minced
1 medium tomato, blanched, peeled, seeded, and chopped
½ cup each julienne-cut carrot and white radishes

In small mixing bowl combine soy sauce, vinegar, fish sauce, cornstarch, sugar, and pepper; add water and stir to dissolve cornstarch and sugar. Set aside.

On sheet of wax paper or a paper plate dredge fish in flour, thoroughly coating all sides. In 8-inch nonstick skillet heat oil over medium heat; add fish and cook, turning once, until golden brown on each side, 2 to 3 minutes each side. Carefully transfer fish to warmed platter; cover with foil and keep warm.

To same skillet add scallions and garlic and sauté for 1 minute; add remaining vegetables and sauté, stirring frequently, until carrot and radishes are tender-crisp, 2 to 3 minutes. Stir reserved soy sauce mixture and add to vegetables; cook, stirring constantly, until sauce is thickened, 2 to 3 minutes. Pour vegetable sauce over fish and serve immediately.

Each serving provides: 4 Protein Exchanges; ½ Bread Exchange; 2¼ Vegetable Exchanges; 1½ Fat Exchanges; 35 calories Optional Exchange
Per serving: 299 calories; 28 g protein; 8 g fat; 28 g carbohydrate; 1,460 mg sodium; 71 mg cholesterol

*This sauce can usually be found in the section of the supermarket that stocks Oriental products; if fish sauce is not available, increase soy sauce to 2 tablespoons.

Pork Adobo

A pungent dish from the Philippines.

1¼ pounds boneless pork shoulder, cut into 2-inch cubes
1 cup water
½ cup white vinegar
2 tablespoons soy sauce
6 garlic cloves, minced
¼ teaspoon pepper
1 tablespoon plus 1 teaspoon vegetable oil

On rack in broiling pan broil pork 6 inches from heat source until rare, 5 to 6 minutes; transfer to 3-quart saucepan. Add water, vinegar, soy sauce, garlic, and pepper and stir well to combine; over high heat, bring to a boil. Reduce heat, cover, and let simmer until pork is fork-tender, 30 to 40 minutes. Using slotted spoon, transfer pork to plate; set aside. Increase heat to high and cook pan juices, stirring occasionally, until liquid is reduced by half; remove from heat and reserve.

In 10-inch nonstick skillet heat oil over medium-high heat; add pork cubes and cook, turning meat frequently, until well browned on all sides, 4 to 5 minutes. Add reserved pan juices and stir well; cook until sauce is heated, about 1 minute.

Each serving provides: 4 Protein Exchanges; 1 Fat Exchange
Per serving: 346 calories; 28 g protein; 24 g fat; 4 g carbohydrate;
    748 mg sodium; 111 mg cholesterol

Tangy Korean Liver

MAKES 2 SERVINGS

An unusual variation on the standard liver and onions.

2 teaspoons vegetable oil
½ cup chopped onion
1 tablespoon sesame seed
1 garlic clove, minced
10 ounces calf or beef liver, cut into thin strips
2 teaspoons all-purpose flour
⅓ cup water
1 tablespoon plus 1 teaspoon soy sauce
½ teaspoon granulated sugar
⅛ teaspoon pepper

In 10-inch skillet heat oil; add onion, sesame seed, and garlic and sauté until seeds are golden. Add liver and sauté until done to taste *(do not overcook)*. Sprinkle with flour and stir quickly to combine; gradually stir in water. Add soy sauce, sugar, and pepper and, stirring constantly, bring to a boil. Continue stirring and cook until sauce is thickened, 1 to 2 minutes.

Each serving provides: 4 Protein Exchanges; ½ Vegetable Exchange; 1 Fat Exchange; 45 calories Optional Exchange
Per serving: 302 calories; 30 g protein; 14 g fat; 15 g carbohydrate; 993 mg sodium; 425 mg cholesterol

Korean Spinach

MAKES 2 SERVINGS

May be served warm or chilled.

2 teaspoons Chinese sesame oil
1 garlic clove, minced
12 ounces fresh spinach leaves (stems removed),
    rinsed well
1 tablespoon soy sauce
1½ teaspoons sesame seed
½ teaspoon cider vinegar
Dash pepper

In 9-inch nonstick skillet heat oil over medium-high heat; add garlic and sauté until golden brown, about 1 minute. Add spinach and sauté, stirring frequently, until spinach has wilted and cooked through, 3 to 4 minutes; add remaining ingredients and combine thoroughly. Serve immediately or let cool, then cover and refrigerate until chilled.

Each serving provides: 1 Vegetable Exchange; 1 Fat Exchange;
    15 calories Optional Exchange
Per serving: 105 calories; 7 g protein; 6 g fat; 9 g carbohydrate;
    786 mg sodium; 0 mg cholesterol

Thai-Style Noodles

MAKES 4 SERVINGS

An excellent way to use up leftover pork.

¼ cup dried Chinese black mushrooms (stems removed)
1 cup hot water
1 tablespoon plus 1 teaspoon peanut oil
¼ cup chopped scallions (green onions)
3 garlic cloves, minced
4 ounces julienne-cut cooked pork
¼ cup julienne-cut drained canned bamboo shoots
2 tablespoons Oriental fish sauce (nuoc nam nhi)*
1 tablespoon red wine vinegar
Dash pepper
2 cups cooked vermicelli (very thin spaghetti)

Place mushrooms in small bowl and add hot water; let soak for 10 minutes. Drain mushrooms, discarding water; slice mushrooms and set aside.

In wok or 10-inch skillet heat oil over medium heat; add scallions and garlic and sauté until scallions are softened, about 1 minute. Add pork, bamboo shoots, fish sauce, vinegar, pepper, and sliced mushrooms and sauté, stirring frequently, for 2 to 3 minutes; add vermicelli and sauté, stirring frequently, until spaghetti is lightly browned, about 3 minutes.

Each serving provides: 1 Protein Exchange; 1 Bread Exchange;
  ½ Vegetable Exchange; 1 Fat Exchange
Per serving: 202 calories; 11 g protein; 9 g fat; 22 g carbohydrate;
  687 mg sodium; 26 mg cholesterol

*This sauce can usually be found in the section of the supermarket that stocks Oriental products; if fish sauce is not available, substitute soy sauce.

Hawaiian Sweet Potatoes

MAKES 4 SERVINGS

Tropical fruits and brown sugar make this side dish special.

12 ounces pared sweet potatoes, cooked
⅓ cup pineapple juice (no sugar added)
½ teaspoon ground cinnamon, divided
1 medium banana, peeled and thinly sliced
½ cup canned crushed pineapple (no sugar added)
1 teaspoon firmly packed dark brown sugar

Preheat oven to 400°F. In bowl combine potatoes, juice, and ¼ teaspoon cinnamon and mash. Spray 7-inch flameproof pie plate or 1-quart flameproof casserole with nonstick cooking spray; using a spoon, spread potato mixture in sprayed plate (or casserole) and make a well in the center, about ½ inch in depth and 4 inches in diameter. Arrange banana slices along the inside edge of potato well, overlapping slices slightly; spoon crushed pineapple over center of well, inside the ring of bananas. Sprinkle fruit with brown sugar and remaining ¼ teaspoon cinnamon; bake until fruit is heated through, 10 to 15 minutes. Turn oven control to broil and broil until fruit is browned, 2 to 3 minutes.

Each serving provides: 1 Bread Exchange; 1 Fruit Exchange; 5 calories Optional Exchange
Per serving: 158 calories; 2 g protein; 1 g fat; 38 g carbohydrate; 10 mg sodium; 0 mg cholesterol

Banana-Tapioca Pudding

MAKES 2 SERVINGS

A tropical dessert from the South Pacific islands.

1 medium banana, peeled and cut into quarters
Dash lemon juice
1 cup skim milk
2 tablespoons pearl tapioca
1 teaspoon granulated sugar
¼ teaspoon vanilla extract
⅛ teaspoon salt
1 egg, beaten
2 teaspoons shredded coconut, toasted

In blender container combine banana and lemon juice and process until smooth; transfer to small saucepan and add milk, tapioca, sugar, vanilla, and salt. Mix well; over medium-high heat, bring to a boil. Reduce heat to low and cook, stirring constantly, until tapioca is tender and turns clear, 15 to 20 minutes. Remove from heat and beat about ½ cup of mixture into beaten egg; slowly pour egg mixture into saucepan, stirring rapidly to prevent lumping. Return pan to low heat and cook, stirring, just until mixture thickens, about 3 minutes *(do not overcook)*. Divide into 2 dessert dishes and sprinkle each portion with 1 teaspoon coconut; let cool, then cover and refrigerate for at least 1 hour.

Each serving provides: ½ Protein Exchange; 1 Fruit Exchange; ½ Milk Exchange; 50 calories Optional Exchange
Per serving: 185 calories; 8 g protein; 4 g fat; 31 g carbohydrate; 238 mg sodium; 139 mg cholesterol

Coconut-Baked Bananas

MAKES 4 SERVINGS

Bring the taste of Hawaii to your table with this delicious dessert.

3 medium bananas
½ cup orange juice (no sugar added)
2 tablespoons plus 2 teaspoons reduced-calorie margarine, melted
1 tablespoon firmly packed dark brown sugar
¼ teaspoon ground cinnamon
⅛ teaspoon ground nutmeg
1 tablespoon plus 1 teaspoon shredded coconut

Peel bananas and cut each in half crosswise, then cut each half in half lengthwise; transfer banana quarters to shallow 2-quart casserole.

Preheat oven to 350°F. In small bowl combine juice, margarine, sugar, cinnamon, and nutmeg, mixing well; pour over bananas and bake until bananas are heated through, about 5 minutes. Sprinkle bananas with coconut and bake until coconut is golden brown, about 5 minutes longer.

Each serving provides: 1 Fat Exchange; 1½ Fruit Exchanges; 40 calories Optional Exchange
Per serving: 146 calories; 1 g protein; 5 g fat; 28 g carbohydrate; 93 mg sodium; 0 mg cholesterol

Hawaiian Cheese-Filled Papaya

**MAKES 2 SERVINGS,
½ PAPAYA EACH**

*A novel dessert
from the
islands.*

⅓ cup pot-style cottage cheese
¼ cup drained canned crushed pineapple (no sugar added)
1 tablespoon golden raisins
1 medium papaya, cut in half and seeded
1 teaspoon margarine, melted
1 teaspoon sugar, mixed with ¼ teaspoon ground
   cinnamon
1 teaspoon shredded coconut

Preheat oven to 375°F. In blender container process cheese until smooth; transfer to small mixing bowl and add pineapple and raisins, stirring to combine. Fill each papaya half with half of the cheese mixture and drizzle each with half of the melted margarine; sprinkle half of sugar mixture over each, then sprinkle each with ½ teaspoon coconut. Place filled halves in 8 x 8 x 2-inch pan and bake until heated through, 20 to 25 minutes; serve warm.

Each serving provides: ½ Protein Exchange; ½ Fat Exchange; 1½ Fruit
   Exchanges; 15 calories Optional Exchange
Per serving: 141 calories; 5 g protein; 3 g fat; 26 g carbohydrate;
   31 mg sodium; 2 mg cholesterol

Brown Cow

MAKES 2 SERVINGS

A delicious drink for two, or whip it up in quantity for your next luau.

1 medium banana, peeled and cut into pieces
½ cup skim milk
2 tablespoons coffee liqueur or dark rum
½ teaspoon vanilla extract
Dash aromatic bitters (optional)
1 cup crushed ice
2 tablespoons thawed frozen dairy whipped topping

Chill 2 goblets. In blender container combine all ingredients except ice and topping; process at high speed until smooth. Add ice, ⅓ cup at a time, processing until mixture becomes frothy; add topping and, using an on-off motion, blend into mixture. Pour into chilled goblets and serve immediately.

Each serving provides: 1 Fruit Exchange; ¼ Milk Exchange; 65 calories Optional Exchange
Per serving: 131 calories; 3 g protein; 1 g fat; 22 g carbohydrate; 32 mg sodium; 1 mg cholesterol

Hawaiian Iced Tea

MAKES 4 SERVINGS

Pineapple and rum give this summertime favorite its typical tropical touch.

3½ cups water
4 tea bags
1 mint sprig
⅔ cup pineapple juice (no sugar added)
½ cup light rum
3 tablespoons lemon juice
Granulated sugar substitute to equal 8 teaspoons
  sugar (optional)

In large teakettle or 2-quart saucepan, over high heat, bring water to a boil; pour into 1-quart heatproof container. Add tea bags and mint and let steep until tea is very dark in color, 4 to 5 minutes; using slotted spoon, remove and discard tea bags and mint. Add pineapple juice, rum, lemon juice, and if desired, sugar substitute; stir well to combine. Cover and refrigerate until chilled.

Each serving provides: ½ Fruit Exchange; 70 calories Optional Exchange
Per serving without sugar substitute: 98 calories; 0.3 g protein; 0.1 g fat;
  7 g carbohydrate; 3 mg sodium; 0 mg cholesterol
With sugar substitute: 102 calories; 0.3 g protein; 0.1 g fat;
  8 g carbohydrate; 3 mg sodium; 0 mg cholesterol

Soviet Russia
and the Ukraine

Had you been a tsar, the Cossacks might have procured your favorite dish the hard way: by chopping holes in the ice to harpoon passing fish and thus get...caviar. This imperial delicacy, which is actually the roe of sturgeon, is one of the world's most expensive foods. In its place, we offer Poor Man's Caviar made with eggplant, a very tasty appetizer. The Russians attach great importance to these pre-meal bites, and their Pirozhki (tiny pies made with various fillings) make exotic hors d'oeuvres.

Because this enormous land blends both European and Asian tastes, there isn't just one Russian cuisine; there are many. From the agriculturally rich Ukraine, once known as the "bread basket of Europe," comes grain for the hearty dark Russian breads and the traditional Kasha, which can be served at breakfast or as an entrée accompaniment, side dish, or stuffing. Yogurt and kéfir (fermented milk), Russian staples today, originated with the nomadic tribes of the eastern steppes.

In the legendary sub-zero winters, meals need to be hot and nourishing, although borshch, the national soup (based on cabbage and beets), may be served either hot or cold. Entrées like beef Stroganoff bear the names of noblemen, but Kotlety Pozharskie, a popular ground chicken dish, was named for the innkeeper who invented it.

The Russians share with the rest of the world a love for desserts. One of their favorites is Kisel, a tart pudding usually made from berries. (Our version uses apples.)

For the proper ambience, keep a samovar simmering for tea — and drink the tea from glasses in true Russian style.

From Russia with Gusto

Poor Man's Caviar*

Pumpernickel Triangles

Chicken with Prune Sauce*

Kasha*

Steamed Red Cabbage

Kisel*
(Apple Pudding)

Tea

Borshch Ukraïnsky

MAKES 6 SERVINGS

Sour cream is the crowning touch for this Ukrainian-style beet soup.

1 pound 7 ounces boneless chuck steak
1 tablespoon vegetable oil
1 quart plus 1 cup water
4 cups shredded green cabbage
2 cups shredded beets
2 medium tomatoes, blanched, peeled, seeded, and chopped
1 cup sliced carrots
½ cup chopped onion
1 tablespoon granulated sugar
1½ teaspoons cider vinegar
1 packet instant beef broth and seasoning mix
9 ounces pared potatoes, cut into cubes
2 tablespoons tomato paste
1 tablespoon each chopped fresh parsley and dillweed
½ teaspoon salt
Dash pepper
¾ cup sour cream

On rack in broiling pan broil steak, turning once, until rare; cut into 1-inch cubes.

In 4-quart saucepan heat oil; add meat, in batches, and sear on all sides. Carefully pour in water; add vegetables, sugar, vinegar, and broth mix and bring to a boil. Reduce heat, cover, and let simmer for about 1 hour. Stir in remaining ingredients except sour cream, cover, and let simmer until potatoes are tender, about 30 minutes longer. Ladle borshch into soup bowls and top each portion with 2 tablespoons sour cream.

Each serving provides: 3 Protein Exchanges; ½ Bread Exchange; 3⅛ Vegetable Exchanges; ½ Fat Exchange; 85 calories Optional Exchange
Per serving: 367 calories; 30 g protein; 17 g fat; 20 g carbohydrate; 464 mg sodium; 90 mg cholesterol

Chicken with Prune Sauce

MAKES 2 SERVINGS

The lemony prune sauce gives a piquancy to the chicken.

1½ pounds chicken parts, skinned
1 teaspoon vegetable oil
¼ teaspoon salt, divided
Dash pepper
¼ cup each chopped onion, celery, and carrot
½ cup plus 2 tablespoons water, divided
1 small parsley sprig
½ bay leaf
4 large pitted prunes
¾ teaspoon lemon juice
¼ teaspoon granulated sugar
1 teaspoon each margarine and all-purpose flour

Using paper towel, pat chicken parts dry. In 12-inch nonstick skillet heat oil; add chicken, sprinkle with ⅛ teaspoon salt and the pepper, and sauté until lightly browned on all sides. Remove from skillet and set aside. In same skillet combine vegetables and sauté until soft but not browned; return chicken to skillet. Add ¼ cup water and the parsley and bay leaf and bring to a boil. Reduce heat, cover, and let simmer until chicken is tender, about 20 minutes. During last 10 minutes that chicken is cooking, in small saucepan combine prunes, lemon juice, sugar, and ¼ cup water; cook until prunes are tender, about 5 minutes.

Remove chicken to warmed serving platter, reserving vegetable mixture; discard parsley and bay leaf. Arrange prunes around chicken, reserving cooking liquid. Cover platter with foil and keep warm.

Set fine sieve over a bowl and pour vegetable mixture into sieve; using back of spoon, press down on vegetables to release liquid. Reserve liquid, discarding solids.

In small saucepan heat margarine until bubbly and hot; add flour and cook, stirring constantly, for 2 minutes. Gradually stir in reserved vegetable liquid; add prune liquid and remaining 2 tablespoons water and ⅛ teaspoon salt.

(CONTINUED)	Stirring constantly, bring to a boil and cook until thickened; pour over chicken and prunes. Each serving provides: 4 Protein Exchanges; ¾ Vegetable Exchange; 1 Fat Exchange; 1 Fruit Exchange; 10 calories Optional Exchange Per serving: 278 calories; 32 g protein; 9 g fat; 18 g carbohydrate; 431 mg sodium; 99 mg cholesterol

Cucumber and Turnip Salad

MAKES 2 SERVINGS *A salad that points up the versatility of the turnip.*	**1 cup each thinly sliced pared turnips, cooked, and sliced pared cucumber** **1½ teaspoons lemon juice** **3 tablespoons sour cream** **1½ teaspoons white vinegar** **1 teaspoon olive oil** **¼ teaspoon each granulated sugar and salt** **Dash pepper** In salad bowl combine turnips, cucumber, and lemon juice; cover and refrigerate for 30 minutes. In small bowl combine remaining ingredients; pour over turnip mixture and toss. Each serving provides: 2 Vegetable Exchanges; ½ Fat Exchange; 55 calories Optional Exchange Per serving: 99 calories; 2 g protein; 7 g fat; 8 g carbohydrate; 318 mg sodium; 9 mg cholesterol

Codfish Cakes
with Mustard Sauce

**MAKES 2 SERVINGS,
2 FISH CAKES EACH**

*The dill-flavored
tangy mustard sauce
is the perfect
complement to
codfish.*

10 ounces cod fillets, cut into 2-inch pieces
¼ cup chopped onion
1 slice white bread, made into crumbs and soaked in
    1 tablespoon skim milk
3 tablespoons chopped fresh dill, divided
Salt and pepper
2 teaspoons all-purpose flour
1 tablespoon each Dijon-style mustard and water
1 teaspoon each pickle relish and lemon juice
2 teaspoons vegetable oil, divided
1 tablespoon plus 2 teaspoons chopped fresh parsley

In work bowl of food processor combine fish and onion
and process until smooth; add soaked crumbs, half of the
dill, ¼ teaspoon salt, and dash pepper and process until
smooth. Form mixture into 4 equal patties and sprinkle
each side of each patty with ¼ teaspoon flour; cover and
refrigerate for 30 minutes.

In small bowl combine mustard, water, relish, lemon
juice, and 1 teaspoon oil, mixing well; stir in parsley, dash
each salt and pepper, and remaining dill. Set aside.

In 9-inch skillet heat remaining teaspoon oil; add fish
cakes and cook, turning once, until golden brown, about
3 minutes on each side. Serve fish cakes with mustard sauce.

Each serving provides: 4 Protein Exchanges; ½ Bread Exchange;
    ¼ Vegetable Exchange; 1 Fat Exchange; 20 calories Optional Exchange
Per serving: 219 calories; 27 g protein; 6 g fat; 13 g carbohydrate;
    746 mg sodium; 71 mg cholesterol

Kotlety Pozharskie

MAKES 4 SERVINGS

Turn your dinner into a Russian repast with these fried chicken patties.

4 slices white bread
¼ cup skim milk
1¼ pounds skinned and boned chicken breasts, cut into small pieces
1 tablespoon plus 2 teaspoons margarine, divided
½ teaspoon salt
⅛ teaspoon pepper

Into small bowl crumble 2 slices bread; add milk and let soak for 5 minutes.

In work bowl of food processor combine chicken with soaked bread and process to a paste; add 2 teaspoons margarine and the salt and pepper and process just until combined. Moisten hands with cold water and form mixture into 4 equal patties, each about ¾ inch thick, shaping patties to resemble cutlets or chops.

Process remaining 2 bread slices into crumbs and transfer to sheet of wax paper or a paper plate; dredge patties in crumbs, using all of the crumbs and coating thoroughly.

In 12-inch skillet heat remaining tablespoon margarine over medium heat until bubbly and hot; add patties and cook, turning once, until chicken is done and crust is golden, about 5 minutes on each side.

Each serving provides: 4 Protein Exchanges; 1 Bread Exchange; 1 Fat Exchange; 15 calories Optional Exchange
Per serving: 269 calories; 35 g protein; 7 g fat; 13 g carbohydrate; 551 mg sodium; 83 mg cholesterol

Russian Krupnik

MAKES 4 SERVINGS

This very hearty beef-barley stew is wonderful accompanied by a mixed green salad.

8 ounces beef for stew (cubes)
1 quart water
1 cup carrot chunks (1-inch pieces)
½ cup each celery and onion chunks (1-inch pieces)
1 ounce uncooked pearl barley, rinsed
¾ ounce sorted uncooked lentils, rinsed
3 packets instant beef broth and seasoning mix
1 bay leaf
¼ teaspoon pepper
½ cup frozen green baby lima beans, thawed, or drained canned green lima beans
2 ounces drained canned chick-peas

On rack in broiling pan broil meat 5 to 6 inches from heat source, turning to brown all sides, until rare. Transfer to 3-quart saucepan and add remaining ingredients except lima beans and chick-peas; cover and let simmer over medium-low heat, stirring occasionally, until meat is fork-tender, 45 to 50 minutes. Stir in lima beans and chick-peas, cover, and cook until heated through, 2 to 3 minutes. Remove bay leaf before serving.

Each serving provides: 2 Protein Exchanges; ½ Bread Exchange;
   1 Vegetable Exchange; 10 calories Optional Exchange
Per serving with frozen lima beans: 209 calories; 19 g protein; 5 g fat;
   23 g carbohydrate; 703 mg sodium (estimated); 39 mg cholesterol
With canned lima beans: 202 calories; 18 g protein; 5 g fat;
   22 g carbohydrate; 717 mg sodium (estimated); 39 mg cholesterol

Sautéed Liver, Potatoes, and Mushrooms

MAKES 2 SERVINGS

Dried mushrooms add a unique flavor to this hearty skillet meal.

6 small dried whole mushrooms
½ cup water
2 teaspoons margarine, divided
½ cup sliced onion (separated into rings)
6 ounces peeled cooked potatoes, cut into ¼-inch-thick slices
Salt
2 teaspoons all-purpose flour
10 ounces sliced calf liver
¼ teaspoon tomato paste (optional)
2 tablespoons sour cream

In a sieve wash mushrooms thoroughly. In small saucepan combine mushrooms and water; bring to a boil over medium heat and cook until mushrooms are tender, about 15 minutes. Set aside.

In 9-inch skillet heat 1 teaspoon margarine until bubbly and hot; add onion and sauté until softened. Add mushrooms (reserving liquid) and potatoes; sprinkle with ¼ teaspoon salt and sauté until vegetables are lightly browned. Remove from skillet and keep warm.

Combine flour with ⅛ teaspoon salt and evenly sprinkle liver slices with seasoned flour. In same skillet heat remaining teaspoon margarine until bubbly and hot; add liver and cook, turning once, until done to taste. Add reserved cooking liquid and, if desired, tomato paste; stir to combine and bring to a boil. Add potato mixture and sour cream and stir to combine; cook until heated *(do not boil)*.

Each serving provides: 4 Protein Exchanges; 1 Bread Exchange; ¾ Vegetable Exchange; 1 Fat Exchange; 45 calories Optional Exchange
Per serving with tomato paste: 405 calories; 32 g protein; 14 g fat; 39 g carbohydrate; 590 mg sodium; 432 mg cholesterol
Without tomato paste: 404 calories; 32 g protein; 14 g fat; 39 g carbohydrate; 585 mg sodium; 432 mg cholesterol

Kasha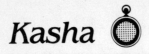

MAKES 4 SERVINGS

A staff of life in Russia.

4 ounces uncooked kasha (buckwheat groats)
1 egg, lightly beaten
1 tablespoon plus 1 teaspoon reduced-calorie margarine
1 cup chopped onions
1½ cups each chopped mushrooms and boiling water
¾ teaspoon salt
⅛ teaspoon pepper

In small bowl combine kasha and egg. Heat 10-inch skillet over high heat; add kasha mixture and cook, stirring constantly, until kasha is dry and grains are separated *(be careful not to burn)*. Remove to bowl and set aside.

In same skillet heat margarine until bubbly and hot; add onions and sauté until softened. Add mushrooms and sauté for 3 minutes; stir in kasha, boiling water, salt, and pepper. Cover and let simmer until water has been absorbed and grains of kasha are separate and fluffy, 15 to 20 minutes.

Each serving provides: 1 Bread Exchange; 1¼ Vegetable Exchanges; ½ Fat Exchange; 20 calories Optional Exchange
Per serving: 155 calories; 6 g protein; 4 g fat; 26 g carbohydrate; 483 mg sodium; 69 mg cholesterol

Poor Man's Caviar

MAKES 4 SERVINGS

Serve with thin-sliced bread, crispbread, melba toast, or saltines.

1 large eggplant (about 1½ pounds)
1 tablespoon plus 1 teaspoon olive oil, divided
1 cup diced onions
½ cup diced green bell pepper
2 garlic cloves, minced
2 medium tomatoes, blanched, peeled, seeded, and
    finely chopped
½ teaspoon each salt and granulated sugar
¼ teaspoon pepper
1 tablespoon plus 1½ teaspoons lemon juice

Preheat oven to 400°F. On rack in roasting pan bake eggplant, turning once or twice, until soft and skin is charred, about 45 minutes. Let cool until easy to handle, then remove and discard skin and chop pulp; set aside.

In 10-inch skillet heat 2 teaspoons oil; add onions and sauté until soft but not browned. Add bell pepper and garlic and sauté for 5 minutes; transfer mixture to a mixing bowl. Add eggplant pulp, tomatoes, salt, sugar, and pepper and stir to combine.

In same skillet heat remaining 2 teaspoons oil; add eggplant mixture and, stirring constantly, bring to a boil. Reduce heat to low, cover, and cook for 1 hour, stirring occasionally. Remove cover and, stirring occasionally, cook until mixture is thick, about 30 minutes longer. Stir in lemon juice, transfer to a serving bowl, and let cool; cover and refrigerate for at least 4 hours.

Each serving provides: 3¾ Vegetable Exchanges; 1 Fat Exchange;
    3 calories Optional Exchange
Per serving: 104 calories; 3 g protein; 5 g fat; 15 g carbohydrate;
    286 mg sodium; 0 mg cholesterol

Flat Onion Bread

**MAKES 6 SERVINGS,
1 FLAT BREAD EACH**

*This special skillet
bread has universal
appeal.*

1 tablespoon margarine, melted, divided
¾ cup diced onions
½ packet fast-rising active dry yeast
**¼ cup warm water (see yeast package directions
   for temperature), divided**
½ teaspoon granulated sugar
1 cup plus 2 tablespoons all-purpose flour, divided
¼ teaspoon salt

In small skillet heat 1 teaspoon margarine until bubbly and
hot; add onions and sauté until soft but not browned. Set
aside and let cool.

In small bowl sprinkle yeast over 1 tablespoon water;
add sugar and stir to combine. Let stand until foamy, about
5 minutes. Measure out and reserve 1 tablespoon flour;
pour remaining flour into mixing bowl and stir in yeast
mixture, sautéed onions, salt, and remaining 3 tablespoons
water and 2 teaspoons margarine. Knead dough until
smooth and elastic, about 5 minutes; divide dough into
6 equal pieces. Sprinkle work surface with reserved
tablespoon flour; on floured surface roll each piece of
dough into a circle, about 8 inches in diameter.

Heat heavy 10- or 12-inch skillet until a drop of water
sizzles and evaporates when sprinkled in pan; transfer
1 dough circle to pan and cook until browned on bottom, 3
to 4 minutes; using a pancake turner, turn dough over and
brown other side. Remove to wire rack and let cool. Repeat
procedure 5 more times, making a total of 6 flat breads.

Each serving provides: 1 Bread Exchange; ¼ Vegetable Exchange;
   ½ Fat Exchange; 2 calories Optional Exchange
Per serving: 113 calories; 3 g protein; 2 g fat; 20 g carbohydrate;
   115 mg sodium; 0 mg cholesterol

Rye Crackers

**MAKES 4 SERVINGS,
5 CRACKERS EACH**

*Even crackers can be
homemade—and
these are well
worth it.*

1 cup plus 2 tablespoons rye flour
¼ teaspoon baking soda
1 egg
**1 tablespoon plus 1 teaspoon each granulated sugar and
margarine, melted**
1 tablespoon plain low-fat yogurt
1 egg white

Onto sheet of wax paper or a paper plate sift together rye
flour and baking soda. In mixing bowl beat egg with sugar
until combined; beat in margarine and yogurt. Gradually
add sifted flour, mixing thoroughly; form dough into a ball.

Preheat oven to 350°F. Spray nonstick cookie sheet with
nonstick cooking spray and set aside. On wooden board
roll dough into a 10 x 8-inch rectangle, about ⅛ inch thick;
cut dough into twenty 2-inch squares. Arrange squares on
sprayed cookie sheet and, with tines of a fork, prick each in
several places; brush an equal amount of egg white over
each square and bake until golden, 12 to 15 minutes. Using
a spatula, remove crackers to wire rack and let cool.

Each serving provides: 1½ Bread Exchanges; 1 Fat Exchange; 45 calories
Optional Exchange
Per serving: 160 calories; 5 g protein; 6 g fat; 23 g carbohydrate;
121 mg sodium; 69 mg cholesterol

Pirozhki

MAKES 4 SERVINGS,
4 TURNOVERS EACH

*These beef-filled
turnovers are served
as a savory appetizer
in Russia and
Eastern Europe.*

¾ cup all-purpose flour, divided
½ teaspoon salt
2 tablespoons margarine
2 tablespoons plain low-fat yogurt
2 ounces broiled ground beef, crumbled
1 egg, hard-cooked and minced
1 egg, beaten, divided
2 tablespoons minced onion
¼ teaspoon each dillweed and salt
Dash pepper
¼ cup prepared mustard

Measure out and reserve 1 tablespoon flour. In small mixing bowl combine remaining flour and the salt; with a pastry blender, or 2 knives used scissors-fashion, cut in margarine until mixture resembles coarse meal. Stir in yogurt to form soft dough; shape into a ball, wrap in plastic wrap, and refrigerate for 30 minutes.

In small bowl combine beef, minced egg, half of the beaten egg, and the onion and seasonings, mixing well. Cover remaining beaten egg with plastic wrap and reserve for later use.

Preheat oven to 400°F. Sprinkle work surface with reserved tablespoon flour; on floured work surface roll out dough to form a ¼-inch-thick circle. Using 3-inch-diameter round cookie cutter, cut dough into circles, rerolling and using scraps of dough and forming 16 circles; spoon an equal amount of beef mixture (about 1 rounded teaspoon) onto center of each circle. Fold dough over filling, forming each turnover into a half-moon shape; press edges together to seal. Transfer turnovers to nonstick baking sheet and brush each with an equal amount of remaining beaten egg. Bake until golden brown, 15 to 20 minutes. Arrange on serving platter and serve with mustard.

Each serving provides: 1 Protein Exchange; 1 Bread Exchange;
1½ Fat Exchanges; 5 calories Optional Exchange
Per serving: 240 calories; 11 g protein; 13 g fat; 20 g carbohydrate;
721 mg sodium; 151 mg cholesterol

Syrniki

MAKES 4 SERVINGS,
2 PATTIES EACH

These yogurt-topped cheese patties make wonderful hors d'oeuvres or appetizers.

1 cup pot cheese, forced through a sieve
¼ cup plus 1½ teaspoons all-purpose flour, divided
1 egg
¼ teaspoon salt
1 tablespoon plus 1 teaspoon margarine
¼ cup plain low-fat yogurt
2 teaspoons minced fresh dill

In bowl combine cheese, ¼ cup flour, and the egg and salt, mixing thoroughly; cover and refrigerate for 2 hours.

Form cheese mixture into 8 equal patties; sprinkle both sides of each patty with an equal amount of remaining flour. In 12-inch skillet heat margarine over medium heat until bubbly and hot; add patties and cook until browned on bottom. Turn patties over and brown other side. To serve, top each patty with 1½ teaspoons yogurt and sprinkle with ¼ teaspoon dill.

Each serving provides: 1 Protein Exchange; 1 Fat Exchange; 45 calories Optional Exchange
Per serving: 136 calories; 10 g protein; 6 g fat; 9 g carbohydrate; 437 mg sodium; 72 mg cholesterol

Varenyky with Raspberry Sauce

MAKES 4 SERVINGS, 3 DUMPLINGS EACH

These cheese dumplings are wonderfully enhanced by the fruit sauce.

¾ cup all-purpose flour, divided
½ teaspoon salt
1 egg, beaten, divided
¼ cup ice water
⅔ cup pot-style cottage cheese
1 tablespoon plus 1 teaspoon granulated sugar, divided
1 tablespoon sour cream
⅛ teaspoon ground cinnamon
2 cups very ripe raspberries*
1 gallon water

Measure out and reserve 1 tablespoon flour. In large mixing bowl combine remaining flour and salt; make a well in center of flour and pour half of the egg and the ice water into well. Gradually, thoroughly incorporate the egg and water into the flour, forming a smooth dough; form into a ball, wrap in plastic wrap, and refrigerate for 30 minutes. Cover remaining egg with plastic wrap and set aside until ready to use.

Set fine sieve over a medium bowl and force cheese through sieve into bowl; add 1 teaspoon sugar and the sour cream and cinnamon and mix well.

Sprinkle work surface with reserved tablespoon flour; on floured surface roll dough to form a ¼-inch-thick circle. Using 3-inch-diameter round cookie cutter, cut dough into circles, rerolling and using scraps of dough and forming 12 circles; using pastry brush, brush each circle with an equal amount of remaining beaten egg. Spoon an equal amount of cheese mixture (about 1 rounded teaspoon) onto lower half of each circle; fold top half over to enclose filling and, using tines of fork, press edges firmly to seal. Cover loosely with clean damp towel or plastic wrap and set aside.

In blender container process raspberries until smooth. Set fine sieve over a 1-quart saucepan and force raspberry puree through sieve into pan; add remaining tablespoon sugar and cook over medium heat, stirring occasionally, for 5 to 10 minutes. Remove from heat and set aside.

(CONTINUED)   In 6-quart saucepot bring water to a boil. Reduce heat to medium and drop 6 dumplings into water; let simmer until dumplings rise to surface, 5 to 8 minutes. Remove dumplings to warmed serving platter and keep warm. Repeat cooking procedure with remaining 6 dumplings. For each portion, serve 3 dumplings topped with ¼ of the sauce.

Each serving provides: ½ Protein Exchange; 1 Bread Exchange; 1 Fruit
    Exchange; 45 calories Optional Exchange
Per serving: 180 calories; 9 g protein; 3 g fat; 30 g carbohydrate;
    296 mg sodium; 72 mg cholesterol

*Frozen raspberries (no sugar added) may be substituted; after measuring, let thaw.

Kisel

MAKES 2 SERVINGS

A thick and creamy apple pudding.

**2 small tart apples, cored, pared, and cut into
½-inch-thick slices**
¾ cup water
1 tablespoon granulated sugar
¾ teaspoon potato starch, dissolved in 1½ teaspoons water

In small saucepan combine apples and water; bring to a boil. Reduce heat and let simmer until apples are tender, 10 to 15 minutes. Set sieve over a bowl and force apple mixture through sieve into bowl; return mixture to saucepan, stir in sugar, and bring to a boil. Stir in dissolved potato starch and cook, stirring constantly, until slightly thickened, 2 to 3 minutes. Let cool to lukewarm, then pour into 2 dessert dishes; cover and refrigerate for at least 4 hours.

Each serving provides: 1 Fruit Exchange; 35 calories Optional Exchange
Per serving: 84 calories; 0.1 g protein; 0.3 g fat; 22 g carbohydrate;
    0.1 mg sodium; 0 mg cholesterol

Blini

Traditionally, these delicious little pancakes are made with buckwheat and all-purpose flours mixed with sour cream, and are served with sour cream and caviar or jam.

⅓ cup plus 2 teaspoons all-purpose flour
1½ teaspoons granulated sugar
½ teaspoon double-acting baking powder
Dash salt
1 egg
¼ cup sour cream, divided
1 teaspoon each margarine, melted, and vegetable oil
1 tablespoon plus 1 teaspoon reduced-calorie strawberry spread (16 calories per 2 teaspoons)

Into bowl sift together dry ingredients. In small bowl beat together egg, 2 tablespoons sour cream, and the margarine; add to dry ingredients and blend thoroughly.

In 12-inch nonstick skillet heat oil; drop batter into skillet by rounded tablespoonfuls, forming 8 pancakes, each about 3 inches in diameter. Cook until browned on bottom; turn pancakes over and brown other side. Serve each portion of pancakes with 1 tablespoon sour cream and 2 teaspoons strawberry spread.

Each serving provides: ½ Protein Exchange; 1 Bread Exchange; 1 Fat Exchange; 100 calories Optional Exchange
Per serving: 252 calories; 6 g protein; 13 g fat; 27 g carbohydrate; 245 mg sodium; 150 mg cholesterol

Spain and Portugal

Fish for interesting recipes from the Iberian Peninsula. Fronting on the Atlantic and the Mediterranean, Spain and Portugal feature a wealth of seafood specialties, from our Catalan Tuna Steaks and Portuguese Clams to Ali-Oli, the savory garlic-flavored mayonnaise served as an accompaniment to fish dishes. The Spanish national dish is Paella, saffron-flavored rice and assorted fish and shellfish mixed with various other ingredients like sausages and/or poultry, depending on the province. (The word "paella" refers to the oval-shaped pan in which the food is customarily cooked and served.)

Omnipresent in Spanish cooking are garlic, olives, olive oil, and tomatoes. In fact, the enterprising Spanish are said to have invented tomato sauce. Portuguese cooking tends to be plainer, but it too depends on these pungent ingredients—witness our Portuguese Steak.

Although cold soups are often thought of in connection with Spanish menus, hot soup-stews, such as our Caldo Gallego, are relished in the winter. These combinations include nourishing pieces of meat or poultry, as well as the ever-popular garbanzos (chick-peas).

The superb Iberian fruits lend themselves to luscious dessert concoctions, such as our Tart Ibiza or Amor Frio, a Spanish-style cream. The name literally means "cold love"—but what you'll love is being able to enjoy such desserts without paying for them in pounds.

You can toast your figure-saving efforts with a spritzer based on one of Spain's fine red wines.

An Iberian Offering

Melon and Asparagus Valenciana[*]

Paella[*]

Basque Green Beans[*]

Amor Frio[*]
(Spanish Cream)

Red Wine Spritzer

Melon and Asparagus Valenciana

MAKES 2 SERVINGS

Traditionally, Spanish meals start with a first course of fruit and vegetables.

4 lettuce leaves
¼ small cantaloupe, pared, seeded, and cut into thin wedges
½ medium tomato, thinly sliced
6 medium asparagus spears, blanched and chilled
1 egg, hard-cooked
2 teaspoons each apple juice (no sugar added) and reduced-calorie mayonnaise
⅛ teaspoon salt

On serving plate decoratively arrange lettuce leaves, melon and tomato slices, and asparagus spears.

Cut egg in half horizontally; remove yolk to bowl. Thinly slice white and arrange slices over tomato. Mash yolk until smooth; stir in juice, mayonnaise, and salt. Serve dressing along with salad.

Each serving provides: ½ Protein Exchange; 1½ Vegetable Exchanges; ½ Fat Exchange; ½ Fruit Exchange; 3 calories Optional Exchange
Per serving: 98 calories; 6 g protein; 5 g fat; 11 g carbohydrate; 220 mg sodium; 139 mg cholesterol

Caldo Gallego

MAKES 4 SERVINGS,
ABOUT 1⅓ CUPS
EACH

*This sausage and
vegetable soup is
popular in both
Spain and
Portugal.*

2 teaspoons olive oil
½ cup chopped onion
3 garlic cloves, minced
1 quart water
2 packets instant beef broth and seasoning mix
1 packet instant chicken broth and seasoning mix
6 ounces pared and diced potato
1 cup seeded and diced canned Italian tomatoes
½ cup diced carrot
1 bay leaf
6 ounces cooked veal sausage, sliced
4 ounces drained canned chick-peas (garbanzo beans)
1 cup cooked chopped kale
1 tablespoon minced fresh parsley
½ teaspoon oregano leaves
¼ teaspoon pepper

In 3- or 4-quart saucepan heat oil over high heat; add onion
and garlic and sauté until onion is translucent, 1 to 2
minutes. Add water and broth mixes and stir until
dissolved. Reduce heat to low and add potato, tomatoes,
carrot, and bay leaf; cover and let simmer until vegetables
are tender, 35 to 40 minutes. Add remaining ingredients
and cook until sausage and chick-peas are heated through,
about 5 minutes longer. Remove and discard bay leaf
before serving.

Each serving provides: 2 Protein Exchanges; ½ Bread Exchange;
  1½ Vegetable Exchanges; ½ Fat Exchange; 10 calories Optional Exchange
Per serving: 236 calories; 18 g protein; 9 g fat; 23 g carbohydrate;
  1,349 mg sodium (estimated); 43 mg cholesterol

Ali-Oli

This is a Spanish version of a garlic-mayonnaise sauce from Provence. It is similar to mayonnaise but is heavily flavored with garlic and is traditionally served with fish.

2 eggs
4 to 8 small garlic cloves, peeled and crushed*
1 cup olive oil
2 tablespoons lemon juice
½ teaspoon salt
Dash white pepper

In blender container combine eggs and garlic and process until pureed (mixture should be smooth). Remove center of blender cover and, with blender running at high speed, slowly add oil in a thin stream. When oil is well combined, turn off motor. Scrape down sides of container, add remaining ingredients, and process until blended (mixture should be the consistency of mayonnaise). Transfer to resealable plastic container, cover, and refrigerate until ready to use.

Each 1-teaspoon serving provides: 1 Fat Exchange
Per teaspoon: 44 calories; 0.3 g protein; 5 g fat; 0.1 g carbohydrate;
  26 mg sodium; 11 mg cholesterol

*The number of garlic cloves to use depends upon how strong a garlic flavor you want.

Portuguese Clams

MAKES 2 SERVINGS

A wonderful mix of colors and flavors.

1 teaspoon olive oil
¼ cup diced onion
½ ounce Canadian-style bacon, finely chopped
4 garlic cloves, minced
½ cup diced red bell pepper
¼ cup diced green bell pepper
1 cup tomato juice
½ cup seeded and diced canned Italian tomatoes
1½ ounces cooked ground pork, crumbled
2 tablespoons each dry vermouth and bottled clam juice
1 teaspoon each chili powder and lemon juice
½ teaspoon each drained capers, minced fresh parsley, and
   red wine vinegar
18 small littleneck or cherrystone clams, scrubbed

In 10-inch skillet heat oil over medium-high heat; add onion, bacon, and garlic and sauté until onion is translucent. Add red and green peppers and cook until peppers are softened, 2 to 3 minutes. Add remaining ingredients except clams; stir well to combine. Reduce heat to low and let simmer for 15 to 20 minutes to blend flavors. Increase heat to high and add clams to skillet; cover and let steam until clam shells open, 10 to 12 minutes. Serve immediately.

Each serving provides: 4 Protein Exchanges; 1½ Vegetable Exchanges;
   ½ Fat Exchange; 45 calories Optional Exchange
Per serving: 262 calories; 25 g protein; 9 g fat; 19 g carbohydrate;
   676 mg sodium; 82 mg cholesterol

Gambas al Ajillo ⏱

MAKES 2 SERVINGS

Turn simple into special with this shrimp in hot garlic sauce.

1½ garlic cloves, peeled
1 tablespoon olive oil, divided
Dash crushed red pepper
5 ounces shelled and deveined large shrimp
1 tablespoon dry sherry
1 teaspoon lemon juice
⅛ teaspoon salt
Dash freshly ground pepper

Chop ½ garlic clove; using mortar and pestle, or in a small bowl using back of spoon, mash garlic to a smooth paste. Using small wire whisk, gradually beat in 1 teaspoon oil, beating until mixture resembles consistency of mayonnaise; set aside.

In 8-inch nonstick skillet heat remaining 2 teaspoons oil over high heat; add whole garlic clove and red pepper and sauté until garlic turns golden brown, about 1 minute *(be careful not to burn)*. Remove and discard garlic. Add shrimp to pan and cook, turning once, until shrimp turn pink, 1 to 2 minutes on each side. Add sherry, lemon juice, salt, and pepper and sauté 1 minute longer. Add garlic "mayonnaise," stir to combine, and serve immediately.

Each serving provides: 2 Protein Exchanges; 1½ Fat Exchanges; 10 calories Optional Exchange
Per serving: 140 calories; 14 g protein; 7 g fat; 2 g carbohydrate; 219 mg sodium; 85 mg cholesterol

Gambas con Salsa Verde

MAKES 2 SERVINGS, 4 SKEWERS EACH

Herbs and wine combine in this unique skewered shrimp with green sauce.

½ cup fresh parsley leaves, rinsed and patted dry
¼ cup fresh cilantro leaves (Chinese parsley), rinsed and patted dry
2 tablespoons water
1 tablespoon white wine
4 garlic cloves, chopped
2 teaspoons each chopped shallots, drained capers, and olive oil
1 teaspoon lemon juice
⅛ teaspoon salt
Dash pepper
8 large shrimp (6 ounces)

In blender container combine all ingredients except shrimp and process until smooth, stopping motor and scraping down sides of container as necessary.

Shell and devein shrimp, leaving tail "feathers" on. Onto each of eight 12-inch wooden or metal skewers, starting at tail end, thread 1 shrimp lengthwise; transfer skewers to nonstick baking sheet and broil for 1 to 2 minutes. Turn shrimp over and spread each with ⅛ of the green sauce; broil until shrimp are firm, 1 to 2 minutes longer *(do not overcook or shrimp will toughen)*. Serve immediately.

Each serving provides: 2 Protein Exchanges; 1 Fat Exchange; 10 calories Optional Exchange
Per serving: 133 calories; 15 g protein; 5 g fat; 5 g carbohydrate; 304 mg sodium; 85 mg cholesterol

Catalan Tuna Steaks

MAKES 2 SERVINGS

Try this wonderful light, delicate Spanish entrée; it's very flavorful as well as colorful.

2 tablespoons each dry white wine and minced fresh parsley
2 teaspoons olive oil
1 teaspoon each lemon juice and drained capers
2 garlic cloves, minced
10 ounces boneless tuna steaks
1 very small eggplant (about 6 ounces)
1 each medium red and green bell pepper
1 small onion (about 3 ounces), peeled and ends removed
3 large plum tomatoes, blanched, peeled, seeded, and cut into 1 x ¼-inch strips

In medium bowl combine wine, parsley, oil, lemon juice, capers, and garlic; add tuna and turn to coat with marinade. Cover with plastic wrap and refrigerate for 1 hour.

On baking sheet broil eggplant, peppers, and onion 3 inches from heat source, turning frequently, until vegetables are charred on all sides. Remove from broiler and let stand until cool enough to handle.

Preheat oven to 350°F. Fit strainer into small bowl and peel eggplant and peppers over bowl, allowing juice from vegetables to drip into bowl; remove and discard stem ends and seeds from peppers. Cut eggplant and peppers into 2 x ¼-inch strips; remove charred layer from onion and cut onion into wedges. Drain tuna, reserving marinade. Transfer broiled vegetables with juices to 8 x 8 x 2-inch baking pan; add tomatoes and reserved marinade. Bake until vegetables are heated, 10 to 15 minutes; set aside and keep warm.

Turn oven control to broil. On rack in broiling pan broil tuna, turning once, until fish begins to brown, 4 to 5 minutes on each side. Transfer to serving plate, pour any juices from bottom of broiling pan over tuna, and serve with baked vegetables.

Each serving provides: 4 Protein Exchanges; 5¼ Vegetable Exchanges; 1 Fat Exchange; 15 calories Optional Exchange
Per serving: 350 calories; 40 g protein; 11 g fat; 21 g carbohydrate; 78 mg sodium; 81 mg cholesterol

Chicken Sofrito

MAKES 2 SERVINGS

Ground toasted almonds elegantly crown this delicious stir-fried chicken.

2 teaspoons olive oil, divided
½ cup finely chopped onion
¼ cup finely chopped green bell pepper
2 garlic cloves, minced
1¼ cups seeded and finely chopped drained canned
    Italian tomatoes
¾ cup water
½ cup sliced mushrooms
1 ounce julienne-cut Canadian-style bacon (thin strips)
2 tablespoons sherry
1 packet instant chicken broth and seasoning mix
1 teaspoon oregano leaves
¼ teaspoon each salt and pepper
⅛ teaspoon ground red pepper
9 ounces skinned and boned chicken breasts, cut into
    3 x ½-inch strips
4 pimiento-stuffed green olives, sliced crosswise
½ ounce shelled almonds, lightly toasted and ground

In 10-inch skillet heat 1 teaspoon oil over medium-high heat; add onion, bell pepper, and garlic and sauté until onion is translucent, 2 to 3 minutes. Add remaining ingredients except chicken and olives and stir to combine. Reduce heat to low, cover, and let simmer, stirring occasionally, for 15 minutes.

While tomato mixture is cooking, in separate 10-inch nonstick skillet heat remaining teaspoon oil over medium-high heat; add chicken and stir-fry until golden brown on all sides. Transfer to sauce, add olives, and stir to combine. Increase heat to medium and cook until chicken is cooked through and sauce is thickened, 5 to 6 minutes. Serve sprinkled with ground almonds.

Each serving provides: 4 Protein Exchanges; 2½ Vegetable Exchanges;
   1 Fat Exchange; 75 calories Optional Exchange
Per serving: 342 calories; 37 g protein; 12 g fat; 17 g carbohydrate;
   1,339 mg sodium; 81 mg cholesterol

Portuguese Steak ⏱

MAKES 2 SERVINGS

Serve with a salad and potatoes or rice.

3 garlic cloves, chopped
1 teaspoon red wine vinegar
¼ teaspoon pepper
2 bone-in beef top loin steaks (5 ounces each)
½ teaspoon each olive oil and margarine
2 slices prosciutto (½ ounce each)
¼ cup canned beef broth
1 tablespoon plus 1 teaspoon red wine
1 teaspoon lemon juice

Using a mortar and pestle, or in a small bowl using back of spoon, mash garlic with vinegar and pepper to form a smooth paste. Spread ¼ of mixture onto each steak; transfer to rack in broiling pan and broil 5 to 6 inches from heat source for 4 to 5 minutes. Turn steaks over, brush with remaining garlic mixture, and broil 4 to 5 minutes longer or until done to taste.

While steak is cooking, in 10-inch skillet combine oil and margarine and heat over medium heat until margarine is bubbly and hot; add prosciutto and sauté for 30 seconds. Transfer to plate, set aside, and keep warm. In same skillet combine broth, wine, and lemon juice and bring to a boil. Reduce heat to low and let simmer, stirring occasionally, for 2 to 3 minutes.

To serve, top each steak with 1 slice prosciutto and half of the sauce.

Each serving provides: 3½ Protein Exchanges; ½ Fat Exchange;
  15 calories Optional Exchange
Per serving: 233 calories; 31 g protein; 9 g fat; 2 g carbohydrate;
  349 mg sodium; 85 mg cholesterol

Paella

MAKES 8 SERVINGS

Don't let this traditional Spanish medley scare you off; if all the ingredients are prepared in advance, it is quite simple to complete and makes an elegant dinner-party dish.

¼ cup olive or vegetable oil, divided
13 ounces chicken cutlets, cut into cubes
1 cup diced onions
3 small garlic cloves, minced
1 cup red bell pepper strips (3 x ¼-inch strips)
2 medium tomatoes, blanched, peeled, seeded, and chopped
12 ounces large shrimp
6 ounces uncooked regular long-grain rice
1 teaspoon each salt and crumbled whole saffron
3 cups boiling water
1½-pound lobster, cut into pieces (green sacs removed)
4 ounces diagonally sliced smoked beef sausage
8 each small clams and small mussels, scrubbed
1 cup fresh or frozen peas*
Garnish: lemon wedges

In 8-inch nonstick skillet heat 2 tablespoons oil; in batches, add chicken and cook until browned on all sides. Remove from skillet and set aside.

In same skillet heat remaining 2 tablespoons oil over medium-high heat; add onions and garlic and sauté until onion is golden, 2 to 3 minutes. Reduce heat to medium-low, add peppers and tomatoes, and cook, stirring occasionally, until liquid evaporates and mixture becomes a thick paste, about 30 minutes *(be careful not to burn)*.

Preheat oven to 400°F. Shell and devein shrimp, leaving tail "feathers" on; set aside. In paella pan or 14-inch non-stick skillet that has a metal or removable handle combine rice, tomato mixture, salt, and saffron; pour in water, stir to combine, and bring to a boil. Remove from heat and arrange chicken, shrimp, lobster pieces, sausage, clams, mussels, and peas over rice. Set pan on bottom oven rack and bake until liquid is absorbed and rice is tender, about 20 minutes *(do not overcook)*. Remove pan from oven and let stand for 5 minutes. Serve garnished with lemon wedges.

(CONTINUED)	Each serving provides: 4 Protein Exchanges; 1 Bread Exchange; 1 Vegetable Exchange; 1½ Fat Exchanges; 10 calories Optional Exchange Per serving: 335 calories; 30 g protein; 11 g fat; 26 g carbohydrate; 650 mg sodium; 127 mg cholesterol *If frozen peas are used, thaw after measuring.

Basque Green Beans

MAKES 2 SERVINGS

An interesting sauce flavors these crunchy beans.

1 teaspoon olive oil
½ cup thinly sliced red bell pepper
1 ounce Canadian-style bacon, chopped
2 garlic cloves, minced
¼ cup canned chicken broth
1 tablespoon plus 1 teaspoon dry sherry
1 teaspoon each minced fresh parsley and lemon juice
¼ teaspoon pepper
⅛ teaspoon salt
1½ cups whole green beans, blanched

In 8-inch nonstick skillet heat oil over medium-high heat; add bell pepper, bacon, and garlic and sauté until peppers are tender-crisp, 2 to 3 minutes. Stir in broth, sherry, parsley, lemon juice, pepper, and salt; add beans and cook, stirring occasionally, until liquid is reduced by half and beans are heated through, 2 to 3 minutes.

Each serving provides: ½ Protein Exchange; 2 Vegetable Exchanges; ½ Fat Exchange; 15 calories Optional Exchange
Per serving: 103 calories; 6 g protein; 4 g fat; 11 g carbohydrate; 447 mg sodium; 7 mg cholesterol

Tortilla Paisana ⏱

MAKES 2 SERVINGS

This Spanish country omelet is an excellent way to use up leftover potatoes.

1 ounce julienne-cut boiled ham (thin strips)
¼ cup thinly sliced onion
2 teaspoons vegetable oil, divided
4½ ounces peeled cooked potatoes, thinly sliced
⅛ teaspoon each salt and paprika
Dash pepper
½ cup diced asparagus spears, blanched
¼ cup each frozen peas, thawed, and julienne-cut
    drained canned pimientos (thin strips)
3 eggs, beaten

Spray 10-inch nonstick skillet that has a metal or removable handle with nonstick cooking spray and heat; add ham and onion and cook over medium heat, stirring occasionally, until onions are softened, 3 to 4 minutes. Remove from skillet and set aside.

In same skillet heat ½ teaspoon oil; add potatoes, sprinkle with seasonings, and sauté over medium heat, turning occasionally, until lightly browned on both sides. Remove potatoes from skillet. Add remaining 1½ teaspoons oil to skillet; return potatoes and arrange in bottom of pan. Top with ham mixture, asparagus, peas, and pimientos; pour in beaten eggs and cook over medium heat until bottom of omelet is golden, 3 to 4 minutes.

Transfer pan to broiler and broil 5 inches from heat source until eggs are set and omelet begins to brown. Using spatula, loosen edges of omelet and carefully slide onto warmed plate.

Each serving provides: 2 Protein Exchanges; 1 Bread Exchange; 1 Vegetable Exchange; 1 Fat Exchange
Per serving: 256 calories; 16 g protein; 14 g fat; 17 g carbohydrate; 446 mg sodium; 419 mg cholesterol

Amor Frio

MAKES 4 SERVINGS

Spanish cream, a delicious orange pudding that will turn any dinner into a fiesta.

2 small oranges, peeled
2 tablespoons dry sherry
1 cup skim milk
2 eggs, separated
2 tablespoons granulated sugar
½ envelope unflavored gelatin
¼ teaspoon ground cinnamon, divided
Dash salt
2 teaspoons lemon juice
1 teaspoon grated orange peel
¼ cup thawed frozen dairy whipped topping

Over small bowl to catch juices, section oranges and cut sections into ½-inch pieces, adding orange pieces to bowl; add sherry and toss lightly to combine. Cover and refrigerate.

In double boiler combine milk, egg yolks, sugar, gelatin, ⅛ teaspoon cinnamon, and the salt and cook over hot water, stirring constantly, until mixture thickens, about 5 minutes. Pour into medium bowl, cover, and refrigerate, stirring occasionally, until chilled, about 30 minutes.

Set aside 4 orange pieces for garnish; add remaining orange mixture, lemon juice, and orange peel to gelatin mixture. Fold in whipped topping. In medium mixing bowl, using electric mixer at high speed, beat egg whites until stiff peaks form; gently fold into gelatin mixture. Spoon into 4 sherbet glasses, cover, and refrigerate until set, about 3 hours. To serve, garnish each portion with 1 reserved orange piece and sprinkle evenly with remaining cinnamon.

Each serving provides: ½ Protein Exchange; ½ Fruit Exchange; ¼ Milk Exchange; 50 calories Optional Exchange
Per serving: 140 calories; 6 g protein; 4 g fat; 19 g carbohydrate; 101 mg sodium; 138 mg cholesterol

Tart Ibiza

A Spanish wine tart, beautifully garnished with luscious grapes.

CRUST
¾ cup all-purpose flour
⅛ teaspoon salt
2 tablespoons plus 2 teaspoons margarine
¼ cup plain low-fat yogurt

FILLING
4 eggs, separated
¼ cup granulated sugar
3 tablespoons lemon juice
1½ teaspoons grated lemon peel
½ cup dry white wine
24 large seedless green grapes, cut into halves

To Prepare Crust: Preheat oven to 375°F. In mixing bowl combine flour and salt; with pastry blender, or 2 knives used scissors-fashion, cut in margarine until mixture resembles coarse meal. Add yogurt and mix thoroughly to form dough; form into ball.

Between 2 sheets of wax paper roll dough, forming a circle about ⅛ inch thick; fit dough into 9-inch pie plate and flute edges. Using tines of fork, prick bottom and sides of crust; bake until lightly browned, 15 to 18 minutes.

To Prepare Tart: In double boiler combine egg yolks, sugar, lemon juice, and peel; stir in wine. Cook over hot water, stirring constantly, until mixture is thick enough to thinly coat the back of a spoon; set aside.

In medium mixing bowl, using electric mixer at high speed, beat egg whites until stiff peaks form. Gently fold whites into yolk mixture. Spoon into prepared crust and bake until golden brown, about 15 minutes. Remove to wire rack and let cool. Decoratively arrange grapes over tart.

Each serving provides: ½ Protein Exchange; ½ Bread Exchange;
  1 Fat Exchange; 65 calories Optional Exchange
Per serving: 173 calories; 5 g protein; 7 g fat; 21 g carbohydrate;
  121 mg sodium; 137 mg cholesterol

Torta de Arroz

**MAKES 8 SERVINGS,
⅛ OF 9-INCH CAKE
EACH**

*An apricot glaze and
almond garnish make
this Spanish rice
cake special.*

3 cups evaporated skimmed milk
2½ cups skim milk
1 tablespoon plus 1 teaspoon granulated sugar
1 tablespoon dry sherry
1 teaspoon each grated orange peel and vanilla extract
¾ teaspoon ground cinnamon
½ teaspoon grated lemon peel
¼ teaspoon each ground nutmeg and salt
8 ounces uncooked regular long-grain rice
4 eggs, separated
½ cup reduced-calorie apricot spread
   (16 calories per 2 teaspoons)
1 ounce sliced almonds

In 4-quart saucepan combine milks, sugar, sherry, orange peel, vanilla, cinnamon, lemon peel, nutmeg, and salt and cook over medium-high heat, stirring frequently, until mixture comes to a boil. Reduce heat to medium-low and stir in rice; cook uncovered, stirring occasionally, until rice is tender, 40 to 50 minutes. Remove from heat and let cool.

Preheat oven to 375°F. Spray 9-inch tube pan with nonstick cooking spray; set aside. In medium mixing bowl, using electric mixer at high speed, beat egg whites until stiff but not dry. Stir egg yolks into rice mixture; fold in whites and pour into pan. Set pan into 14 x 10 x 2-inch baking pan and pour water into baking pan to a depth of about 1½ inches. Bake in middle of center oven rack for 50 to 60 minutes (until cake is browned and springs back when pressed with finger). Remove pan from water bath and let cake cool in pan for 5 minutes; invert cake onto serving plate and let cool for 10 to 15 minutes longer.

In small saucepan heat apricot spread over low heat, stirring frequently, until melted; drizzle over cake. Sprinkle cake with sliced almonds.

Each serving provides: ½ Protein Exchange; 1 Bread Exchange; 1 Milk
   Exchange; 65 calories Optional Exchange
Per serving: 303 calories; 15 g protein; 5 g fat; 47 g carbohydrate;
   254 mg sodium; 142 mg cholesterol

Appendix

Pan Substitutions

It's best to use the pan size that's recommended in a recipe; however, if your kitchen isn't equipped with that particular pan, chances are a substitution will work just as well. The pan size is determined by the volume of food. When substituting, use a pan as close to the recommended size as possible. Food cooked in too small a pan may boil over; food cooked in too large a pan may dry out or burn. To determine the dimensions of a baking pan, measure across the top, between the inside edges. To determine the volume, measure the amount of water the pan holds when completely filled.

When you use a pan that is a different size from the one recommended, it may be necessary to adjust the suggested cooking time. Depending on the size of the pan and the depth of the food in it, you may need to add or subtract 5 to 10 minutes. If you substitute glass or glass-ceramic for metal, it is recommended that the oven temperature be reduced by 25°F.

The following chart provides some common pan substitutions:

Recommended Size	Approximate Volume	Possible Substitutions
8 x 1½-inch round baking pan	1½ quarts	10 x 6 x 2-inch baking dish 9 x 1½-inch round baking pan 8 x 4 x 2-inch loaf pan 9-inch pie plate
8 x 8 x 2-inch baking pan	2 quarts	11 x 7 x 1½-inch baking pan 12 x 7½ x 2-inch baking pan 9 x 5 x 3-inch loaf pan two 8 x 1½-inch round baking pans
13 x 9 x 2-inch baking pan	3 quarts	14 x 11 x 2-inch baking dish two 9 x 1½-inch round baking pans three 8 x 1½-inch round baking pans

Sugar Substitutes

The use of sugar substitutes on the Weight Watchers food plan has always been optional. Natural sweetness is available in the form of fruits and honey. You may also use white and brown sugar, fructose, molasses, syrup, jams, jellies, and preserves. The use of sugar substitutes is completely optional, and we believe that the decision about using them should be made by you and your physician.

Nutrition Notes

Nutrition is defined as the process by which we utilize foods in order to maintain healthy bodily functions. Foods provide the nutrients necessary for energy, growth, and repair of body tissues, as well as for regulation and control of body processes. You need about forty different nutrients to stay healthy. These include proteins, fats, carbohydrates, vitamins, minerals, and water. It is the amount of proteins, carbohydrates, and fats in foods that determines their energy value (caloric content). The objective of daily menu planning is to provide yourself with basic nutrients while staying within your caloric limit.

Proteins are necessary for building and maintaining body tissues. Poultry, meat, fish, eggs, milk, and cheese are the best sources of protein. Fats and carbohydrates provide energy in addition to assisting other body functions. Fruits, vegetables, cereals, and grains are rich in carbohydrates. Margarine, vegetable oils, poultry, meat, and fish supply the fats we need.

Vitamins and minerals are also essential for the body's proper functioning. Sodium is especially important for maintaining body water balance and therefore has a significant effect on weight control. Sodium occurs naturally in some foods, and additional amounts are often added in processing prepared foods.

Variety is the key to success. No single food supplies all the essential nutrients in the amounts needed. The greater the variety of food the less likely you are to develop either a deficiency or an excess of any single nutrient, and the more interesting and attractive your diet will be.

Metric Conversions

If you are converting the recipes in this book to metrics, use the following table as a guide:

Temperature
To change degrees Fahrenheit to degrees Celsius, subtract 32° and multiply by five-ninths.

Weight

To change	To	Multiply by
Ounces	Grams	30.0
Pounds	Kilograms	.48

Volume

To Change	To	Multiply by
Teaspoons	Milliliters	5.0
Tablespoons	Milliliters	15.0
Cups	Milliliters	250.0
Cups	Liters	.25
Pints	Liters	.5
Quarts	Liters	1.0
Gallons	Liters	4.0

Length

To Change	To	Multiply by
Inches	Millimeters	25.0
Inches	Centimeters	2.5
Feet	Centimeters	30.0
Yards	Meters	.9

Oven Temperatures

Degrees Fahrenheit	=	Degrees Celsius
250		120
275		140
300		150
325		160
350		180
375		190
400		200
425		220
450		230
475		250
500		260
525		270

Symbol	=	Metric Unit
g		gram
kg		kilogram
ml		milliliter
l		liter
°C		degrees Celsius
mm		millimeter
cm		centimeter
m		meter

Dry and Liquid Measure Equivalents

Teaspoons	Tablespoons	Cups	Fluid Ounces
3 teaspoons	1 tablespoon		½ fluid ounce
6 teaspoons	2 tablespoons	⅛ cup	1 fluid ounce
8 teaspoons	2 tablespoons plus 2 teaspoons	⅙ cup	
12 teaspoons	4 tablespoons	¼ cup	2 fluid ounces
15 teaspoons	5 tablespoons	⅓ cup less 1 teaspoon	
16 teaspoons	5 tablespoons plus 1 teaspoon	⅓ cup	
18 teaspoons	6 tablespoons	⅓ cup plus 2 teaspoons	3 fluid ounces
24 teaspoons	8 tablespoons	½ cup	4 fluid ounces
30 teaspoons	10 tablespoons	½ cup plus 2 tablespoons	5 fluid ounces
32 teaspoons	10 tablespoons plus 2 teaspoons	⅔ cup	
36 teaspoons	12 tablespoons	¾ cup	6 fluid ounces
42 teaspoons	14 tablespoons	1 cup less 2 tablespoons	7 fluid ounces
45 teaspoons	15 tablespoons	1 cup less 1 tablespoon	
48 teaspoons	16 tablespoons	1 cup	8 fluid ounces

Note: Measurements of less than ⅛ teaspoon are considered a Dash or a Pinch.

Index

B

Bacon, Canadian-style
Basque Green Beans, 349
Boerenkass Soup, 37
Braised Lettuce with Vegetables, 133
Canadian Corn Chowder, 266
Canadian Yellow Split-Pea Soup, 267
Cuban Black Bean Soup, 73
"Down Under" Brussels Sprouts, 28
Fish Fillets "Out of Oven," 40
Grüne Bohnen mit
Zwiebel und Speck, 149
Haitian Rice and Beans, 81
Himmel und Erde, 151
Hungarian Sauerkraut, 97
New Zealand Bacon and Egg Pie, 26
Oysters Rockefeller, 265
Portuguese Clams, 342
Rabbit Flemish Style, 44
Stuffed Steak Rolls, 22
Bagna Cauda, 195
Baked stuffed peaches
(Pesche Ripiene), 205
Bamboo shoots
Sukiyaki, 226
Thai-Style Noodles, 310
Bananas
Banana Fritters, 15
Banana-Tapioca Pudding, 312
Brown Cow, 315
Coconut-Baked Bananas, 313
Frozen Tropical Banana-on-a-Stick, 87
Hawaiian Sweet Potatoes, 311
West Indies Banana Bread, 88
Barley
Russian Krupnik, 324
Scotch Broth, 53
Basil
Soup au Pistou, 125
Basque Green Beans, 349

Baumkuchen, 155
Bean Curd Appetizer, 109
Bean sprouts
Cucumber and Bean Sprouts with
Sesame Dressing, 216
Beans, dry
Boston Baked Beans, 271
Caldo Gallego, 340
Cassoulet, 130
Couscous, 6
Cuban Black Bean Soup, 73
Haitian Rice and Beans, 81
Hummus, 256
Lebanese Meatball Soup, 249
Minestra di Pasta e Ceci, 196
Russian Krupnik, 324
Sancocho de Frijoles, 84
Soup au Pistou, 125
Tostadas, 236
See also Legumes
Beans, green, *see* Green beans
Beef
Beef à la Lindstrom, 292
Beef-barley stew
(Russian Krupnik), 324
Beef casserole
(Carbonnades de Boeuf), 46
Beef-filled turnovers (Pirozhki), 330
Beef Siciliana, 199
Beef-Spinach Soup, 305
Borshch Ukraïnsky, 319
Carbonnades de Boeuf, 46
Carpetbagger Steak, 21
Cornish Pasties, 54
Portuguese Steak, 347
Sailor's Beef, 293
Sauerbraten, 148
Smørrebrød, 290
Steak and Kidney Pie, 58
Steak au Poivre, 128
Steak Rancheros, 239
Steak Teriyaki, 225

G

S